THE
EXPANDED
VOICE *the Art of*

Thomas Traherne

by

Stanley Stewart

THE HUNTINGTON LIBRARY
SAN MARINO, CALIFORNIA
1970

PUBLISHED WITH THE ASSISTANCE OF THE
UNION PACIFIC RAILROAD FOUNDATION FUND

Library of Congress Catalog Card Number 71-111800
PRINTED BY ANDERSON, RITCHIE AND SIMON
DESIGNED BY MARY STODDARD

TO THE MEMORY OF MY FATHER

MARK HANNATH STEWART

TABLE OF CONTENTS

ACKNOWLEDGMENTS

I am happy to express my appreciation for the help and encouragement of many friends and colleagues during the years this study was being prepared. The Research Committee of the University of California, Riverside, generously supported my efforts, and the Staff of the Henry E. Huntington Library and Art Gallery was consistently most helpful. My debt to Miss Mary Isabel Fry goes back over many years. I want also to give my warm thanks to Robert F. Gleckner, John M. Steadman, James Thorpe, and Howard D. Weinbrot, who patiently read the full-length manuscript and offered advice. James M. Osborn graciously extended me the privilege of consulting and of quoting from the manuscript of "Select Meditations." It has been said that one's success is measured by the kinds of debts one acquires. For the good of this book (and its readers), I surely hope this is so. For two of my deepest debts alone would augur well; I greatly appreciate the help given to me by Carol L. Marks and Joan Webber, both of whom took time out from their own work to answer questions, and to send me copies of manuscripts and galleys of their work in progress. They taught me much about an author whom I greatly admire. I have tried to write a book they will enjoy reading.

S. S.

University of California, Riverside
August 1969

THE
EXPANDED
VOICE *the Art of*
Thomas Traherne

INTRODUCTION

I

"And therefore I will only tell thee what he was...." When Thomas Traherne lay on his deathbed, he willed some few pounds to each of his servants, his best hat and books to his brother, and then, taking no note of the disposition of five tenement houses in London, he died, leaving little apparent mark in the world.[1] In a way, this last omission signifies a defining feature in the character of this talented man (whom obscurity would envelop for more than two centuries), a quality which today might earn him some such fashionable label as an "alienated being," or as an artist prone to "manic" episodes. George Herbert, also on his deathbed, handed a manuscript of *The Temple* to a friend, intending that it be delivered to Nicholas Ferrar and (we may believe) that Ferrar should see the work published. In contrast, Traherne took no more notice of his unpublished literary work than he did of what little wealth he had acquired. Even the implementation of his charity (he wanted the tenements given to the city for the poor) he left to his brother, Philip. Traherne died much as he seems to have lived: a man more in the world than of it.

Unfortunately, we know very little about Traherne's life. We cannot even say for sure which of the Thomas Trahernes or Treherons or Trehernes was the historical figure whose literary achievement is the subject of this book. In the *Times Literary Supplement* in 1927, M. L. Dawson argued that Anthony à Wood, at whose account we shall look shortly, must have been mistaken in his biographical sketch.[2] Dawson believed that Traherne must have come from a family with some means and considerable connections, specifications which fit the scion of the "Treherne" family of Lugwardine, who for three hundred years owned Middle Court. This argument has merit on several grounds. First, Traherne mentions a tapestry in one of his poems, and Middle Court was known to have such a tapestry. Again, the only place specifically mentioned in the poetry is Lugwardine. Even more striking is the fact that

3

Thomas Traherne's nephew offered upon his entrance to Cambridge the coat of arms of this ancient and well-to-do family. Finally, the major attractiveness of Dawson's argument is that it seems to fit the facts of Traherne's success in later life, a success awarded in the seventeenth century to very few shoemakers' sons.

But there are even better reasons to reject this view.[3] Upon his death, Traherne gave away five houses, an economic maneuver which, at that time, would have been hard for anyone but a commoner to accomplish. Though the baptismal records of neither Hereford nor Lugwardine reveal any trace of the birth date of *the* Thomas Traherne, the best evidence seems to support the description drawn by that indefatigable Oxonian, Anthony à Wood. He states that Traherne was of modest parentage (a view fitting his recorded presence at Brasenose College) from the town of Hereford near the Welsh border, birthplace of many of the best poets of the Caroline and Jacobean period.

Moreover, this description is confirmed by the few scattered documents which remain: Traherne's will, the record of his attendance at Oxford, another of his appointment at Credenhill, mention in the diary of a friend, the prefatory reminiscence of a friend, and two more or less contemporary accounts of his life. The first biographical sketch appeared in Anthony à Wood's *Athenae Oxonienses*, in which Wood includes Traherne in "The History of Oxford Writers." The entry is brief:

THOMAS TRAHERNE a *Herefordshire* man born, was entred a Communer of *Brasn.* Coll. on the first day of *March* 1652, took one degree in Arts, left the house for a time, entred into the sacred function, and in 1661 he was actually created Mast. of Arts. About that time he became Rector of *Credinhill* commonly called *Crednell* near the City of *Hereford*, afterwards Domestick Chaplain to S. *Orlando Bridgman* Lord Keeper of the *Great Seal*, and Minister of *Tuddington* called by some *Teddington*, near *Hampton Court* in *Middlesex*, and in 1669 Bach. of Divinity. He hath written,

> Roman forgeries . . . *Lond.* 1673. oct.
> Christian Ethicks . . . *Lond.* 1675. oct.

He died at *Teddington* before mention'd, in the house of S. *Orl. Bridgman*, and was buried on the tenth day of *Octob.* in the

Church there, under the reading desk, in sixteen hundred seventy and four. This Person who always led a single and a devout life, was well read in primitive antiquity as in the Councils, Fathers, &c.[4]

Similarly, in 1696, in his *Miscellanies*, under the rubric of "Apparitions of a Man's Own Self," voluble John Aubrey includes slim mention of Traherne in describing what he considers to be evidence of *"Hermetick Philosophy"*:

Mr. *Trehern* B.D. (Chaplain to Sir *Orlando Bridgman* Lord Keeper) a Learned and sober Person, was the Son of a Shoe-maker in *Hereford*: [O]ne Night as he lay in Bed, the Moon shining very bright, he saw the Phantome of one of the Apprentices sitting in a Chair in his red Wastcoat, and Headband about his Head, and Strap upon his Knee; which Apprentice was really abed and asleep with another Fellow-apprentice in the same Chamber, and saw him. The Fellow was Living 1671. Another time, as he was in Bed he saw a Basket come Sailing in the Air along by the Valence of his Bed; I think he said there was Fruit in the Basket: It was a Phantome. From himself.[5]

Two bits of information here are worth remembering, since they helped in identifying Traherne as the author of *Centuries of Meditations* and *Poems of Felicity*. As we can see from Wood, these works were unknown in connection with Traherne's name, and so they remained until the turn of the twentieth century, when, quite by accident, William T. Brooke came upon two manuscripts in a London bookstall.[6] Thinking the poetry in one of these volumes to be much like Henry Vaughan's, Brooke showed the manuscripts to Alexander Grosart, the prominent bookman and editor. Convinced the poems were Vaughan's, and hoping to bring out a completely new edition, Grosart bought the manuscripts. Circumstances including Grosart's death forestalled this possibility, and eventually the material fell into the hands of another famous bookman, one with whom Traherne's name has been linked ever since: Bertram E. Dobell. Dobell studied the manuscripts closely, coming to regard them as the work of someone other than Vaughan. Here the few facts known about Traherne come into the picture.

At this juncture, Brooke led Dobell to a volume entitled *A Serious and Pathetical Contemplation of the Mercies of God, in Several Most Devout and Sublime Thanksgivings for the Same* (1699), an anonymous book with which he had become acquainted, and a portion of which he had once anthologized. Recognizing the author of this work and of the uncovered manuscripts to be one and the same, Dobell was on the threshold of one of the century's great literary discoveries. In the Preface to the anonymous *Thanksgivings*, the author is identified as having once been *"removed out of the Country to the service of the late Lord Keeper* Bridgman, *as his Chaplain.*"[7] The entry in *Athenae Oxonienses* brought the connection between Bridgman and Traherne to light, and in 1903 Dobell published for the first time an edition of Traherne's poetry. Five years later he brought out the prose work under the fortuitous title *Centuries of Meditations*.

Beyond the sketchy portraits in Wood and Aubrey we have little more than speculation to go on. Gladys Wade's more or less standard biography depends almost wholly on extrapolations from local history ("the significance of the date and the place of his birth")[8] and on inferences derived from the text of Traherne's writings. Miss Wade accepts "as literal facts Traherne's own references and allusions in his *Centuries of Meditations* and in the two autobiographical cycles in his poems."[9] No doubt something of Traherne's self shows through in his writings (if not his, whose would?), but it is quite another matter to extract from an author's work actual events in his life. Even though the speaker in *Centuries of Meditations* seems blissful and secure, it does not follow that his creator was so blessed: "He [Traherne] became one of the most radiantly, most infectiously happy mortals this earth has known."[10]

As far as Traherne's biography goes, the facts and justifiable inferences are few. His friendship with one Edward Harley points to early years of schooling at the Hereford Cathedral grammar school, where the young commoner may have won a scholarship to Brasenose.[11] Such an inference would help explain how the son of a shoemaker got sufficient funds to survive at Oxford when even the advantaged undergraduates were practicing the fine art of wheedling money out of parents. Even so, this possibility need not be construed as a denial of the numerous hints that Traherne also enjoyed the generous concern of a wealthy relative or patron. Even with a scholarship, probably the commoner would have needed help. In any event, Traherne enrolled at Brasenose College, Oxford, on March 1, 1652.[12]

Though we know precious little about the actual events in Traherne's life at this time, we do know something about the kind of education he must have received. The intellectual climate of Oxford during the Interregnum was exceedingly intense. During the preceding decade all the old political, religious, and philosophical conflicts had been brought into the open. The university became physically as well as metaphorically the battleground of competing world views.[13] The military triumph of Parliament had led to the installation of Puritan overseers at Oxford. But these stern people failed to silence dissent; faculty and students debated the major issues of the Reformation, taking particular delight in questioning the views of their new overlords. The situation was dangerous, for Oxford was under the control of the Presbyterians, whom the university had resisted. Oxford had been King Charles's last outpost. The king had used the buildings on campus to store ammunition, and later he chose the university press to print arguments in his defense. Even after his defeat, Oxford remained the underground center of Royalist literature, issuing forth such Royalist works as Denham's *Coopers Hill*.[14]

The civil war merely translated into violent action the split which had inexorably widened in the earlier decades of the century. From shortly after the time of Henry VIII, England had been torn between two politico-religious poles: Puritan and Roman Catholic, with a third group between seeking a *via media*. Puritans feared a return by the established church to Rome. That fear was intensified not only by wild rumor of subversive elements at court and in the church, but also by such hard facts as the Papal Bull of 1570 excommunicating Queen Elizabeth, the Gunpowder Plot of 1604/5, and the intermittent capture of Jesuit priests.[15] Reaction to Archbishop Laud's imperious manner and high-church sympathies were typical of the hysterical thinking which sometimes accompanied the Catholic issue.[16] The vestiarian controversy raged throughout the period, and during the Interregnum, John Evelyn was only one of many persons arrested for using the *Book of Common Prayer*.[17] The papist bogeyman appeared in rumored royal liaisons with Spain, in suspected *double-entendres* in the Sunday sermon—even, finally, in the observation of one's devotions on the Lord's Day.

Meanwhile, the Anglicans viewed with equal distress the growing Puritan reliance on individual and often eccentric opinion in matters of doctrine; and they resented the congenital Puritan mistrust of church traditions.[18] Leaders of the Church of England perceived in the Puritan emphasis on the individual's reading of Scripture a kind of *hybris*, a self-centered quality with far-reaching religious and political implications. If every man were equally qualified to read and understand Scripture, and if that understanding alone could guide him to the sole salvation, what would become of the holy church? And if man alone were competent in this most august of issues, what logical arguments could be advanced in defense of man's governors?

From early in the century, groups at the far left had broken from the Anglican communion. Small in actual power, they were nevertheless thought to be a serious menace to public order. John Selden cataloged the manifold splits in Christendom in seventeenth-century England; every faction claimed a doctrine worthy of the people's allegiance and (implicitly) laid claim to the support of the sovereign state. From a political point of view, we may subsume these dissenting factions under the general heading of "puritan," since none of them—from Presbyterian to Fifth Monarchy men—were willing in the long run to live peaceably with the Act of Uniformity.[19] They argued that the thrust of the Reformation was toward reliance on the self rather than on church hierarchy, and away from the established liturgy toward spontaneous prayer and praise. Radical reformers saw in every clerical bow, and in the cadences of the *Book of Common Prayer*, the satanic trappings of the Whore of Babylon.

It was only logical that loyal Anglicans were caught painfully in the middle. By merely adhering to the authorized can-

8

ons of the church, they were liable to attack for their Romish ways. On the other hand, if they went too far in placating the reformer's demands, they would have to sunder what they believed to be the foundations of the church, the primary doctrine of the church enunciated in the creed: "And I beleve one Catholike and Apostolike Churche."[20] For them, the traditions of the past were more than excrescences; they were the sacramental signs of grace within Christ's Church.

On this great issue of church authority Traherne wrote the only one of his works to be published during his lifetime, *Roman Forgeries* (1673). In certain respects, *Christian Ethicks* (1675) may be seen as part of the same controversy. Closely related to the vestiarian controversy was the intellectual split within the church between the Calvinists and the Arminians.[21] Of course, not all high-church Anglicans were Arminians; nor were all Puritans doctrinaire Calvinists. But one could scarcely support what came to be the Presbyterian cause and be an Arminian too. The strong Calvinist position of the Church of England at the turn of the century, seen in the thinking of men like William Perkins, came under heavy fire in the universities. The way was laid for the separation of Presbyterians from the Church of England. Here was by far the greatest intellectual issue of the day: freedom or necessity. While Puritans adhered rather strictly to Calvin's idea of predestination, Anglican sentiment (especially in the universities) was distinctly Arminian. The effects of this issue show very clearly in Traherne's writing, and especially in *Christian Ethicks*.

Traherne's formal education at Oxford covered roughly the last eight years of the Protectorate. Though Cromwell, who acted as chancellor during part of this time, and Dr. Greenwood, the installed principal of Brasenose, were of strong Puritan bent, we cannot assume that the dominant attitude of the college or of the university was Puritan.[22] It was not. Most of the faculty and student body were staunchly Anglican as well as Royalist. They looked upon their Presbyterian superiors as interlopers, sustained in their authority not by logic or achievement but by military force. Many scorned their new masters for their stolid Puritanism, openly satirizing the dress and even the stern countenances of the Presbyterians. Hence, though the

Parliamentarians had quelled the intellectual attack on Calvinism on the surface, the divisiveness of the basic issue ran to the very center of the body politic. Though the *Book of Common Prayer* was banned, students and faculty continued its use. And on the far left, students openly defied all religious conformity. For example, one young man in open debate defended the proposition that he or any other layman possessed as legitimate a warrant as any member of the church hierarchy for interpreting Scripture.[23]

Many of the greatest works of the Renaissance deal with education, with theories of the value of education and the proper means of teaching. We think of Erasmus' *The Education of a Christian Prince*, of Castiglione's *Book of the Courtier*, of Ascham's *The Scholemaster*. But later in the Renaissance, though this interest remained and even intensified, the tone of its expression began to change radically. Men like Bacon, Descartes, and Milton criticized the scholastic structure of the curriculum, which they considered unrelated to the problems of human life. Though a nascent Pelagianism in such Renaissance thinkers as Erasmus[24] lent to humanistic ideas of education a kind of pragmatism or this-worldliness, nevertheless the greatest influence on young minds continued to be the Aristotelianism of the medieval schools. Critics found this especially true in the emphasis on formal logic, and in the way that subject was taught. Everywhere they looked, reformers saw the methods and materials of scholasticism, these often perpetuated by law as well as by the congenital resistance of the university to change. Thus, the lectures, the disputations, the declamations—the three major enterprises of the university— all revealed the dialectical systemization of the Middle Ages.[25] The undergraduate was required[26] to attend these lectures (three times weekly during the freshman year) and debates, which proceeded in the manner of Abelard from "questions" and "sentences," followed by incredibly honed responses intended to cut the ground out from under the defender. In public and in private, the student had to listen, take notes, and before taking his degree, participate in at least two disputations.[27]

The topics debated were, of course, a priori theses. Induction was disparaged in comparison with the syllogism.[28] This is what so troubled the critics of contemporary education: to debate properly one needed to know little more than how to debate properly. Despite the fact that in 1571 Elizabeth changed the curriculum, placing greater emphasis in the freshman year on rhetoric, and putting off the study of philosophy until the fourth, even that first year engaged the student with the aridities of logic.[29] The student learned that the aim, regardless of the topic or side of the question assigned to him, was to get his opponent to trap himself in the web of his own argument. Only if the opponent could be forced, during a minor aspect of an argument, to consent to a premise in the other argument, could one force him, point by point, to contradict his original thesis completely. He must be made to consent to the very opposite of the thesis he had propounded, not because of any evidence which had been introduced (for none had) but because of either a slip with his own language or the superior subtlety of the opposition. And all of this had a quasi-ritual aspect about it. The most important disputations, called quadragesimals, took place during the Lenten season.[30]

Though Bacon and Milton are the best-known critics of education of their time, they were by no means the only ones. René Descartes made rather devastating remarks on his university education: "I had discovered in college that one cannot imagine anything so strange and unbelievable but that it has been upheld by some philosopher."[31] He found his education all but useless, giving it up as soon as he was old enough. As for logic, he writes: "I noticed that as far as logic was concerned its syllogisms and most of its other methods serve rather to explain to another what one already knows, or even, as the art of Lully, to speak without judgment of what one does not know, than to learn new things."[32] Herbert of Cherbury, Thomas Hobbes, Abraham Cowley, and many others join in the indictment of the irrelevancies of university training.

We tend to see the educational shifts in the seventeenth century with too much hindsight. To reformers like Bacon, the cards seemed badly stacked against effective change. This explains the tone of impatience in so much written on the subject. In 1644, in "Of Education," Milton writes:

And for the usual method of teaching arts, I deem it to be an old error of the universities not yet well recovered from the scholastic grossness of barbarous ages, that instead of beginning with arts most easy—and those be such as are most obvious to the sense—they present their young unmatriculated novices at first coming with the most intellective abstractions of logic and metaphysics.[33]

And this view was relevant enough to justify a second edition of the work in 1673, the year Traherne published *Roman Forgeries*. Even the teaching of logic was atavistic. In his book on logic, written in the manner of Peter Ramus (the teaching of whose techniques was banned by statute), Milton's destruction of form and matter, and his wish to advance the simplifying formulae of Ramus, represent more than cavils. Resisting the teaching of method in a vacuum, he insists that learning must have a practical aim. Even the form of an art is in "the actual teaching of something useful."[34] Finally, "All agree, besides, that what is taught should be useful in the life of man."[35]

Milton's essay and Cowley's "Of Experimental Philosophy" may be seen as practical implementations of Bacon's program presented in *The Advancement of Learning*. These efforts were to have their effect in turning the interests of the universities from the felt arrogance of the kind of theology and philosophy which had held sway for centuries: ". . . for the Theologians fetch out as though from the heart of logic canons about God and about divine hypostases and sacraments as if these had been furnished for their use; yet as nothing is more alien from logic or in fact from reason itself than the ground of these canons, as prepared by the theologians."[36] Increasingly this attitude prevailed in education. Even in the Middle Ages logic had its detractors.[37] But now the great shift in emphasis was under way. Administrators expanded the science courses: geography, cosmography, navigation, astronomy, and others.[38] In 1619, Sir Henry Savile founded special professorships in geometry and astronomy, and others in the natural sciences and in history and music followed.[39] Private money began to erode ties between university and crown. Thomas Bodley made the gift which led to the naming of the great library at Oxford. In 1664, Thomas Traherne contributed to the Brasenose College fund. Students began to do more reading—the library offset to some degree the scholastic influence of lectures and disputations.[40] The hegemony of church and crown was beginning to lose its grip on the schools. As Mark Curtis has effectively shown, many students were coming up to Oxford with no thought in their minds of a clerical career.[41]

This fact in itself is of considerable significance. The emerging *ambiance* of the university was secular and cosmopolitan. Parents appear to have dissuaded their sons from aiming at the less lucrative life of the clergy. By the time Traherne entered Brasenose, the impact of reform had long been felt. Though logic occupied a place of importance, the curriculum was more weighted toward rhetoric, literature, and the sciences. Traherne shows an interest in science, especially astronomy. He has with justice been called the poet laureate of the Cambridge Platonists.[42] But with equal justice, Marjorie Nicolson has linked Traherne with the scientific aspect of the seventeenth-century enlightenment.[43] His work reflects the broadened training of the scholar at mid-century, not only in the rational theology of *Christian Ethicks* but also in the wide range of literary and scientific interests.

In 1656 Traherne took his Bachelor of Arts degree and a few months later was appointed to the living at Credenhill, a parish near Hereford, where he was born. It is not clear whether he took up residence at once, but he did continue toward the postgraduate degree. In 1661, after completing the Master of Arts, Traherne settled into priestly duties as rector. He became fast friends with one Susanna Hopton, whom he probably met while at Oxford.[44] They seem to have enjoyed a rather close contact over the years, and Mrs. Hopton appears to be the spiritual novice and select audience in several of Traherne's major works. In the preface to *A Serious and Pathetical Contemplation* a friend recalls the Traherne of the Credenhill years:

He was a Divine of the *Church* of *England*, of a very comprehensive Soul, and very accute Parts, so fully bent upon that Honourable Function in which he was engaged; and so wonderfully transported with the Love of God to Mankind, with the excellency of those Divine Laws which are prescribed to us, and with those inexpressible Felicities to which we are entitled by being created in, and redeemed to, the Divine Image, that he dwelt continually amongst these thoughts, with great delight and satisfaction, spending most of his time when at home, in digesting his notions of these things into writing, and was so full of them when abroad, that those that would converse twith [sic] him, were forced to endure some discourse upon these subjects, whether they had any sense of Religion, or not.[45]

Beyond this, the friend writes, through the years in which the Church of England "laid in the dust, and dissolved into *Confusion* and *Enthusiasme*," Traherne fell "in love with the beautiful order and *Primitive* Devotions of this . . . excellent [Anglican] Church."[46] He insists that regardless of the situation, Traherne never faltered from the devotional offices of the Church of England.

So he remembers Traherne as a man whose time and conversation were filled with the love of God. We find no analogue to "The Collar" in Traherne's poetry, and unlike Donne, Traherne was not forced into the clergy by circumstance, much less by the crown. His anonymous friend tells us something significant about Traherne when he says:

To tell thee who he was, is I think, to no purpose: And therefore I will only tell thee what he was, for that may possibly recommend these following Thanksgivings, and Meditations to thy use.[47]

It is a strategy Traherne would have liked, for he uses it himself in both *Christian Ethicks* and the *Centuries*. When Traherne died in 1674, he was remembered for his piety and learning. They buried him beneath the lectern in the chapel at Teddington, from which he had read the gospels. Unlike Milton and Marvell, Traherne had played no part in the dramatic political events of his time. Unlike Donne, he achieved no acclaim as a preacher. He was neither spokesman for nor martyr to any cause. His name as poet drew no epitaphs from the pens of famous authors. Nor was his funeral a state occasion like Cowley's. But Traherne was a most interesting figure, even in this century so rich in gifted men. His thinking, at once sophisticated, original, and reactionary, anticipates ideas developed later by men as different as Blake, Wordsworth, Thoreau, and

Freud. *Christian Ethicks* alone would justify the scholar's interest in Traherne.

But Traherne wrote marvelously in other veins. Even now, a major literary work, "Select Meditations," has not seen print; much of interest in Traherne's thinking remains in manuscript. Already in print are a wide variety of works ranging from solid scholarship to lyric poetry. It is probably as a poet that Traherne's achievement is least properly appreciated. Many scholars of the period have not yet heard of, much less read, *Roman Forgeries*. Yet here is where our study begins. *Roman Forgeries* was the book that Anthony à Wood remembered when he spoke of Traherne as a person "well read in primitive antiquity as in the Councils, [and the] Fathers."[48] And in its own way, *Roman Forgeries* is a remarkable document.

THE
RHETORIC
OF
ROMAN
FORGERIES

II

"... next to the
Holy Bible,
the very *first....*"
—*Roman Forgeries*

In the first chapter we considered not who but "what" Traherne the poet was: commoner, student, divine of the Church of England, roles institutionally joined at Brasenose College, Oxford. More than any of his writings, *Roman Forgeries* (1673) reflects his involvement with the academy. Its subject, the canonical basis of church authority, may have emerged as part of his graduate work; as we have seen, theological and religious issues were preferred topics of undergraduate debate. Miss Wade thinks the book may be something like a master's thesis;[1] certainly it bears the trappings of the university disputation. Traherne invites the reader to believe that his work grew out of a heated argument with a fellow student, which he describes in the front matter of the work; like the diffident speaker of *Religio Medici*, he enters the public lists for the purpose of setting the record straight.

Traherne gives a lively description of this episode. He has just emerged from the Bodleian Library when a friend approaches him to inquire if he will speak to his cousin, a Roman Catholic who has "spent many thousand pounds in promoting Popery" and has heard of Traherne's ability as a defender of Anglicanism. The two are introduced and immediately fall to debating the exact number of martyrs legitimately claimed by Rome. Since Traherne holds that Rome may properly claim as martyrs only those "that die for *Transubstantiation,* the *Popes Supremacy,* the Doctrine of *Merits, Purgatory,* and the like,"[2] the issue hangs on the meaning of the term "catholic." His opponent insists upon the authority of ecumenical councils and

16

church fathers, but Traherne strenuously rejects this argument on the singular grounds that the ancient documents of Rome are forged:

As for his *Councils, Antiquities*, and *Fathers*, I asked him what he would say, if I could clearly prove, that the Church of *Rome* was guilty of *forging* them, so far, that they had published *Canons* in the *Apostles* names, and invented *Councils* that never were; forged *Letters* of the Fathers, and *Decretal Epistles*, in the name of the first Bishops and Martyrs of *Rome* . . .? [Sig. B7ᵛ]

The opponent's answer (*"Tush, these are nothing but lyes . . ."*) provides Traherne with his major opening in the dispute, and he lays down this challenge:

Sir, answered I, you are a Scholar, and have heard of *Isidore Mercator, James Merlin, Peter Crabbe, Laurentius Surius, Severinus Binius, Labbe, Cossartius*, and the *Collectio Regia*, Books of vast Bulk and Price, as well as of great Majesty and Magnificence: You met me this Evening at the *Library door*; if you please to meet me there tomorrow morning at eight of the Clock, I will take you in; and we will go from Class to Class, from Book to Book, and there I will first show you in *your own Authors*, that you publish for good *Records*; and then prove, that those *Instruments* are downright frauds and *forgeries*, though cited by you upon all occasions. [Sig. B8]

Since Traherne is recording the conversation, perhaps we should in fairness allow for some coloring of the description in his own favor. But even if we do so, his opponent's response must appear rather droll: *"What if they be Forgeries? what hurt is that to the Church of Rome?"*

Allowing for bias, the episode indicates that Traherne was considered an eager participant in theological debate. Besides revealing a stridency of character not at all consistent with the current stereotype of Traherne, the passage also depicts the author as a serious student. But this incident and Traherne's proclaimed familiarity with library research are not all that mark *Roman Forgeries* as a work of scholarship. This treatise itself is immensely learned, and in its preparation Traherne read widely among the early documents of church history. His textual research is very much a product of the new university. University research in the way we now think of it received its greatest impetus in the seventeenth century. Previously, research depended on the largesse of either the church or the crown.[3] The church, in turn, had primarily sponsored study in theology, metaphysics, and logic. But private patrons in increasing numbers opened the door to more varied and more sophisticated subjects and approaches.

Although Traherne's interest in the first 420 years of church history has its antiquarian aspect, it manifests also a more philosophical turn of mind than we might at first think. It expresses an attitude close to the primitivism of the Earl of Shaftesbury. It is this attitude, I think, which leads critics to think of Traherne as pre-Romantic. In Romanticism, institutions corrupt, and one seeks in antiquity a hint of the proper, simple relations binding man to nature. In much the same way, Traherne believes that by returning to the fountainhead of church differences one provides the basis for resolving differences: by establishing truth in religion he establishes the rational grounds on which he and his friend's cousin may stand together as "catholics." But in order to do this he must refute Catholicism without reference to doctrinal issues. Here is the major innovation and rhetorical strategy justifying Traherne's venture into religious polemics. Corruption came (with civilization) after "the first 420 years" (sig. B6) of idyllic, catholic Christendom.

Of course Traherne seeks a rhetorical advantage by his supposed exclusion of doctrinal issues. If successful, he infirms the Catholic position without really attacking it, and so manages to move theological debate from the embattled doctrinal center to the less enflamed domain of textual criticism. From the outset we sense Traherne's implied role as the dispassionate observer and worthy arbiter who, though participating in the debate, operates under such valid rules as to render him a fair and competent judge. He means to strengthen this reasoned stance by focusing on the Council of Nicaea, an accord admired by Catholics as well as Protestants. Again, the disputant is one whom no reasonable person is able graciously to suspect; Traherne invokes the most powerful of persuasive weapons, the single authority his opponent must refuse to assail:

This Note *is the more* weighty, *because the* Nicene Council *is con-fessed* on both sides, *(by us for its own sake and its conformity to the Scriptures, by the Papists, for the* Popes, *that have ratified it,) to be of great* Authority; *next to the* Holy Bible, *the very first, and most indisputable that is.*" [Sig. A7]

Traherne had learned his job well. As we can see, he all but equates the Nicene Council with Holy Writ, and he does so in such a way as to enlist the popes in his effort to undercut the doctrine of supremacy.

Here we have the crux of Traherne's effort to limit his scope of study: the primitive condition of the church was one of uto-pian unity and order in which the apostles ruled in *"equal hon-our and power."* Christ himself ordained *"the Primitive Order and Government of the Church"* (p. 7) as a harmony among equal parishes and bishoprics, intending that bishops function solely "for the better Regiment of the Church" (p. 8). They were to facilitate uniformity, not to subjugate the congrega-tion. Where differences between a member and the hierarchy arose, ecumenical councils were held to adjudicate them, with each bishop exercising an equal voice. The voice of truth with-in the church was the voice of Scripture reinforced by the agreements issuing from these councils. Accordingly, the prim-itive church basked in the perfect light of unity in consensus.

It followed from this that the means of restoring this pristine order lay in establishing accurate records of the early councils. Traherne's textual strategy is based on the conviction of a prim-itive democracy, of a universal church abiding in harmony and truth; we can see a clear connection between this mythological view of early Christendom and Traherne's conception of an-gelic infancy. In both views, time corrupts; history is the inter-necine enemy of the church, just as it is of the soul. Implicitly, doctrinal disputes are the issue of degenerate age. Thus history records the evidence of a collective fall from an innocent state of Christian consensus. On the face of it Traherne appears to bypass all doctrinal or theological disputes, and therefore to impute to himself the emotional attitudes of the prelapsarian church. But this apparent focus on the textual issue actually functions as only part of his persuasive rhetoric. Though he insists that doctrinal issues arose after the period with which he is concerned, the reader soon recognizes that Traherne does not maintain this purely textual focus. But the fact that he purports to do so is interesting in itself, for it shows him attempting to modulate the vocabulary and tone of the controversy he has entered. His method purports to be an instance of that ecumenism which characterized the early church.

The textual approach had of course been tried before, but for the most part the verbal conflict between Protestant and Catholic proceeded along theological and metaphysical lines, and in a manner singularly divisive and vitriolic. *Roman Forgeries* cannot be fully appreciated unless we see it in contrast to the full stridency of tone in the debate at large; its taproots are in the emotional alluvium of the Council of Trent.[4] At a time when pressures toward reform were building both within and without the Roman Catholic Church, the Tridentine Council aimed not only at reform but at reconciliation. The Fifth Lateran Council (1512) had reiterated the supremacy doctrine, and Luther's arguments increased the breach between moderate and conservative elements of the Roman Church. With the upsurge of nationalism, especially in Germany, the Tridentine Council, which lasted from 1545 to 1563, was finally forced to settle for a clarification and strengthening of church doctrine. Though marriage, ordination, and other offices came under consideration, four particulars were of greatest importance: the sacrament of Mass, abuses in offering Mass, the morals of the clergy (which included church administration and its relation to the body politic), and the offering of the cup to the laity (left, finally, to the pope's discretion).

Even before the Council of Trent had dispersed, John Jewel, Bishop of Salisbury, in the first work of the kind to which *Roman Forgeries* belongs, hurled back the answer of the Church of England. Following the publication of Jewel's *An Apologie or Answer in Defence of the Church of England* (1562), the debate raged for over a century without serious change in either terms or tone. Jewel's little book (translated from the Latin by Lady Anne Bacon in 1564)[5] was the first systematic statement of the doctrinal position of the Church of England. Greatly admired for its lucidity, the *Apologie* did not all of itself enflame the passions which would mark the following controversy. Nevertheless, though a learned man, Jewel was an intense one whose character and ambition militated against any cool dispatch in argument. So when Thomas Harding answered his *Apologie* in 1565, Jewel responded—in a most tendentious work—and the round of doctrine and invective began, with each contribution seeming to increase in length.

At this time Harding, who had fled to the Continent, made matters worse by dedicating his response to Jewel's *Apologie* to Queen Elizabeth. The queen, after all, cannot have been thought receptive to Harding's point of view, and if we may judge from Jewel's answer, Harding's reply must have been taken as a personal insult to Elizabeth. Meanwhile, the situation in England was exacerbated by the Papal Bull of 1572, which excommunicated Queen Elizabeth and (in effect) absolved in advance any regicide successful in his attempt to assassinate her. Furiously, Jewel spoke out again (in a work also dedicated to Queen Elizabeth), arguing that the "maigne grounde of his [Harding's] whole plea . . . [was] That the Bishop of Rome . . . can never erre," which doctrine led to the belief that the pope, alone, can unify the church, and, further, that to separate oneself from the pope was heresy, removing all hope of salvation.[6] As we might expect, Jewel's *Defence* fell on receptive ears; indeed all future representations of the Anglican position emphasized the issue of papal supremacy, which is virtually the whole concern of John Rainolds' 750-page *Summe of the Conference Betwene John Rainoldes and John Hart* (1584); it was an issue which roused the people to heights of anger if not folly. From the very beginning the debate was rife with *argumentum ad hominem*; *Roman Forgeries* is part of a grand tradition of personal abuse. For instance, Jewel and Harding were by their temperaments ideally suited to be adversaries; contemporaries at Oxford, their lives reveal notable parallels, which seem to have increased their antagonism.[7] Both had been forced by polar reverses of religious sentiment at court to flee the country, and during Mary's reign, Jewel, though a successful teacher, lost his fellowship. Despite the fact that under pressure he signed the Articles of the Catholic faith, when he later fled to the Continent he was also under suspicion for having signed the Articles. Directly after Elizabeth's ascension Jewel returned to England and in a sermon delivered at St. Paul's Cross during Lent of 1560 set forth a challenge to Catholic theologians, which is the prototype of the works which followed. This passage is typical:

If any one of all our adversaries be able cleerely and plainely to prove, by such authority of the Scriptures, the old Doctors, and Councels, as I said before, by such that it was then lawfull for the Priest to pronounce the words of consecration closely and in silence to him selfe: Or that the Priest had then authority to offer up Christ unto his Father: Or to communicate and receive the Sacrament for another as they doe: Or to apply the vertue of Christs death and passion, to any man by the meane of the Masse: Or that it was then thought a sound doctrine, to teach the people, that the Masse *ex opere operato*, that is, even for that it is said and done, . . . Or that ignorance is the mother and cause of true devotion and obedience: These be the highest mysteries, and greatest keies of their religion, and without them their doctrine can never be maintained and stand upright. If any one of all our adversaries be able to avouch any one of all these articles, by any such sufficient authority of Scriptures, Doctors, or Councels, as I have required, as I said before, so say I now againe, I am content to yeild unto him and to subscribe. But I am well assured that they shall never be able truely to alleage one sentence.[8]

Others rushed to enter the lists; as an example of how involved one could become in this controversy, on the Continent the most brilliant Jesuit partisan, Jacques Gretser (1561-1625), spent the greater part of his adult life writing over 150 works in this polemical mode, heaping "beaucoup de véhémence et d'aigreur contre ses adversaires."[9]

With the turn of the century the controversy, which had been almost wholly doctrinal, witnessed a new turn: William Crashaw introduced the problem of textual authority. Numerous books on the subject began to appear, but none of these had greater impact on young Thomas Traherne than the learned Dr. Thomas James's *A Treatise of the Corruption of Scripture, Councels, and Fathers, by the Prelats, Pastors, and Pillars of the Church of Rome, for Maintenance of Popery and Irreligion* (1611). As the primary influence on the subject, tone, and structure of *Roman Forgeries*, this work deserves special attention.

Dr. James, who served as the first librarian to Sir Thomas Bodley, was (like Jewel) an Oxford fellow. In 1600, James published a catalog of the manuscript holdings of Oxford and Cambridge, to which he appended critical notes on the text of Cyprian's *De unitate ecclesia* and Augustine's *de fide*. This bibliographic feat is indicative of his entire intellectual life, for James was absolutely determined to accomplish a thorough investigation of the texts of the Fathers, which he believed would once and for all vindicate the Anglican Church.

Several severely critical letters written in 1610 by Thomas Bodley indicate that James had tried to get released time from his work as librarian to further his research. Bodley refused that request.[10] More and more James's research project became his obsession. It is worth mentioning in this connection that in 1614 Dr. James tried to obtain financial aid for research assistance. In a broadside entitled *The Humble Supplication of Thomas James . . . for the Reformation of the Ancient Fathers Workes, by Papists Sundrie Wayes Depraved*, James outlined eleven specific requests. As near as I can tell, this *Supplication* is comparable to the now familiar proposal for research funds. It is also an announcement of research in progress.

James tells his reader that the projected research will take five years "without interruption or cessation," and since his book was published before these five years were out, it seems likely that he had already launched upon his research when he issued the *Supplication*.[11] He wanted at least six divinity students—industrious ones—"elected" to carry on the work with him, to collate all available texts, and then, on the basis of that collation, to publish an index which would "shew the corruptions of the printed copies of either Papists or Protestant Editions." One may well admire his patience, for at a convocation at Oxford ten years later, James repeated the same plea, hoping to get scholars commissioned to work in libraries—public and private—throughout England and Europe, to establish authentic (and, of course, antipapal) texts.[12]

The Corruption of the Fathers is divided into five parts, the first of which is written in a highly elliptical, almost tabular form. In effect, it is a summary refutation of 187 separate documents, including works supposedly written by Clement, Abdias, Dionysius, Cyprian, Ambrose, Jerome, and others.[13] James sets out to show them *"Bastard Treatises which* [the Fathers] *themselves never saw"* (sig. *3). He puts this section to telling use in a seven-page table, *"wherein is declared the use that Papists make of these Bastard Treatises"* (I, 73-79). The implication is hard to miss: since the treatises are counterfeit, it follows that the doctrines based upon them are false, too. As a matter of course, then, the Apocrypha has no authentic place in Scripture. Furthermore, no grounds remain for the Roman beliefs that the Bible is hard to understand, that tradition is necessary, that Peter was appointed supreme head of the church, that the Roman bishop is infallible, that Mary was without sin, that there were more than two sacraments, that the sacraments confer grace, that faith alone is insufficient for salvation, that there was any scriptural basis for belief in transubstantiation or the canonizing of saints or the omniscience of angels. Confession, worship of images and saints, private communion, the doctrine of merits, purgatory, prayer for the dead, free will—scarcely one idea, practice, or habit of mind associated with the Roman Catholic Church escapes James's doggedly negative scrutiny and protest.

Parts II and III are more lengthy considerations of particular aspects of the topic. According to James, the third chapter of Cyprian's *De unitate ecclesia* (a frequently cited source for proponents of papal supremacy) had been strategically altered. Cyprian never meant "one chair" to apply to the bishopric of Rome (II, 1-9). The only copy favoring the Romish reading lay in "an old *Abbey at Cambron, written by some blind monke or other*: for he could not see this clause that the Apostles were *endewed with like fellowship both of honour and power, but hath cleane left it out; and instead of these words, but the beginning doth come from unity: he hath put in these, but the primacie is given to Peter"* (II, 5). In 1626 Dr. James published an expanded discussion of the Cyprianic canon as a separate volume, indicating his continued interest in the textual aspect of the controversy.

Like his Elizabethan predecessors, James seldom sustains a

very lofty tone. In the grand manner he gives way to personal spleen. For example, in discussing a Bavarian manuscript of Cyprian supposedly used by Catholics to authenticate the Vatican version, he writes: "You see the world goes harde with the *Jesuite*, when this copie must bee se[n]t from *Bavaria* to justifie the *Cambron*, and both of them brought to testifie for the *Roman*, the *Roman* for the supremacie" (II, 6-7).

Here we see a ploy used over and over again by Anglicans, one which Traherne would also use to advantage. The attack on the Jesuits was designed to delight a far-from-dispassionate English audience. No matter how most Englishmen felt about toleration in the abstract, they deviated little from a uniformly vigorous dislike of the aggressive Society of Jesus. The feelings of James's audience, then, become part of a purportedly scholarly discussion. In the rhetoric of the situation, if the Jesuits were involved, the entire line of Roman dispute must be corrupt: "These [Jesuits] were hired to speak anything, and have more cunning in them, then that we should rely upon them alone. For, say, Is there more credit to be given to these two copies, (which, whether there be any such, or so ancient, must rest upon the faith of a *Jesuit*) than all the *Manuscript* copies throughout the world? which, *without doubt*, saith one of their owne side, *bee some hundreds*" (II, 7). Hence, the character of a Jesuit, familiar to all good Englishmen, provided the final and most crushing blow, not only to any claim for the Cyprianic text, but (implicitly) for papal supremacy: "Is *Cyprian* for their supremacie, in his Booke *de unitate* . . .? Are these sentences found in any of those choice copies? Not in one: their deep silence proves as much" (II, 8).

Part III, in which James attacks the Latin Bibles (especially Jerome's), need not concern us here. In general, the discussion is just more of the same. But in Part IV, James deals with "the open and secret abuses done unto the holy Fathers of the Church" by means of the "indices Expurgatory." James returns to the fountainhead of the controversy, to the Council of Trent: "So then . . . the *Councel of Trent*, seeing the danger that was likely to happen unto their church, if books indifferently of all sorts should be permitted to be read, sollicited the *Pope*: who appointed certaine *Cardinals general Inquisitors* at

25

Rome" (IV, 9), to which were soon added others at the diocesan level. The main purpose of this repressive move by Rome was to counteract the widespread influence of Wycliff and Luther (IV, 10). And in the Papal Bull of March 24, 1564, the *Index* became official church policy. This strategy differs considerably from that employed earlier in James's treatise. For the substance of his argument shifts from the textual issue to the more typical raillery of the sixteenth-century polemicists Jewel and Harding.

James handles the issue of censorship with a clever rhetorical maneuver. The English practice of licensing books precluded any attack on censorship itself, even if James had been opposed to it in principle. He is at pains to make clear that one must separate the *Index* from any discussion of censorship: "Our quarrell is not so much unto the *Catalogues of bookes forbidden*: wherein also they doe wrong us greatly, forbidding books which themselves have printed; . . . although we grant, it is lawfull, nay very behoofefull and expedient, that men should be restrained from reading som books; as books against the State, lewd, profane, or tending unto Atheisme, which are expresly forbidden in all religions, and in all countries." (IV, 22). He aims to encapsulate the issue of censorship by subsuming it under the heading of textual criticism. Thus, in the second half of Part IV he indicts "the Divinitie books first set-forth, and approved, then censured by Papists" (IV, 49; see also IV, 22). By replacing the question of censorship with an indictment of inconsistency, of ill-principled expedience, James attempts to attack the *Index* and defend censorship at the same time. He manages also to turn the reader's attention away from the councils, which he readily admits he cannot adequately treat.

Further, the appeal for further research into the councils is part of the rhetoric of James's work. Implicitly, added textual research would justify the author's spleen, even when, under its sway, he ventures beyond the prescribed limits of his discussion. James takes as a typical case the Council of Basle, which did not register the supposed appeal of "that famous Linwood," a doctor of laws, which had supposedly proclaimed the supremacy of the state in matters of civil law. According to James, this appeal had been perniciously suppressed, proving once and for all the need for sound records of church councils: "It may bee easily conjectured, by this one fact, what wrong hath beene done unto Religion by the particular setting-forth of the Councells; and chiefly by forging false, or suppressing the true Acts." (II, 101). One step had already been suggested (the preservation of Crabbe's edition of the councils), but even Crabbe's "best of all" versions had to be redone. James called for someone to undertake the very effort of *Roman Forgeries*: "But, what pitty is it, since the *Councels* have been so many times published by our Adversaries, to our great disadvantage (as by *Zerlin*, *Crabbe* . . . and now lately by *Paul* the fift) that no *Protestant* hath, as yet, taken any paines, if not to restore the bodie of the *Councels* unto its former health and integritie; yet to keepe it from decaying and growing worse and worse" (II, 102). Miss Wade neglects to point out that James had a particular person in mind when he made this broad appeal: Dr. Ward of Sidney-Sussex College, Cambridge, who had begun research into this area some time before, but had not seen fit to expose his views to the world.[14] So far as I know, until Traherne came along, no one did.

I do not mean to suggest any duplicity in James's interest in future research. He was a serious scholar, and regardless of how the degenerate aspects of the historical issue reflect themselves in his rhetoric, we can see in his work many indications of the kind of thinking which would become the rational hallmark of the Cambridge Platonists. James was not content with the scurrilous quality of argument in matters of religion. He was especially uncomfortable with the intransigent hatred of Catholics, which had become acceptable in the academies. Though he never emphasizes this issue directly, James reveals a conception of the way in which the church's claims over men's lives must continually be examined and reexamined in the light of reason. The drift in the university was clearly in this direction: religious faith could never be secure until squarely grounded on reason. This seems to be the implicit point when James writes:

The triall of religion, is like the triall of a *Nisi prius*, at the *Common Law*; you have pretended witnesses and evidences on your side, to informe your Counsel and perswade the Jurie: your writers are your Atturnies and Lawyers, that pleade the case, and in-force the proofes before the tribunall seate of each mans conscience, that is uprightly and indifferently minded: now as you have your Counsell, so wee have ours, to speake for us. Admit the question were about the Popes Supremacie (a point to be debated by the Counsell of both sides): let us see your evidences, and heare your best witnesses that can speake most directly to the matter. [IV, 27-28]

The point is that religious differences must be resolved in an atmosphere like that of a courtroom. Love and hatred breed prejudice, whereas what was needed was evidence: witnesses who were real witnesses, not "pretended" ones. Granted, James would hardly serve as a model of objectivity today. But we have the advantage of just such contributions to intellectual dialogue: the legal imagery points away from the passion and hatred of more "committed" men.

The comparison between theological and legal disputes fits well with the general secularization taking place in the academy and in society at large. Not only does it suggest that arguments cannot be foisted on councils and synods from above, thus foreclosing debate and dismissing the need for reason, but the comparison also suggests that revelation has no proper place in the ordering of church affairs. Trial by common law proceeds according to human rules and is subject to human error. Tyranny cannot set aside the workings of God's providence; man must proceed with his own aims and capacities and limits, using reason and sensation alone to arrive at truth in religion and justice in the body politic. This secular view will have immense impact on the author of *Christian Ethicks*.

In its context, the rhetoric generates considerable power. Comparison between legal and theological procedures suggests that religious constraints on a parishioner amount to invasion of his rights as a citizen. In the seventeenth century this argument would not have been lost on the more literate advocates of royalism: when the subjects' rights are invaded, the sovereignty of the crown is usurped (James, IV, 31-33). Equipped with hindsight, we can see how this line of argument led in a direction totally anathematic to Traherne: to the logical atomism of Thomas Hobbes. However much he resisted the full implications of rational theology, Traherne shared with James and Hobbes many of the views which were part of the secularization of the time. Certainly Hobbes would have approved of the royalist bent of Traherne's attack on the Council of Sinuessa:

How absurd, for them to judg the Pope, whom they continually teach no man can judg? How much more absurd for the Council to meet to depose him, who if he were pleased to declare their sentence null, all was in vain? It is just as if a *Rebellious* Parliament should meet on their own Heads, to call their King to account, upon preference of his Crimes. If this be admitted, all must be Disorder and Confusion in the Kingdom. [P. 232]

Ironically, though Hobbes and Traherne are polar opposites in philosophy and temperament, the rationalism which is the one thing they seemed to share went hand in hand with a conservatism in politics and religion. Neither man put much faith in doctrinal disputes.

Perhaps this is why Traherne writes only once in the polemical mode of *Roman Forgeries*. In a sense, however, he never fully separates himself from the major aim of this work: certainty and truth in man's spiritual life are the persistent themes and desiderata of *Christian Ethicks* and the *Centuries*. But Traherne will ignore the doctrinal implications of these issues, and he never again submits to the assumptions and rhetorical limits of argumentative prose. All polemical writing holds a common admiration for clarity in syntax and diction. Implicitly, such a linguistic norm tends to value the formal, representational ideas of truth. Yet, as Descartes understood so well, truth in the sense of certainty implied psychological overtones; all the best arguments he had encountered in the universities failed to convince him. He sought a new method, independent of all others. In a similar way Traherne appears uneasy with the formal restraints of disputation. Even if the argument of *Roman Forgeries* were true, how would this fact aid man in restoring the church to innocent harmony? If I am not mistaken, Traherne is ill at ease with the ringing challenge of his Roman Catholic antagonist: "*What if they* [the Roman documents] *be Forgeries? what hurt is that to the Church of Rome?*" (sig. B8).

The assumptions of *Roman Forgeries* lead Traherne toward

the hostile terrain of secularism. If accepted fully—if all man needed to make him happy were accurate texts and neatly framed arguments—one had no legitimate quarrel with the archsecularist Thomas Hobbes. But certainty in the way that Traherne comes to think of it has no necessary connection with such criteria as consistency. (Even today, with the presence of the *Journal of Symbolic Logic*, psychiatrists continue in practice.) The methods of *Roman Forgeries* were determined largely by criteria inherited from men like James, Harding, and Jewel. Hence, a radical uneasiness pervades the work. For though the author's theme is of the past glory of ecumenism, his rhetoric is bound by the fury of its own time. In *Roman Forgeries*, Traherne writes as a student, and no situation is more defined by history than the student/teacher relationship. Traherne imitates, he echoes the same questions and he shares the same assumptions of his mentors.

Thus, Thomas James instructs the careful textual sleuth to look for three kinds of errors: scrivener's errors, printer's errors, and intentional alterations, pointing to the last of these—usually the product of Roman collations disguised as scholarly diligence—as the most problematic. The scholar had no choice but to employ even greater diligence in ferreting out and revoking these emendations (presumably by making emendations of his own). When James himself could "proceed no further; being tired out, and almost spent," he left instructions to younger scholars who might be persuaded to further the project, including a strong reassertion of his method: "I have made true report of that which I have found; and I have found nothing, but in certaine Authors which my selfe have seene" (V, 26). Like Bacon, placing his final trust in the truth of the senses, James ends his major work with a statement reminiscent of the motto of the Royal Society:

To ground my maine proofes upon other mens reports, *in fide aliena*, were to make a faire flourish at the first, and to suffer my selfe to be foiled with shame enough at the end . . . therefore I will end with the words of that famous Keeper of the *Vatican Librarie*, *Caesar Baronius*, in his *Roman Martyrologe. Ponant qui velint, ad libitum*, &c. *Let other men do as they list; Nobis certè, nisi ex certis Auctoribus, quicqua[m] affirmare, Religio est. I hold it a*

Religion, to say nothing which I cannot proove; and to prove nothing, but out of certaine, knowne, and sufficient Authors. [V, 26]

We are not surprised when his pupil, Traherne, proclaims his own familiarity with primary sources:

I desire the Reader to note, that I do not trust other mens information, but mine own eyes; having my self seen the *Collectors of the Councils,* and searched into all their *Compilers* for the purpose: Neither do I use our own, but their most affectionate and Authentick Writers, the circumstances of the things themselves (in their most approved Authors) detecting the Forgeries. [Sig. B6ᵛ]

As we read the work carefully we see how completely Traherne accepts the major assumption that in textual research man possessed the vehicle for establishing truth in religion. The purpose of *Roman Forgeries* is to do just that: to finish James's work on the councils and thereby to settle once and for all the question of church authority. Further, Traherne's strategy follows James's almost exactly. He seeks to establish by his own senses the truth of his major premise, imputing to that premise and all that followed a kind of scientific certainty. Major premise: the Catholic records of the councils are corrupt; minor premise (challenged by his Catholic opponent at the Bodleian): any church which refers to corrupt documents for its authority cannot be the repository of true doctrine. The deduction follows necessarily.

We cannot, of course, remove this syllogistic formula from the rhetorical strategy of the work as a whole. It is like Traherne's insistence that he will exclude doctrinal issues. He never does exclude these issues, but even more important, by his purported exclusion he implies that these issues have already been decided, against the Roman cause. It is an effective persuasive device to imply that one may safely assume the previous exposure of the opponent's position. Similarly, the clever debater learns to blur the differences between fact and favorable interpretation. Traherne resorts also to the staple of this controversy, *argumentum ad hominem*:

Had we time, we might make many curious reflexions upon these passages of *Baronius*: He afterwards talks of another *Isidore,* called sometimes *Mercator*, and sometimes *Peccator*; but of what Parents, what Calling, what City, or what Country he was, he mentioneth nothing. So that this *Child*, among all those *Isidores* and *Fathers* that are found out for it, must rest at last in one that is *unknown*. [P. 58]

References to the parentage of popes, and to popes as parents (of forged documents as well as other popes) are quite frequent in the work. These and other evidences of abusive language remind us of an important rhetorical point: Traherne was preaching to the converted. Despite the predictable sympathy of his audience, he puts each chapter together in such a way as to suggest a polemical tour de force. One of the shortcomings of the work inheres in the fury of his argument, which is inappropriate when we consider the assumptions shared by the author with his audience.

Though the stock trappings of religious controversy are present in *Roman Forgeries*, so are the evidences of Traherne's serious aim, namely, religious certainty. He is so anxious to still the turbulence of the religious issue in his time that he gets to his main point twice before his argument begins. In "A Premonition" he directly confronts his reader with Canon 5 of the Nicene Council, which is certainly his most powerful and most frequently cited evidence. Because of *"the Tenor of the undoubted Canons of"* this council, Catholics and Protestants alike had vested it with absolute authority (sig. A3). Canon 5, which Traherne quotes in its entirety, deals with excommunication and the means available for appeal. He lays special emphasis on the injunction to parish priests and bishops that no man who has been "cast out by some, be . . . received by others" (sig. A4). Each outcast member had the right of appeal open twice a year:

But let the Councils be held, the one before *Quadragesima* before Easter, that all dissention being taken away, we might offer a most pure Gift unto God: and the second about the middle of *Autumn*. [Sig. A4ᵛ]

Here is the substantive point of the argument: while *"the Council had said in terms*, The last Appeal shall be made to Councils,"* it still provided for any excommunicated member to be heard before *Quadragesima*. Thus, if the council decided in his favor, he could take communion in his own church by Easter (sig. A5).

For Traherne, since any man might err, tyranny and certainty were mutually exclusive. The value of councils rested in their recognition of human frailty and in their abiding humility. In the early church, bishops gathered to assure by their common voice that any eccentric judgment of a local church official could not bar a member of the congregation from Easter communion. Ideally, such decisions represented not secular power but communal judgment: the reasoned opinion of the congregation. Traherne is determined to see that such a system could not justly be contravened:

No Evasion (I think) can possibly be made there from; when it is once noted and understood. For the Bar put in against the Pope, is not here in Words, *but* Things. [Sig. A6]

It is always possible for men to quarrel about the meaning of words. Traherne admits that language can be twisted, making the pope an exception to the rule that only councils have the power to revoke excommunication. But primitive churchmen had placed their meaning—with certainty—beyond words. Time and distance—real things—precluded any legitimate appeal to Rome:

Whereas, if after the Sentence of the Council, *the business were to be carried to the Court of* Rome; *Suits and Quarrels could not be ended against* Easter, *but would be lengthened in many Provinces, beyond* Easter; *both by reason of the* Seas *and* Regions, *to be passed over . . . before they* [the appellants] *could come from their own Countries to the* Roman Chair; *and by those Prolatory delays they might find there.* [Sig. A6ᵛ]

Perhaps the repeated emphasis on Canon 5 of the Nicene Council indicates the relative strength of Traherne's view here as compared to the more general strategy of *Roman Forgeries*. In addition to the front matter, the book is divided into twenty-four chapters and an appendix. The first three chapters are introductory, dealing with the types of forgery, the history of the early church, and a general purview of the supposedly

33

forged documents of the Roman church. But beginning with the fourth chapter Traherne treats, seriatim, either discrete documents or particular authors. He will mention a document, usually quote from it, and repeat the point made concerning the work treated in the preceding chapter. The unfortunate result is that the arguments become increasingly predictable: the Vatican document is a forgery because it was written by or discovered by or concerned with a person dead long before or long after the supposed date of authorship.

Traherne handles most of his examples in just this way. But his repertoire has some flexibility. For example, when he discusses James Merlin, his main criticism is that promised evidence from the Nicene Council is never produced:

I had a long time coveted a sight of these Canons, and finding them numbred in such *an Annotation of Synods, the Acts whereof are contained in this book*, I was much comforted with hope of seeing them: But when I turned to the place, I found them not! [Pp. 77-78]

But as I have suggested, Traherne rises to his most vindictive tone when he can point to an apparent anachronism. This is his constant theme on the subject of Isidore. And when he discusses an epistle from Athanasius to Pope Mark requesting a copy of the seventy canons of the Nicene Council (his own had been burnt), he comments with typical wryness: "*Mark* was dead 9 years before the Burning happened; howbeit, he sent them a Gracious Answer, with 70 Canons" (p. 71).

Traherne's broad strategy takes its rise from Vincentius Lirinensis, a proponent of the view that Scripture and Scripture alone was the arbiter of doctrinal disputes (sig. B2). Vincentius sought merely to restrain new heresies from corrupting patristic teachings. In contrast, Traherne argues that once a false interpretation gains adherents, history will give it sway. The entire issue of exegesis—even the text itself—becomes clouded by claims and counterclaims. When this happens, the wise man either ignores the controversy or seeks the guidance of Scripture as elucidated by the ancient universal councils. As for the Fathers, as Dr. James had shown, from them one learned that truth was not invincible, that error could and did prevail

34

within the later church. Having gained the upper hand, error succeeded in corrupting the Fathers, and sought now to corrupt both Scripture and the councils (sig. B2ᵛ).

In this connection Traherne frequently reminds his audience of a logistics problem. While throughout the Middle Ages the Roman see exercised full control over the housing and reproduction of manuscripts, Protestants had only recently acquired access to a limited number of early materials. Since Eastern libraries had long since fallen to Islam, it happened that almost every important text was in the hands of Rome. One might expect such a point to weaken the textual approach chosen by Traherne for his attack. Instead, he turns this admission to his own use: one had only to show that Rome, in possession of all written matter, was disposed to violate her own conscience, in order to prove her guilty of heresy and blasphemy. No greater proof of this was needed than the papal complicity in the falsification of patristic and concilar writings: the trajectory of Traherne's rhetoric appears to be conveniently curved.

All things conspire to fit the plan of *Roman Forgeries*. The Vatican monopoly of manuscripts is evidence of bad faith, which is (in turn) proof that the documents monopolized are forgeries. Traherne's utopian view of the primitive church is part of the general assumption that corruption intruded after the first 420 years of the church as a direct response to papal ambition. The leitmotif of corrupt tradition is a major one here: "It is sufficient to prove, that all the *Streams* Are infected by the *Poyson* that is thrown into the *Fountain-head*; and to expatiate downwards, would overswell the Book" (sig. B6-B6ᵛ). One of the four sources of heresy was the pretense of "*unwritten Traditions*" (sig. B10), a perpetual Roman theme. According to Traherne such claims were always based on the distortion or outright fabrication of documents:

They bring forth a vast multitude of Apocryphal and Spurious Writings, which themselves have feigned, to the amazement of Fools; and that those may admire them, that know not the Letters (or Records) *of the Truth.* [Sig. B1ᵛ]

Even disagreements within the Roman church must be recognized as part of a plan to subvert truth:

All other Controversies are but superficial blinds, more freely exposed to her Enemies debates, that mens eyes may be turned another way from this *Arcanum*, which is with all endeavour hidden from the people: And for this cause they find it better to buy up the *Editions*, than answer the *Discoveries;* which makes Dr. *James* his Treatise, and *Blondels Pseudo-Isidorus*, so rare among the people. [Sig. B5ᵛ]

For Traherne, issues such as textual purity and church authority cannot be separated; if the church employs "forged" documents (the term is loaded, of course), then, *ipso facto*, she is guilty of blasphemy. The argument runs like this. One may think of many kinds of forgery: a lease, a will, a deed may be forged (pp. 1-6). One may forge the king's seal. Of such felonies the state takes note, exacting punishment. But certainly the forgery of church documents is of a higher and more dangerous order; the former acts are criminal, the latter sacrilegious. The gravest offense of all would be the counterfeiting of Scripture. Now, suppose the Church of Rome were guilty of these offenses, and suppose further that with reference to them money has changed hands. It follows for Traherne that the church stands guilty of sacrilege and simony, too. When Traherne described his Catholic opponent as "obdurate," he knew the subtle overtones of that word: obdurate, obstinate, presumptuous, reprobate. To him, the Roman church was steeped in the unpardonable sin (cf. James, III, 2).

Incomparably the best example of her presumption was one of the two great claims separating the Church of England from Rome: papal supremacy. As Traherne sees it, church history began with Christ's injunction to his apostles recorded in the synoptic Gospels (Matt. 27:19-20; Mark 16:15-18); priests and bishops were the lineal descendants of the apostles only in the sense that together they administered the offices of the church in the unity of Christ's love. It was natural, however, that as the church grew, serious rifts required arbitration and settlement. It was for such a purpose that the bishops convened in the first ecumenical Council of Nicaea. They met in the innocence of democratic harmony, and the bishop of Rome was "expresly noted to be equal to that of the other Patriarchs" (p. 8). But soon the church would fall from this innocence in-

to the secular wilderness of imperial power. Though Canon 5
announced the primacy of councils, the church began to respond to pressures of geography, commerce, and politics. The
fall was complete when the centrally located bishop of the dio-
cese of Rome "invaded the Jurisdictions of his *Fellow-Patri-
archs*" (p. 10).

It is not hard to see that this is a comment of historical interpretation rather than of textual criticism. Nevertheless, it is
one of Traherne's most important points. The major rift occurs
when the pope jettisons the fifth canon of the Nicene Council
and receives appeals from excommunicated members of other
dioceses. When men could appeal the excommunication imposed by local bishops for the simple reason that they possessed
the means to make the expensive and arduous journey to Rome,
the altar cloth was soiled with commerce, "seared with trade."
Giving way to the same secular interests, other patriarchs
helped accomplish the usurpation of their own authority. As
the see *"openly* Espoused" the "Cause of Malefactors" (p. 10),
the resulting scandalous conditions gave rise to the Sixth Council of Carthage. To this fateful congress of churchmen Zozimus
sent a delegation "with two *Canons* fathered upon *Nicene*
Council" (p. 12).

The Traherne of *Roman Forgeries* is at his best with close-up
material which lends itself to irony and sarcasm. If the pope
had excommunicated the African church, and if the latter had
remained separated for a hundred years, then she must be described as a Protestant church. Such a state of affairs would
render Rome's claim to universal recognition a self-proclaimed
absurdity. On the other hand, if the documents decreeing
separation were false, then the church stood self-convicted of
an additional forgery. The line of paradox extends: if the African church had recognized the pope's supremacy, what motive
would exist for excommunication? In the same way, Roman
martyrologies list hundreds of African saints and martyrs,
many from the century of supposed cleavage (St. Augustine,
to name only the most visible). The question arises of how a
being excommunicated from the true church can become
either a saint or martyr of that church.

Traherne looks upon the Sixth Council of Carthage as the

37

great moment of crisis in the church. Though one thousand priests and all the emissaries from the four centers of ecclesiastical authority other than Rome dutifully repudiated the Vatican documents, corrupt forces pressed inexorably for supremacy. Later advocates of Rome moved even to obscure St. Augustine's denial of papal supremacy. This occasion elicits one of Traherne's more clever maneuvers. He insists that those assembled at Carthage found the notion of papal supremacy "so absurd and monstrous . . . that . . . they thought no man impudent enough to affirm it" (p. 15). With the key word "impudent" Traherne strikes a familiar chord, though one having little to do with the records of the council. Not only does the passage level all bishops including the pope to mere humanity, but such a word as "impudent" would not be lost on his audience, with its imputation of that puff of vanity they had learned to associate with the Whore of Babylon. Excommunication, as the most serious administrative power of the church hierarchy, was rightly exercised only after the checks of numerous perspectives at the councils. Yet the Bishop of Rome, acting independently, proceeded to excommunicate the entire African church.

Using James and Stillingfleet to prove his case, Traherne urges the significance for the Protestant side of St. Augustine's presence at the Sixth Council of Carthage. This is part of his manipulation of the idea of authority: whenever possible, one ought to record any reservations of any kind about Catholic documents when expressed by Catholics. The "Appendix" to *Roman Forgeries* is an extended effort in this direction. We will remember how stridently Traherne protests his use of authorities and texts condoned by Rome (a major rhetorical thrust of his encounter at the Bodleian). The strategy does more than insinuate the speaker's good will and moderation. It implies that he and his audience have grounds for agreement, that perhaps a third party is responsible for any misunderstanding between them. In the same way Traherne will insist that most Catholics are sincerely devout in themselves. They are victims of a sinister hierarchy—"seduced" by the criminal designs of church officials (p. 309). Even open disclaimers by Catholic editors concerning Vatican texts figure in the defrauding of the credulous faithful. For example, in Binius such disclaimers are made in small print not intended to be read (p. 157). Even when the opposition agrees with him, the debater warily attacks his motives. If need be, inferred motives may be used to banish the example of consent completely.

Traherne's interest in the physical or logistics aspects of his problem is a special instance of his belief that the Roman patriarchs sought to keep men ignorant. Were not the manuscripts "Chained up in Monasteries and Libraries" where no one could without prior authorization consult them (p. 36)? And what was the major purpose of "their *Indices Expurgatorii*" (sig. B6)? Had not printing and the proliferation of texts gone hand in hand with the Reformation (p. 37)? Again, the line of Traherne's argument—in typical scholastic fashion—arches admirably to meet itself: Rome was the champion of ignorance because ignorance was the bastion of her power. Only forms of corruption could have kept men ignorant for so long; therefore, Rome's success as a secular power is evidence of her corruption in using force to perpetuate ignorance in order to sustain herself in power. This drift of argument represents a special case of *argumentum ad hominem*. Taking his lead from Thomas James, who harked back to the rhetoric of proclaiming the pope as Anti-Christ (IV, 8), Traherne discerns on the pope's forehead the Mark of the Beast (p. 159). This level of invective differs from the more typical and tame sexual imputations about illegitimacy and adultery.

In retrospect, we can see that this rhetoric either proceeds from or lends to a conspiratorial view of history: "I go on thus . . . that you might see the Conspiracy of the Members with the Head, and the general Guilt of that Church . . ." (p. 120). The conspiracy theme is strong in the idiom of this great religious controversy. Traherne interprets church history from the Sixth Council of Carthage to the Reformation as the unfolding drama of a developing tyranny, perpetuating itself by the bondage of the peoples' ignorance, by intimidating, silencing, or burning all dissenters. The great bogeyman of Anglican rhetoric was the Jesuit, and Traherne generously spices his work with digressive asides on this nefarious group. Abuse of the Jesuits in a work like *Roman Forgeries* must have served as something like the gunfight in a western movie: a predictable element, because the audience looked for it and even insisted upon it. The Jesuit was a familiar rogue, known to the English by his portraits in the "Characters" and broadsides, sermons and plain gossip of the time. Such portraits were calculated to please an audience reared on exaggerated and often apocryphal stories handed down from men supposedly present at the sacking of the monasteries: infant bones beneath the floors and the like (see pp. 85, 100, 125). Then, too, one had the oppressive and more pertinent reminder of the nightmarish Gunpowder Plot. *Roman Forgeries* ends on the ominous note of just such an alarum:

> This dangerous Intimation is sufficient hint for *Jesuitical* Souls: He declares his Principle, that he is an *Enemy* to some, contrary to our Saviours Order: and gives order to his Disciples to guess at his meaning, and without any publick notice to execute the same. *Hatred* removes its Object; he hates, *and they must do his Will without Admonition.* If they mistake his meaning, provided they do it out of Zeal, he can easily connive at it: which suits with their Practices, of Poysoning Emperours, Murdering Kings, attempting on Queens, their Massacre at *Paris*, the Gunpowder-Treason, &c. The *Instruments* of which Acts, are by such Records rather favoured than discouraged; and some of them Canonized, rather than punished in the See of *Rome*. [P. 316]

It would be wrong to think that *Roman Forgeries* offers no more to readers than simple invective. Though frequently the most incisive passages get lost in the stilted rhetoric of the book, careful reading turns up passages of considerable crispness and intensity. In the section on Binius, for example, we find a very interesting development. The discussion begins typically, with a long quotation:

> *Horum quinquaginta priores*, &c, saith he, *Only the first fifty of these (the last of which is of dipping thrice in Baptism) containing nothing but sound Apostolical Doctrine, and approved by Ancient Bishops, Councils, and Fathers, are received as Authentick*, Cap. 3. Dist. 16. *And according to that common Rule of the Holy Fathers, because the Author of them is unknown, they are rightly believed to flow unto us by Apostolical Tradition. The residue by Pope Gelasius*, Can. Sanct. Dist. 15. *are accounted Apocryphal, both be-*

*cause their Author is unknown, as also because the 65 and the
last Canon, it is evident, that some of them are craftily put in by the
Grecians, and some of them corrupted by Hereticks.* [P. 162]

Traherne answers vigorously, and in a manner transcending
any sectarian issue:

I. If the Tradition of the Apostles, though committed to *writing*,
be capable of corruption; what security can we have of *Oral Tradition*, which is far more loose, and liable to danger?

The question here had been the subject of Donne's Third
Satyr, and it is an important issue in Browne's *Religio Medici*:
How does a man of intellect and conviction perceive the truth
among the competing claims of numerous churches and
churchmen for his allegiance? Traherne emphasizes the "how,"
the epistemological aspect of the question.

Though frequently Traherne seems merely to be arguing in
a circle, a serious epistemological interest informs certain of his
best points. For example, his major quarrel with the Council of
Sinuessa seems to be the fact that Catholics support it. Hence,
Traherne states that "*Binius* and his fellowes, *Baronius*, *Labbe*,
and the *Collectio Regia* ... embrace this Council" solely on the
grounds that "it cannot be rejected without Prejudice to the
Authority of the *Roman Chair*" (p. 219). Traherne never
presses this circular argument; instead, he indicts his opponents
for arguing a circle. "But the Impossibility of the Thing is an
argument *ad Hominem*, that may perhaps be more convincing.
For as they hold that no man may condemn a Pope, So do they
hold that no man, but he, can call a Council" (p. 210; see p. 224
on "Nonsence and Tautologies").

Though the argument has thus far been routinely polemical,
Traherne makes a final and significant point: no single trace of
the city of Sinuessa remains. Why, then, must one believe in the
authority of a document supported by nothing more than its
own existence? Rome explains that the city had been destroyed
by earthquake. But why are there no other mentions of this city
anywhere? The question is not trivial, for it implies that Traherne has in mind a criterion for inclusion of texts within the
canon, and that this criterion is comparable to that in other

disciplines in the academy. The skepticism of the late Renaissance is closely related to the emerging new university and to the new science. With Traherne, as with Bacon and Browne, the worlds of faith and knowledge were not the same. But even here the philosophical issue becomes obscured by invective, as Traherne's rhetoric reverts from the ironic to the sardonic:

It is an unlucky Chance that this City should be swallowed up by an *Earth-quake*: As ominous almost as the *Burning of the Nicene Canons* by the *Arrians*. That other Place[s] have been lost we know: but no man knoweth that this City was lost, *nor is the least memory of it to be found.* [P. 225]

On occasion, Traherne uses the sardonic tone effectively, as, for example, in this discussion of the Sixth Council of Carthage:

Here the *Roman Bishop*, nay the meanest *Priest* he shall please to send as his *Legate*, is exalted above all Councils, Bishops, and Patriarchs in the world; he may do, and undo, act, add, rescind, diminish, alter, whatsoever he pleaseth in any Council, when the Causes of the most Eminent Rank of the Church do depend in the same. [P. 24]

Here the diction is extremely abusive in its implications. Traherne's audience would compare the "meanest priest" with the One celebrated as "exalted above all forever" in the Canticles of Morning Prayer. Also, the crisp series of verbs describing the power of the pope's lowliest legate ("do, and undo, act, add, rescind, diminish, alter") cannot have but distantly recalled to the reader's mind the text—and perhaps even the commentary of some Jacobean divine on that text—from the last chapter of Revelation: "If any man shall add unto these things, God shall add unto him the plagues that are written in this book: And if any man shall take away from the words of the book of this prophecy, God shall take away his part out of the book of life, and out of the holy city, and from the things which are written in this book" (22:18-19).

Traherne's colorful diction ("Popish Hirelings," "*Jesuitical* Souls") is one of the stylistic features of *Roman Forgeries* (p. 316). Like many literary men of his time, Traherne loved the play on words: he can see the popes between John VIII and

Leo IX as "*Apostatical,* rather than *Apostolical*" (p. 4), and so on. He is also fond of anaphora, a device which he will use with great success in *Centuries of Meditations*: "If a *Beggar,* If a Lease, a Bond, a Will, or a Deed," "If .... If .... If ..." (pp. 2-3). And at times, even in *Roman Forgeries,* we come across evidences of prose style worthy of the author of the *Centuries*:

If Lyes were always consistent, *Truth* would be amazed. God doth infatuate the Counsels of his Enemies, and turn their Wisdom into Foolishness. They run into inconveniences, sometimes so great, that they cannot be remedied. Could a Lye shun all inconvenience, and see to its Interest on every side, it would be as wise and perfect as Truth itself. [P. 302]

From a rhythmic point of view, this paragraph unfolds by a series of neatly balanced phrases, each subtly shifting in the number of major stresses. The first sentence has two members with three stresses each. The second is made up of balanced members with four stresses on each side of the major juncture. The following sentence, which shifts from the declamatory sense of the previous two, is broken into three parts: three, two, two. The final sentence returns to a declamatory tone. It is divided into three parts, and is the most complex of the three. Depending on how one reads the first dependent clause, we have a stress pattern of either 4-4 or 3-4, producing in either case a kind of syncopation carrying over to the final clause. The juncture, however, calls for a major stress on "it," producing the culminating member in iambic pentameter.

Beyond the rhythmic complexity, we find here and elsewhere in *Roman Forgeries* examples of Traherne's effective use of balance and antithesis. At times, he uses antithesis with precision: "They confess the *Fraud,* but make no *Restitution*" (p. 308). Again, Traherne will spice a passage with an idiomatic expression, as he does in his discussion of the "Forgers" just mentioned: "All their Drift is to save their *Skin.*" The neat balance (two major stresses on each side of the weak copula) heightens the impression of this almost racy idiom.

We find numerous such examples in *Roman Forgeries*. As a historical document, the work will justify the scholar's interest; but as a literary artifact it will also reward the careful reader.

Miss Wade and others have felt compelled to apologize for *Roman Forgeries*, but in its context the work requires no apology. Compared with polemical treatises like it, *Roman Forgeries* has a sharpness and precision of diction and syntax which is distinguished. Its flaws are the flaws of the received norms of religio-political controversy. Any work which addresses issues of immediate and urgent relevance is apt to date itself; *Areopagitica* is a most glaring exception to the rule. Even today, we hope for good rather than poor writing on those issues of relevance which rouse to anger. It is easy to look upon the invective of *Roman Forgeries* as naïve. It is not so easy for us to disengage ourselves from invective itself, when the issues concern us. In the seventeenth century, religious and political issues were frequently inseparable. In our own time, economics has replaced religion in its close relation to political faction. And who would recognize political dialogue if it proceeded either scientifically or rationally?

History has decreed our separation from the great emotional upheaval of religious differences. But so long as irrational elements govern the rhetorical norms of political confrontation, we can make use of *Roman Forgeries*. For even in the heat of the most powerful divisions of his time, Traherne retained a deep concern for the proper methods of gathering and presenting evidence. For him, the only sure solution to the major problem dividing Christians from each other lay in the truth, which was accessible only through those rational and sense operations shared by all men equally. This explains Traherne's method, his use of the "most affectionate and Authentick Writers" of the Roman church, and his intended scrupulousness as a scholar: "but mine own eyes, having my self seen. . . ."

CHRISTIAN ETHICKS: PHILOSOPHY AND FORM

III

HE that would not be a stranger to the Universe, an Alien to Felicity, and a foreiner to himself, must Know GOD to be an infinite Benefactor, all Eternity, full of Treasures, the World it self, the Beginning of Gifts, and his own Soul the Possessor of all, in Communion with the Deity.
—Christian Ethicks

Though it has its moments and perhaps even a surprising share of stylistic impressiveness, as noted above, probably we learn more about Traherne's education than about his mature prose style from a study of *Roman Forgeries*. He never wrote another polemical piece, and in fact, though his work is frequently laced with evidence of his erudition, Traherne pays little mind to the more topical aspects of political or religious themes. In some ways the literary critic will find Traherne's Commonplace Book more interesting than *Roman Forgeries*.

Commonplace books were a widespread seventeenth-century phenomenon. They were not invented in the period, nor do they disappear with it, but they enjoyed an importance in the Caroline and Jacobean period lacking in any other until (perhaps) our own. Commonplace books and marginalia are a subspecies of the journal or diary, which is the monopoly of no age; recently autobiography as a form has reemerged, and various related types of marginalia have not only returned to popularity but have found their way into other forms. The first chapter of Jonathan Kozol's *The Fume of Poppies* (1958) begins with the description of a course in late eighteenth-century literature from the Harvard *Announcement of Courses* (1956) and is made up of the irrelevancies in the notebook of one student. Several examples of such seventeenth-century notebooks are preserved in the Bodleian Library. In Traherne's time, professors urged their students to store up sayings and passages which struck their fancy or their conscience.[1] In this way, commonplace books are visible artifacts of the memory, mnemonic devices. And like the memory itself, they tend to be both inchoate in structure and often unoriginal in the extreme.

Traherne's Commonplace Book, part of the Dobell Folio (Bodleian MS. Eng. poet. c. 42), is the product of collaboration between the author and his amanuensis.[2] Carol Marks has traced many of its sources, the study of which began early in the century.[3] Traherne drew the major portion of the entries from works by Theophilus Gale, Hermes Trismegistus (in the very popular Everard translation), Thomas Jackson, Henry More, and Isaac Barrow. One is struck by the disparity between the two sections of the manuscript, a disparity immediately visible to the eye. The "Poems" in the first part of the manuscript, written in Traherne's meticulously attractive hand, have the feel of characters carefully drawn rather than penned, even in those places where lines have been struck for revision. In the Commonplace Book we have no such evidence of carefully done work. Here one finds evidences of the anomalies which plague the work in progress: inconsistencies, relocated boundaries, countermanded instructions, a wide range between parts done in a hurried scrawl and others executed with care, and doodles.[4] The entire work seems in the process of physical growth. Thus, the "A" atop the recto of folio 17, preceding "Of Judiciall Astrologie," appears to be the planned beginning of the book. Yet the notebook seems later to have expanded backwards: to make room for "Aristotle's Philosophie," Traherne used both columns on the verso of folio 16. If we take the "Astronomie vid Admiration"[5] on folio 17 as evidence that Traherne planned an entry for "Admiration," then the only space left in the alphabetic scheme of things would be the second column of the recto of the same leaf, since the opposite column is occupied by the last four stanzas of "Goodnesse."

In the same way, space remains to end the notebook with an entry for "World," mentioned in the "Pythagoras" section (fol. 80^v.2). So the work seems to expand and to be expandable in both directions. Similarly, the numerous blank spaces and leaves often correspond to the alphabetic position of topics mentioned but for which no entries exist. Without suggesting that Traherne intended each topic for given slots (he does not uniformly follow the alphabet), we may note that space does exist in the appropriate order for every such heading. Though one entry may be tightly squeezed,[6] plenty of room is available for most. Space occurs between "Neighbor" and "Omnipotencie" for "Obdurateness"; more than a column remains between "Beginning" and "Bounty" for "Blindness," and two such columns fall between "Darkness" and "Death," allowing room for "Deafness," and so on. "Rarity" would have to precede the "R's," but we have precedent for that with "Aristotles Philosophie"; and besides, "Reason" precedes the "R" above "Retirement" already.[7]

Along with the other anomalies we have the great disparity in length of the entries themselves. Many are quite short, like "Circulation," no more than a sentence: "Tris [megistus] defineth Circulation to be a Motion which is always carried about the same."[8] Others go on, column after column. I emphasize the physical flexibility of the Commonplace Book because I think it suggests a quality which asserts itself more and more in Traherne's prose style, a quality of encyclopedic accretion. In the notebook the author presents himself as appreciative reader, thus asserting his dependence on others. Implicitly the act of reading is one of evaluating, selecting, gathering, and preserving, but also of reordering into a new and still expanding whole. As Carol Marks writes, Traherne "jumped from section to section of the book, paraphrasing extensively, adding comments (usually brief, sometimes a good paragraph in length), using his source as a point of departure for an expanded consideration of the same topic, sometimes lending the flavor of his own personality to Gale's aridities."[9] More than a comment on Traherne's eclecticism, this description suggests the way in which the Commonplace Book should be read. For Traherne, reading was no passive performance. As the mind selects, it alters its material, placing the most striking ideas into relief. In effect, Traherne supplies his book with directions to the reader who, like the author, must use the "Word" for an end transcending the moment of perusal. Behind the mask of the antiquarian compositor is the teacher-creator who makes sense out of the seemingly formless mass of raw experience.

Interesting resemblances indicate that the Commonplace Book may have been used in preparing a draft of *Christian Ethicks* (1675), from a philosophical point of view probably Traherne's most important work. Though apparently the author did not copy directly from the notebook, slightly different versions of two passages from Hermes appear in both works and run contiguously in the *Ethicks*.[10] Further, many headings in the notebook remind us of those in the published work: "Essence," "Ethicks," "Liberalitie," "Omnipotence," "Prudence," "Sagacitie," "Virtue." The same is true of the Early Notebook, where the questions summarized in the "Ethica" section ("Quid est Prudentia, Bonum, Intellectus, Liberum Arbitrium, Virtue, Justitia, Temperantia, Magnificentia?") read like "The Contents" of Traherne's own work: "Of Prudence," "Right Reason," "Of Goodness," "Of Virtue," "The Will," "Of Justice," "Of Temperance," "Of Magnificence," and so on.[11] In short, just as Traherne copies from other authors, he also copies from himself copying them.

Just what actual connections of a genetic kind exist between the notebooks on the one hand and the *Ethicks* on the other is hard to tell. But of one thing we may be sure: they are all of them put together in the same way, composed of bits and pieces of other works. At the same time in *Christian Ethicks* we have much more than a commonplace book; the author is no mere scribe, recording interesting or edifying moments from his reading experience. He is not a reader at all. In the early notebooks the compositor who shapes the whole is the project director, the intelligent reader, the critic, but he is, nevertheless, defined and shaped almost wholly by what he reads. In *Christian Ethicks* the author presents himself as the spiritual guide whose purpose it is to mold and shape others: "My Office," he declares, "is, to carry and enhance *Vertue*," and his technique is to draw "out of the *Treasuries* of *Humanity* those Arguments that will discover the great perfection of the *End* of Man..." (p. 3).[12]

As with so many areas of life in the seventeenth century, the subject of Traherne's treatise at the time of his writing was in the midst of upheaval. Probably the two most important works on ethics at that time were Hugo Grotius' *De jure belli et pace* (1625) and the *Leviathan* (1651) of Thomas Hobbes, works which had challenged the received bases of ethical norms. Both works sought to establish public criteria for evaluating social behavior and, as such, represent important departures from those views which presupposed the natural monopoly of religion in ethical disputes. Both works are strongly imbued with the secular influences discussed in the previous chapter. Rhetorically, *Christian Ethicks* must be seen as part of a reaction against these influences. A rebuttal to the legalistic arguments being generated in the academies, Traherne's work has much in common with Roger Coke's criticism of Hugo Grotius, Thomas White, and Thomas Hobbes. In *Justice Vindicated* (1660) Coke attacks the principle which he believes is common to all three men: namely, the view that one may reduce all morality to *"Pacts and contracts of Men in a parity and equal condition."*[13] Such a reduction amounts to a quantitative description of virtue. To Coke, the new legalism in ethics declared that goodness and evil were purely matters of convention or taste. Morality had been cast out; no longer an issue of man's will, it had become a method of describing bodily movements. It seems to me that Traherne's ethical treatise shares many of the conservative elements of this analysis.

Though Traherne had great enthusiasm for certain aspects of what we now call the "new science" (its conception of unlimited space, for instance), still, he had his reservations too. So much has been said about Donne's reaction to Copernicanism that we often miss the point of those famous lines, with which Traherne would likely have agreed:

> And new Philosophy cals all in doubt,
> The Element of fire is quite put out;
> The Sunne is lost, and th' earth, and no man's wit
> Can well direct him, where to looke for it.
> And freely men confesse, that this world's spent,
> When in the Planets, and the Firmament
> They seeke so many new; they see that this
> Is crumbled out againe to his Atomis.

49

'Tis all in pieces, all cohearence gone.
All just supply, and all Relation:
Prince, Subject, Father, Sonne, are things forgot,
For every man alone thinkes he hath got
To be a Phoenix, and that there can bee
None of that kinde, of which he is, but hee.[14]

He could have agreed without joining the "counter-Renaissance" wholeheartedly because, very simply, Donne is not talking about what man has learned about planets. He uses one
instance of scientific discovery because it seems appropriate to
the feelings of disintegration within man which are the subject
of the poem. Man's inner cosmos has lost its center of gravity,
which is always and of necessity in such things as loyalty and
family ties. I say in such things because, again, Donne is dealing
with only one of numerous possible examples of the unity, once
apparent among men, which has disappeared. The explosion in
the mind has rent the fabric of love and cooperation among
men; and in the place of older values one finds the absurd conception of man as deity, bestowing immortality upon himself.
For Donne, the *hybris* implicit here was a logical outcome of
the secular reductionism one recognized on all sides: the universe defined as "just supply, and all relation."

In *Christian Ethicks*, Traherne totally reverses the emphasis.
He never manifests the tone of the First Anniversary because
he completely ignores the quantitative issue of "supply, and . . .
relation." Though an admirer of Bacon,[15] one might say he not
only ignores the senses but the world itself. Further (and perhaps this is more surprising), his ethical discussion explicitly
excludes questions of conduct, which (like the doctrinal issues
supposedly excluded from *Roman Forgeries*) had already been
adequately treated:

I need not treat of Vertues in the ordinary way, as they are *Duties*
enjoyned by the Law of GOD; *that* the Author of *The whole Duty
of Man* hath excellently done: nor as they are *Prudential Expedients*
and *Means* for a mans Peace and Honour on Earth; *that* is in some
measure done by the *French Charron* of Wisdom. [P. 3]

In a work like *The Whole Duty of Man* one might find a good
deal of practical advice, down even to specific instructions on

when and where to pray.[16] But in contrast Traherne shows little interest in the practical and formal aspects of piety. Indeed, he seems to avoid discussion of conduct completely, an aversion which fits well with his antipathy for the growing secularism of his age. After all, conduct is the potential meeting place of that dubious triumvirate of humankind: "Custom, Action, [and] Desire."

Traherne's implicit denial of the secular foundation of ethics goes further than Coke's, which places considerable emphasis on the virtue of justice. Traherne makes no effort to distinguish justice from the other virtues. His own discussion of justice turns on the contrast between its divine and human forms: hence, he treats the fall of angels along with reward and punishment in human society. At times the two realms seem to merge, but toward the end of the section the author veers away from issues of conduct to subject matter and diction closer to St. Teresa's "Conceptions of the Love of God" than to *Justice Vindicated*: "Every soul is the Bride of God: and his own infinite Goodness, which deserves infinite Love, is infinitely Beloved by him. He infinitely tenders it and avoids its least Displeasure" (p. 98). If God's justice is hurled against sin, that is because God's goodness has both temporal and essential priority over sin. Rather than a discussion of classical and secular virtues, Traherne's brief chapter on justice is actually part of a larger "Design . . . to reconcile Men to GOD" (p. 6).

Literary forms of theodicy assume special importance in periods of radical challenge to accustomed epistemological assumptions. *Paradise Lost* is the major poetic evidence that the late Renaissance was just such a period. When one asks how man knows, or what he can know, he manifests the anxiety of one whose suspicion it is that man's knowledge is either trivial or nonexistent. One way to handle such anxiety is seen in the declaration of man as phoenix, potentially godlike, rising from the ashes of his own mortality. This is the thrust of Pico's *Oration on the Dignity of Man*, which Traherne loved and emulated. But the expansive view of human potentialities did not go unchallenged. We need only look at the debate between Luther and Erasmus—or at Calvin's *Institutes*—to see the many ways in which the proposition that man possessed angelic qualities might be qualified or undermined completely in the area of religion.

But neither did the issue rest with the foundations of theology shaken. The Reformation had exposed philosophical assumptions just as vulnerable to skeptical criticism as the supremacy doctrine. The crisis of faith in the established church was no more or less than the harbinger of an all-embracing crisis of faith in knowledge itself. *Roman Forgeries* had dealt merely with one of the piecemeal cavils of perhaps the most significant intellectual disruption in the history of western civilization. It was one thing to challenge the validity of a particular document or truth claim: one could without disturbing the primary assumptions of anyone deny the doctrine of papal infallibility. It was quite another matter to deny the relevance of all councils and of all church tradition excluding Scripture. Perhaps this is why *Roman Forgeries* strikes the modern reader as quaint: while attacking one sect of Christendom, Traherne energetically assumes the importance of those traditional helps toward salvation external to the individual long insisted upon by Rome. More than once he insists that he is a champion of the Catholic church, and in *Christian Ethicks* he insists "that there is not the least *tittle* pertaining to the *Catholick Faith* contradicted or altered in his [text]" (p. 5). Nevertheless, the die had long been cast, and as Erasmus and others so well understood, the question of the place of conscience in salvation was not so far removed from the problem of knowledge in general: By what standard does man have certain knowledge of salvation? Of God? Of anything?

Defenders of tradition were not slow to perceive the gravity of the situation, and they responded in the only way they knew —with the arsenal of scholasticism—by pressing forward the logical dilemmas in which the man of the Reformation found himself. They pointed out, for instance, that rebellion against Rome on the basis of the individual's faith (and Scripture) presumed the infallibility of the individual conscience, the very proposition in reverse which Protestants denied the pope. Further, it was illogical to bring about the total disintegration of the church which one claimed to serve. This argument is part of the conservatism of *Roman Forgeries*; expropriated by the archsecularist Hobbes, it becomes the major underpinning of *Leviathan*, where the individual conscience (and the individual point of view in general) requires the check of an instrument outside the self. If no unquestioned authority or premise exists, then man is left with moral and civil anarchy; this is the view of those who argued in favor of central authority, whether of cross or crown. Finally, how could one advance arguments criticizing Rome, and propose that these arguments be taken seriously, when the universe of rational discourse had been replaced by private conscience and passion? As if in one final act of obeisance to scholasticism, the Protestants also attacked the Catholics with logical antinomies: if only the pope were infallible, then only he could know that he was the pope. Religious wars had generated a renewed philosophical insight: every proposition presented as true depended upon acceptance of another proposition, which, when likewise examined, assumed another, and so on, ad infinitum.

One of the landmarks of the counter-Renaissance was Henry Cornelius Agrippa's pessimistic *Of the Vanitie . . . of Artes and Sciences* (1569). This treatise was designed to test the claim of all philosophers that study of the arts and sciences would "bring unto man some Divinitie . . . so that oftentimes, beyonde the limites of Humanitie, they may be reckoned among the felowship of the Godds."[17] For Agrippa, this belief was both profoundly dangerous and patently false. To prove his point he takes virtually the sum total of the various disciplines one by one, leaving scarcely any man's claim to helpful knowledge untried. But Agrippa's work is not typical of the philosophical debate which dominated the latter half of the century. Agrippa falls back on the association between knowledge and the Fall,[18] and he is openly Philistine in his hatred of academic pretense (somewhat like the Milton of *Paradise Regained*). But the strongest challenge to Florentine eclecticism came not from fundamentalists like Agrippa and Savonarola. Probably the most influential single work of the skeptical reaction was the *Hypotyposes* of Sextus Empiricus, which was published for the first time in the modern world in 1562.

In his *Outlines of Pyrrhonism* Sextus gave voice to the dominant attitude which was to pervade the skepticism of Montaigne. The greatest of Renaissance skeptics, Montaigne, had lines from Sextus Empiricus inscribed on the beams of his study.[19] The antecedent of his arch abdication, "What do I know?" is in Book I of the *Outlines* where Sextus discusses the expressions "I suspend Judgment" and "I determine nothing." The aim in chapters 22 and 23 of that work is to refute the philosophical assumptions of the Dogmatists: "The phrase 'I suspend judgment' we adopt in place of 'I am unable to say which of the objects presented I ought to believe and which I ought to disbelieve'." The substance and tone are intended to impute presumption to anyone who claims sufficient grounds for belief: "Regarding the phrase 'I determine nothing' this is what we say. We hold that 'to determine' is not simply to state a thing but to put forward something non-evident combined with assent. For in this sense, no doubt, it will be found that the Sceptic determines nothing, not even the very proposition 'I determine nothing'."[20]

In the *Apology for Raymond Sebond* we find something of Agrippa's disparagement of particular disciplines, just as we do in Descartes' *Discourse on Method*. But in both of these works the philosophical issue of what constitutes proof is much more important than the separate faults of pedantic studies. The answers given by these two important figures were of course quite different. In his own way Descartes tears down only to reconstruct an expansive and optimistic system: the universe as comprehensible to human ego and intellect. Montaigne is much closer to the Pyrrhonism of Sextus; and his views are not far from those of Englishmen like Greville, Donne, Herbert of Cherbury, Webster, and Ford.

Just as *Roman Forgeries* dealt with a sectarian dispute common to the time, *Christian Ethicks* confronts the most important philosophical problem generated by the Reformation. The work is more deeply a part of the Pyrrhonian crisis than has generally been recognized. Perhaps this is a result partly of the fact that if critics read the *Ethicks* at all, they read it only in relation to some other work such as the *Centuries*. I think, too, that a stereotype of Traherne has tended to blur the actual views represented in the work. For many of his readers Traherne is the simple if not simple-minded man of piety whose literary portrait has been drawn by the anonymous biographer of the *Thanksgivings*.[21] But like Aubrey's life of Herbert, certainly this sketch does not fit the facts of Traherne's extraordinary learning and sophistication. Even the pietistic material of the *Ethicks* must not be taken uncritically but seen in relation to the strategy of the work as a whole. Traherne makes clear right at the outset of the book that he is dealing with an important problem of philosophy, and that his presumably less sophisticated reader may encounter certain "New Notions." The only author Traherne mentions by name in the front matter is Montaigne's most precocious disciple, Pierre Charron. Author of the deeply Pyrrhonist *De la Sagesse* (1601), which was extremely popular in England and which Traherne read and admired, Charron was known to many in his time as a *libertin* and (worse) an *athée couvert*.[22]

The tone of Charron's work never quite reaches the supernal indignation of his mentor, but he goes far in that direction: "Vanity," he writes, "is the most essentiall and proper quality of humane nature. There is nothing so much in man, be it malice, infelicity, inconstancy, irresolution (and of all these there is alwaies abundance) as base feeblenesse, sotishnesse, and ridiculous vanity."[23] Never is this vanity more apparent than in man's pretensions about why and what he knows. Charron does not deny the theoretical possibility of knowledge so much as its application with man in particular: "the fault or reproach is not in learning, no more than that wine or other good drugge is faulty which a man knoweth not how to apply and accomodate to his needs: *non est culpa vini*."[24] Man is capable of knowledge, but prone to self-deception in believing that knowledge comes from the exercise of his faculties of sense and reason. The schoolmen believed that all knowledge began with the senses, which was not true. If the senses provide knowledge, then animals who possessed sense must also possess knowledge.[25] On the other hand, reason was no more reliable than sense.[26] If man would only humble himself, he would know the truth, which was that the truth was not his to know: "We are borne to search the truth, but to possesse it, belongeth to a higher and greater power."[27]

Charron's skepticism is not as complete as Montaigne's; he

seems to aim at a middle position between dogmatic poles: "Some have affirmed that [the senses] never deceive us, and when they seem to doe it, the fault proceedeth from some thing els; and that we must rather attribute it to any other thing than to the senses. Others have sayd cleane contrary, that they are all false, and can teach us nothing that is certaine. But the middle opinion is the more true."[28] We may infer from the Commonplace Book that Traherne was quite interested in this kind of argument. One of the longer entries is given over to "Scepticisme," several longish paragraphs dealing with the history of Pyrrhonism, the types of skepticism, its philosophical implications, and (from Traherne's point of view) its strengths as well as weaknesses.[29] Accordingly, we read that "we must not precipitately Judge," but rather "suspend our assent, as was the practice of Plato and his Successours in the old Academie."[30] Traherne seems to be sympathetic neither with the dogmatics, who argue that their knowledge is certain, nor with the skeptics who insist with equal fervor that all knowledge is impossible: these men "consider a matter but never determine anything."[31]

Traherne allows that certain forms of skepticism may endanger religion, but he also records indications of a sympathy with aspects of Pyrrhonism:

Albeit Scepticisme be a thing of dangerous consequence, yet it is not wholly to be condemned in things natural [?], as it was used in its first Original So Although there are many things, if we will not precipitately erre, we must not precipitately Judge.[32]

In other words, skepticism is a valuable stance toward any truth claims about the natural world. One must discern the boundary between useful and self-deceiving doubt: the former always concerns truth claims with respect to things external to the self, exactly those objects of inquiry excluded from *Christian Ethicks*. In the notebook entry what seems to interest Traherne is the point at which skepticism becomes a self-contradicting dogma, when "suspension of Judgment" ceases to be a technique of restraint in the absence of sufficient reason for assent and becomes instead a habit of mind governing both the means and the end of reflection. He seems to understand that uncertainty may refer to either a species of argument or a propensity of spirit, while the aim of his own effort in this area is to establish the one absolute certainty: the condition entitled "Felicity."

Before considering particular virtues, Traherne dedicates two chapters to the means by which man becomes acquainted with his own innocence. Chapter 4, "*Of the Powers and Affections of the Soul*," concerns the issues of free will and election: How does a man know that he is in "*the Estate of Grace*" and "*the estate of Glory*"? Traherne's answer is partly that of faculty psychology: the intellect or understanding makes man "see" the world, and the will operates freely so that he may "atchieve Glory [in his] actions" (p. 29). Indeed, all the affections or "Faculties of the Soul" operate on the two materials of felicity: anger, appetite, fear, reason, desire, hope, love, joy, all of which are the measure of the world within man. Too much of a particular affection vis-à-vis a particular object can skew the pattern of man's existence, which is to experience "Felicity." The knowledge of his "estate" and the experience of "Felicity" are one and the same thing. In short, knowledge is the end of a self-referential experience over which man exercises control in the form of recognizing and implementing decorum with respect to object and affection: "WHEN our own Actions are Regular [appropriate], there is nothing in the World but may be made conducive to our highest Happiness" (p. 30).

Before there can be felicity there must be knowledge:

WITHOUT *seeing*, it is impossible to enjoy our Happiness, or find out the Way unto it; therefore is *Knowledge* necessary in all estates. [P. 30]

Here is where Traherne's theodicy comes in. In the state of "Innocency" man naturally experienced the "Transcendent Virtues." But it pleased God to require man to exercise his "natural Powers of [his] own Accord" (p. 31), and so "GOD gave [man] Liberty, in the beginning, that [he] might chuse what [he] would." Freedom is part of the decorum of the universe which allows man to create virtue:

All Goodness is spoiled by Compulsion. Our own Actions, springing from an interiour Fountain, deep within the Soul, when voluntarily and freely exerted, are more acceptable; and the Will, whence

57

they spring, is more excellent and perfect. This I would have you note well, for the intrinsick Goodness and Glory of the Soul consists in the Perfection of an excellent Will. [P. 31]

In free will lies the wellspring of felicity, for man has the power "with *Difficulty*" of properly ordering his affections and of experiencing a true acquaintance with felicity. The will is the artisan-sovereign ruling over a Leviathan of all the objects of sense or imagination, and over all the affections which they arouse, thus producing the perfect order of felicity.

Had there been no Fall there would be no need for philosophy: "In *Eden* there was no ignorance, nor any Supernatural Verities to be confirmed by Miracles; Apostles therefore and Prophets . . . were Superfluous there, and so were . . . Schools of Learning, Masters and Tutors" (p. 33). Not only would all "have been instructed by the Light of Nature," but instructive knowledge was part of an existence completely "Innocent, and Just, and Regular." In such a knowledgeable and innocent world, men would need no universities, no commerce, no courts; for institutions, like philosophical debates, are only evidences of strife. This blissful, primitive communism is a concomitant of man's acquaintance with the world, himself, and his "Fellow Citizens throughout the World." In such an estate the only "Dominion" would be "that of Husbands and Fathers, a Dominion as full of sweetness, as so gentle and free a Relation importeth" (pp. 33-34). It follows from this that institutions and the sacraments themselves are the surrogates of "the clear Light of a Diviner Reason, and a free Communion with God in the Right discharge of those Virtues, Divine and Moral, which naturally belong to the Estate of Innocency" (p. 34).

Like all other institutions, the sacraments are tokens of a fallen man. Originally all virtues were combined in man, whose unified being perfectly harmonized with God and nature. In the peace of this instinctive accord with nature man developed a surrogate for divine reason in the form of intellectual capacities. But in the actual world man's knowledge always differs from the perfect light of the original. The anti-institutional values of chapter 4 may give a hint of the "New Notions" of fideism which Traherne apparently shared in some measure with Charron. Both men follow Montaigne in disparaging man's institutional claims to knowledge. Like the *Apology for Raymond Sebond* and *De la Sagesse, Christian Ethicks* is a "discourse on method." But unlike Descartes, Traherne avoids the question of restructuring a new but systematic epistemology. He addresses only the spiritual or psychological dimension of the problem: certainty. All skeptics shared the belief that the proposition "Man is capable of knowledge" was both problematic and important. Descartes seems to be saying that this proposition is not only problematic but does not lend itself to ordinary means of rational or empirical solution. In the fallen world the most monumental erudition could not extricate one from the single enduring fact of fallen consciousness: uncertainty. Indeed, the same discord prevailing in the world of commerce could be seen in the intellectual collisions among factions in the universities.

This emphasis on fallen nature seems to give Traherne something in common with John Calvin. Yet no figure would be less sympathetic with Traherne's attitude toward the Fall. It is one thing to say that man is limited, and quite another to build a system emphasizing that belief:

IT is a great Error to mistake the *Vizor* for the *Face*, and no less to stick in the outward *Kind* and Appearance of things; mistaking the Alterations and Additions that are made upon the Fall of Man, for the whole Business of Religion. And yet this new Constellation of Vertues, that appeareth aboveboard, is almost the only thing talked of and understood in the World. Whence it is that the other Duties, which are the *Soul* of Piety, being unknown, and the *Reason* of these together with their Original and Occasion, unseen; Religion appears like a sour and ungratefull Thing to the World, impertinent to bliss, and void of Reason; Whereupon GOD is suspected and hated, Enmity against GOD and *Atheism* being brought into, and entertained in the World. [P. 34]

One avenue to atheism is overemphasis on man as the passive victim of circumstance, internal or external. Behind the rhetoric of this passage is Traherne's strong interest in the free will controversy.[33] Calvin believed that every movement in the universe was "governed by the secret counsel of God"; and this determinism applies a fortiori to the will: "man will be said to possess free will in this sense, not that he has an equally free election of good and evil, but because he does evil voluntarily, and not by constraint."[34] Emphasis on the corrupt passions of man tended to strengthen the Calvinist position, for man was the victim of psychological faculties over which he had no control. As the humanists tried to point out, determinism allows man no capacity which, by existing apart from the quality of his acts, might enable him to contemplate possible actions with respect to alternative ends: "Whereupon GOD is suspected and hated," says Traherne, and Burton gives the explicit reason that under this view "God should be the author of sin."[35]

It is no wonder that sin and the Fall receive little attention from Traherne: "I do not speak much of *Vice*, which is far the more easie Theme, because I am taken up with the abundance of Worth and Beauty in *Vertue*" (p. 3). This comment relates to the frequently disputed question of Traherne's Pelagianism.[36] As the debate between Luther and Erasmus makes clear, the issue is logical rather than theological. Logically, Luther was right in saying that the abstract conception of free will precludes all ideas of constraint, however minor. Nevertheless, the critics who place Traherne in the line leading from the humanists are right in part: he emphasizes the power of man's will. Probably Traherne was in sympathy with the Arminians at Oxford, who in his day were the main opponents of Calvin.

The Arminians sought a middle ground between the felt secularism of Pelagius on the one hand and the determinism of Calvin on the other. Traherne insists on man's power to know and do the good, but he also differentiates man from God:

I will not deny, but that there are many Disorders and Evils in the World, many Deformities, Sins, and Miseries: but I say two things; first that in the Estate of innocency, wherein all things proceeded purely from GOD, there was no Sin, nor Sickness, nor Death, nor Occasion of Complaint or Calamity. Secondly, that all the Evils that are now in the world, men brought on themselves by the Fall: And there is great need of distinguishing between the works of GOD, and the works of men. [P. 53]

Traherne specifically rejects the notion that man is naturally inclined toward the good. This is the point of his distinction between habit and "Natural Disposition" (p. 25). Though they may seem very different, the Earl of Shaftesbury and Calvin really argue for the same insignificance of human choice; Traherne is at pains to separate all instinctive behavior from dispositions of the will:

THE Powers of the Soul, are not vertues themselves, but when they are clothed with vertuous Operations, they are transformed into Vertues. For Powers are in the Soul, just as Limbs and Members in the Body, which may indifferently be applied to Vertues and Vices. [P. 26]

An "inbred inclination" whether to do well or ill reduces man to a bestial existence, responding to motives and impulses over which he exercises no control. Traherne presses this point by distinguishing infused from acquired habits. The infused habit, even though it may result in the same act or consequence as an acquired habit, cannot possibly result in virtue, for its source (in grace) lies outside of man. Virtue derives only from "Improvement and exercise" of such infused habits, and here the will comes into operation. Graces flow through a passive spirit without the actions of the will: "These Dispositions, because they do not flow from our Choise and industry, cannot be accounted Virtues," for men "are Passive in [their] reception" (p. 25). Beasts lack the quality of discernment, responding automatically to either instinctive or learned impulses; and of course they are incapable of moral decisions (p. 15).

Christian Ethicks is Traherne's *de libero arbitrio*. Doubtless he was steeped in the literature of the subject, which was extremely popular at Oxford and Cambridge in his time. Most of the important intellectuals of the Caroline and Jacobean period had their say on the nature of the will, men like William Perkins, Richard Hooker, Henry More, Peter Sterry, Roger Coke, Thomas Hobbes, Robert Burton, John Milton. Likely all of them had read the classic statements by St. Augustine, St. Thomas, Calvin, Luther, and Arminius. As a divinity student Traherne had been exposed to the controversy, and judging from *Christian Ethicks*, he considered it important. He thought of free will as the *sine qua non* of human dignity:

THAT Vertues might be *ours*, in being wrought by *our selves*; and be Vertues *indeed*, in being wrought with *Difficulty*; that we might be so much the more Laudable and Glorious in our eternal Condition, GOD gave us Liberty, in the beginning, that we might chuse what we would, and placed us in such an Estate; that, having in us only the Seeds and Principles of all Vertue, we might exercise our natural Powers of our own Accord, for the Attainment of that actual Knowledge, Wisdom and Righteousness, wherein the Perfection of our soul consisteth, and by which the Perfection of our Bliss is to be enjoyed. That being Naked by Nature, tho Pure and clean, we might cloath our selves with our own *Habits*, attain the Glory of those Ornaments, in our own Acts, for which we were created; And work our *own* Righteousness, in such a Way as GOD had appointed. [P. 31][37]

This passage, which could easily have been written by Pico, clearly reflects Traherne's libertarianism. But in an important sense Traherne has little in common with humanists like Bacon or Cowley—or even with the Milton who wrote "Of Education." All of these men believed in the advancement of learning; they were concerned with curricula, and all thought of themselves as part of an onrushing development of human knowledge which aimed unerringly at the improvement of society. Traherne is not part of this movement; he never writes an "Ode to the Royal Society," much less a *Novum Organum*. Though he seems to have been interested in the scientific revolution going on around him, he gives small notice to the world in the way Bacon thought of it.

We can distinguish at least two lines of libertarian humanism, and each leads in a different direction. The Baconian path inclines toward space exploration and social work; it is the way of empiricism, and it furnished direction for the modern world. The other line was already narrowing toward extinction in the secular landscape of the Enlightenment: this is the way of solipsism or of mysticism or both. Traherne's solution is far from neither Berkeley nor Descartes: "THE principal objects of our Knowledge are GOD, and a Mans self" (p. 41). His

answer to skepticism is to modify his scope: *Nosce teipsum.*
With Charron, Traherne avoids the issue of how man knows
about the world. His epistemology involves the senses, in that
they operate fully in perceiving and enjoying both the world
and "Felicity." But for Traherne the *reductio* of the scientists
was a species of error by omission. By limiting his range of discourse, Traherne was able to add discrete instances of knowledge at will. Thus, all knowledge is an aspect of the author's
literary and intellectual freedom.

Paradoxically, Traherne's limited range allows a treatise of
personal ethics to be also a *summa* of man's knowledge. Virtue
and knowledge are inextricably related:

KNOWLEDGE is that which does illuminate the Soul, enkindle
Love, excite our Care, inspire the mind with Joy, inform the Will,
enlarge the Heart, regulate the Passions, unite all the Powers of the
Soul to their Objects, see their Beauty, understand their Goodness,
discern our Interest in them, form our Apprehensions of them, con-
sider and enjoy their Excellences. All Contentments, Raptures, and
Extasies are conceived in the Soul, and begotten by Knowledge, all
Laws, Obligations and Rewards are understood by Knowledg: All
Vertues and Graces of the Mind are framed by Knowledge. [P. 39]

This is so because one must know an object before he can desire
or love it. Since all things were made to be enjoyed—by God as
well as man—it follows that perfection of man's knowledge is
essential to "Felicity." Self-knowledge is the beginning of love:
for what a man knows he naturally loves. It would not be wrong
to think of Traherne as a theological hedonist: "For to be
Pleased, and to love are the same thing" (p. 44), he writes. God
was pleased to create the world, and he created everything in it
to please himself.

So the universe flows from the fountain of God's self-love.
Here lay the answer to one of the great paradoxes posed by
skepticism: How is it possible for finite man to be acquainted
with infinite Deity? The answer was, again, through knowledge and love of self:

The Knowledge of a Mans self is highly conducive to his Happiness, not only as it gives him Power to rejoyce in his Excellencies,
but as it shews him his End, for which he was created. For by

Knowing what Inclinations and Powers are in his Soul, he discerns what is agreeable with, and fit for his Essence. . . . If the Powers of his Soul are illimited, his Desire infinite, and his Reach Eternal, if he be able to see and enjoy all Worlds, and all that is above all Worlds in the Image of GOD [p. 42],

then he by definition knows and loves the infinite by knowing and loving the infinite in himself. This view is the Trahernean analogue to Descartes' "*Cogito*." But Traherne rejects the rigors of Descartes just as he does the Pyrrhonism of Montaigne. For him, the proper way to deal with doubt was to replace it with certainty, a mental set totally antithetical to Montaigne's "What do I know?" Traherne's solution is nothing like Calvin's, in that Traherne directs attention away from signs and tokens. God is knowable, and "Felicity" is an accomplished fact of the speaker's existence.

In his address "To the Reader" Traherne suggests that one aim of the *Ethicks* will be to convince the doubtful and put atheism to flight. It was an aim he shared with Charron. The entire strategy of the work is based on the relation of the speaker to his audience. The reader may have doubts, but they are derived from his ignorance. The speaker's role as spiritual guide is predicated upon knowledge in its "experimental" or experiential form. He presents as his credentials "many years [of] earnest and diligent study" among the objects of "Felicity" (p. 3). The pathway to this experience is through intimate acquaintance with the self and the universe: "For by Knowing what Inclinations and Powers are in his Soul [man is] . . . able to see and enjoy all Worlds." Thus, to know the self and to know the universe are identical cognitive acts; in the part inheres the whole:

HE that would not be a stranger to the Universe, an Alien to Felicity, and a foreiner to himself, must Know GOD to be an infinite Benefactor, all Eternity, full of Treasures, the World it self, the Beginning of Gifts, and his own Soul the Possessor of all, in Communion with the Deity. [Pp. 41-42]

This is a theme to which Traherne frequently returns: in the macrocosm the parts all respond to each other in loving harmony, each reflecting the majesty and unity of the whole. The minuscular figure is an appropriate figure of God's image in the soul of man; by a divine geometry the apparently minuscular image of God in the soul is like the multifaceted sand crystal, infinitely extended in its full relation to the universe.

Traherne's philosophy of time enters here. Like Augustine he thinks of all time as eternally present in the soul:

> In all Things, all Things service do to all:
> And thus a Sand is Endless, though most small.
> And every Thing is truly Infinite,
> In its Relation deep and exquisite.
>
> [P. 181]

Each man therefore recapitulates the sum total of the human drama; he is Adam and Noah and Samson and David. In the lines from the poem just quoted I think we perceive an expansive feature characteristic of the structure of the *Ethicks* as a whole. The "Sand is Endless" by virtue of its rich capacity to suggest "its Relation deep and exquisite"; the single object is valuable in that it provides an occasion to recognize and ponder totality. But the connection here is not logical. Structurally, the paragraphs, the sentences, and the chapters of the *Ethicks* do not develop logically. Indeed, we have no basis for predicting the way in which the chapters will unfold, what virtues will be included, and where.

In chapter 3 of *Leviathan* (1651), Thomas Hobbes describes the "TRAYNE of Thoughts" which pass as the succession of ideas in the mind: "When a man thinketh on any thing whatsoever, His next Thought after, is not altogether so casuall as it seems to be. Not every Thought to every Thought succeeds indifferently." In the twentieth century this feature of mental discourse, especially in literature, has been called the stream of consciousness, and in various forms it provides the material of psychoanalysis. Freud believed that every sequence of thoughts, however absurd, has a meaningful explanation in the context of the patient's biography. In this view Freud followed in the footsteps of many, including Thomas Hobbes, who divided his "TRAYNE of Thoughts" into "*regulated*" and "*unguided*" species. The latter of these appeared to be "*without*

65

Designe, and unconstant." In such cases, "the thoughts are said to wander, and seem impertinent one to another, as in a Dream." On the contrary, Hobbes argues that even in this unguided "wild ranging of the mind, a man may oft-times perceive the way of it, and the dependance of one thought upon another." To prove his point Hobbes analyzes an apparent solecism:

For in a Discourse of our present civill warre, what could seem more impertinent, than to ask (as one did) what was the value of a Roman Penny? Yet the Cohaerence to me was manifest enough. For the Thought of the warre, introduced the Thought of the delivering up of the King to his Enemies; The Thought of that, brought in the Thought of the delivering up of Christ; and that again the Thought of the 30 pence, which was the price of that treason: and thence easily followed that malicious question; and all this in a moment of time; for Thought is quick.[38]

The second or *"regulated"* sort of mental discourse includes all ratiocinative forms, which are limited to man, and the more simple (trial and error) judgment of cause and effect by which both man and beast seek desirable ends.

In the context of this analytic structure, the principle of organization in *Christian Ethicks* appears to be as "unguided" as it is "regulated." Succession of one thought to another is frequently alogical, or it may contradict earlier discussion completely. Although in chapter 3 Traherne outlines the plan of discussion, he does not follow it. The main section of the *Ethicks* is the second, which is divided into five parts, treating of the five species of virtue outlined in chapter 3. In the outline itself Traherne more than doubles the number of Theological virtues by adding to the usual triumvirate repentance, obedience, devotion, and godliness. He considers as Intellectual those virtues "seated in the Understanding": intelligence, wisdom, science, prudence, and art. Prudence appears again under Traherne's version of the *"Cardinal Vertues,"* which he calls *"Practical"* or *"Moral."* To prudence, justice, temperance, and fortitude Traherne adds magnificence, liberality, modesty, magnanimity, gentleness, affability, courtesy, truth, and urbanity. He calls goodness, righteousness, and holiness "Divine virtues," and the remaining "Christian virtues" are meekness and humility.

I render the list intact because I think it suggests a quality of Traherne's method of organization. The most noticeable anomaly is the duplication of prudence, which appears under the rubrics of both Intellectual and Moral virtues but seems to be treated only among the "heroic." Then too, Traherne includes a number of virtues in his outline to which he never dedicates a chapter: obedience, devotion, intelligence, science, gentleness, affability, courtesie, urbanity. Just as he omits, he also adds chapters on virtues never mentioned in his outline: mercy, patience, contentment, and most important, gratitude, which takes up the last two chapters and figures importantly in the "Appendix." One senses a lack of parallelism, an inconsistency throughout the work. Why, for instance, should "godliness" be one of the Theological virtues, and holiness not? Are charity and obedience parallel virtues? What is the principle of inclusion and exclusion operating in the work?

We get a hint of Traherne's structural procedure in chapter 3, when after mentioning the predictable virtues, faith, hope, and charity, he writes "To which we may add *Repentence*" (p. 23), going on to add, "to which, if we are making them more, we may add *Obedience*, Devotion, Godliness." Though Traherne follows through on his promise to eliminate certain of the Intellectual virtues, the general effect of his shifts from the outline is additive. And if we examine these additions we see the "way" of them. For instance, chapters 5 through 12 treat what Traherne calls the Divine virtues, knowledge, truth, wisdom, righteousness, goodness, and holiness. Chapters 6 and 7 are digressions on love, which continue the thematic union between knowledge and love, but they have no topical relation to the outline itself. With the beginning of chapter 13, "Of Justice," we appear to be entering a section on the Moral virtues. This expectation is firmly grounded in our previous experience; the "regulated" train of thoughts is stipulated in chapter 3: "THE *Moral Vertues* are either Principal, or less Principal. The *Principal* are four: *Prudence, Justice, Temperance,* and *Fortitude*" (p. 24). But what we find in chapter 13 does not correspond to this "design."

Though the chapter heading provides no reason to suspect a shift, the text begins with this explanation:

THO following the common Course of Moralists, in our Distribution of Vertues, we have seated *Justice* among the Cardinal *Moral*; yet upon second Thoughts we find reason to reduce it to the number of *Divine* Vertues, because upon a more neer and particular Inspection, we find it to be one of the Perfections of *GOD*, and under that notion shall discover its Excellence far more compleatly, then if we did contemplate its Nature, as it is limited and bounded among the Actions of Men. [P. 94]

We might observe that the same point would apply to most of these virtues. But it is sufficient to notice that the shift from the earlier outline comes as an afterthought or insight concerning the restraints implied by the category "Moral." It is just this implied restraint which leads Traherne to distinguish his purpose in writing the *Ethicks* from the aims of Richard Allestree[39] and Pierre Charron. Traherne's comment now makes very clear that the author violates the boundaries he himself has set up on the justifiable grounds of completeness. He exceeds the limits precisely because they are "limited and bounded."

This shift helps explain Traherne's principle of inclusion in the *Ethicks*. Traherne adds discussions of virtues not mentioned in plans laid out in the general outline. In fact, one of these discussions follows "Of Justice," which ends on the thought of divine justice and of God's "Dominion" over the universe. Perhaps, as Hobbes believed, the mind pursued some dimly understood connection between "Dominion" and arbitrary judgment (as if Traherne thought of Providence and Calvin invariably together). In any case, the speaker adds that God's "Dominion ... cannot be Arbitrary (in a loose Construction) because it is infinitely *Divine* and Glorious" (p. 98). Then, as if this is somehow an insufficient refutation of determinism, Traherne launches, unannounced, into a new chapter, "Of Mercy," clearly intended as a companion piece to "Justice." As we can see from the first paragraph of this new chapter, the departure from plan is rooted in thoughts growing out of the already altered topic of Justice:

68

SUCH is the infinite Justice of God, and the Severity of his Displeasure at Sin, his Holiness so Pure, and his Nature so irreconcilable, his Hatred so real and infinite against it, that when a Sin is committed, his Soul is alienated from the Author of the Crime. [P. 99]

Once the first change has been made, the others follow, like parentheses within parentheses. Regardless of what had been proposed, the speaker's thoughts go from God's justice to his mercy. We have generated an addition to the material of the work, which precedes another shift. Following "Of Mercy" Traherne does not resume discussion of the Moral virtues, but turns instead to a completely different category, which occupies the next five chapters: faith, hope, repentance, charity. The connection is again one of appropriate association rather than logic; these virtues appear at this point "because by them alone a Sinner is restored" (p. 106). They are the instruments of God's mercy. One shift or inconsistency provides the occasion for another, and Traherne never revises to bring them into accord with the design of chapter 3.

We see the same thing but even more explicitly in chapter 27, entitled "Of Contentment," a virtue not mentioned earlier. Traherne is mindful of the shift, and he explains it:

THOUGH we have not named it, in our first distribution of Vertue into its several kinds, yet the commendation which Contentment hath in Scripture, imports it to be a Vertue: so does the difficulty of attaining it, and the great and mighty force it is of in our Lives and Conversations. [P. 216]

Emerson claimed that consistency is the hobgoblin of little minds; it is also almost the sole defining characteristic of the true case paranoiac. We have heard of the piety of *Christian Ethicks* but not of its structural inconsistency. Yet both features help to define the speaker. In the preceding chapter he has discussed the offices and rewards "Of Humility." But as he discusses he also manifests that very virtue. "Contentment" intrudes, alters, makes its own place in Traherne's book, just as the speaker in "Of Humility" dismisses "Courtesie," for which space had apparently been planned, with scarcely a mention (p. 215).

And the antinomies generated as the discussion unfolds are defining features of the speaker's virtue. There is no need for great effort to make the *Ethicks* a perfectly rational discourse: "*Contentment is a sleepy thing*" (p. 217).

The underlying principle of organization appears to be additive. As the discussion develops from moment to moment its plan changes, so that inconsistency is one of the features added along with other unplanned material. The additions, the anomalies reflect the sense of wonder which surpasses the orderly norms of public discourse. The speaker as guide must show himself as witness to "the whole Body of GODS Dispensations" (p. 116). The following remark opens the section on hope, but Traherne's mind is still on the theme of timelessness, with which he ended the previous chapter:

JANUS with his two Faces, looking backward and forward, seems to be a fit Emblem of the Soul, which is able to look on all Objects in the Eternity past, and in all Objects before, in Eternity to come. Faith and Hope are the two Faces of this Soul. By its Faith it beholdeth Things that are past, and by its Hope regardeth Things that are to come. [P. 117]

He, the speaker, is the embodiment of both virtues, uniting within himself the seemingly irreconcilable qualities of existence. Janus is the emblem of a man doing the impossible, looking in two opposite directions at once; but he not only includes times past, present, and future—with whatever inconsistence that entails. He also embraces both distant and near; this is, I believe, the rhetorical function of the additive structure—to suggest the "Body" of the speaker, "united" by "Felicity" "in all its parts, being an eternal *Monument*" to the love of God. It is not quite right to see the form as purely accretive. The emphasis is upon the moment-to-moment, dramatic creation of a mythical and comprehensive soul, through whose mind these virtuous thoughts run. This style, which is both additive and dramatic, stresses an unpredictable quality which seems to undermine rational or logical order, and for want of a better word, I shall call it an open form.

The open form of the *Ethicks* as a whole seems to be carried out in the very syntax of paragraphs and sentences. One of

Traherne's most typical techniques is what Puttenham calls the "stacking" figure, the piling up of syntactic elements, especially nouns:

THE Sun is a glorious Creature, and its Beams extend to the utmost Stars, by shining on them it cloaths them with light, and by its Rayes exciteth all their influences. It enlightens the Eyes of all the Creatures: It shineth on forty Kingdomes at the same time, on Seas and Continents in a general manner; yet so particularly regardeth all, that every Mote in the Air, every Grain of Dust, every Sand, every Spire of Grass is wholly illuminated thereby, as if it did entirely shine upon that alone. Nor does it onely illuminate all these Objects in an idle manner, its Beams are Operative, enter in, fill the Pores of Things with Spirits, and impregnate them with Powers, cause all their Emanations, Odors, Vertues and Operations; Springs, Rivers, Minerals and Vegetables are all perfected by the Sun, all the Motion, Life and sense of Birds, Beasts and Fishes dependeth on the same. [Pp. 39-40]

The more one reads Traherne the more he is struck by the incantatory, almost numinous effect of the repetition. Traherne piles up the words and phrases, taking pains to proliferate synonyms, as if the mere weight of the word itself—the word intensified and isolated by the junctures produced in series and periodic sentences—were enough to summon forth the essence of the universe in this small part. Traherne has often been compared to Wordsworth; he has much more in common with Blake or Whitman. He is a radically synechdochic figure. In an interesting essay Northrop Frye suggests that in Romanticism one discerns a marked shift in man's relation to nature, the emergence of an attitude endowing nature with numinous qualities.[40] In Traherne this same quasi-mystical attitude is invested in the word, that miniature epiphany of divine reason in man.

Like all metaphor, synechdoche is paradoxical. Though Traherne's use of language is not witty like Donne's, it is similarly paradoxical. It allows Traherne to encompass multitudes, to contradict himself without altering the validity of his perspective. Though he shares certain of his intellectual interests with the skeptics of his time, epistemologically his conception of experience and knowledge form the bulwark of his ethical stance:

IF we would *be perfect, as our Father which is in Heaven is perfect,* our Power of Knowing must be transformed (into *Act,*) and all Objects appear in the interior Light of our *own* understanding. For tho all Eternity were full of Treasures, and the Whole World, and all the Creatures in it transformed into Joys and our Interest to all never so perfect; yet if we are Ignorant of them, we shall continue as poor and Empty, as if there were nothing but Vacuity and Space. For not to *be,* and not to *appear,* are the same thing to the understanding. [Pp. 36-37]

It follows that the man who fails to express love has no love; without God's love, no universe would exist, and man is a tiny universe. Without love, he would be nothing (*et ad nihil ex nihilo*).

I think this paragraph shows the Traherne of *Christian Ethicks* at his best, which is very good indeed. Intensely Cartesian in substance, the passage is also thoroughly Christian. Beginning with a paraphrase of Scripture ("If we would be perfect . . ."), which is balanced against two parallel clauses, the first of which states a general necessity ("our Power of Knowing must be transformed . . .") while the second and longer member applies that necessity in specific relation to man's faculties, what follows is a marvelous periodic sentence, with the typical Trahernean "For . . ., and . . ." movement from one member to another. Notice that the first two clauses pit a general thematic statement against one slightly more concrete (eternity in contrast to the "Whole World"). The third member of the sentence is linked by the "yet" to the first ("for . . ."): "yet if we are Ignorant of them, we shall continue as poor and Empty, as if there were nothing but Vacuity and Space." The rhythm of the paragraph places greater stress on the second member of this clause (because "poor" is followed by a pause or single bar juncture), and the repetition of "as" makes the closing of the period a parenthetical expansion of the meaning of "Vacuity and Space." The final aphoristic sentence codifies the somewhat repetitious expatiation of the mind (what, for instance, is the logical connection between the first sentence and the last?); it restates or applies the perceptions contained in the paragraph in a more concise manner, one more striking to the intellect. In effect, the style of the paragraph attempts to make the objects of the paragraph accessible to "the interior Light of . . . [the] understanding." The complexity of the syntax of the periodic sentence ought not to "disguise" the fact that the same truth applies in all three sentences: Scripture, rumination, aphorism. A proper spiritual guide will use them all.

Not every paragraph in *Christian Ethicks* is like this one. But here as well as elsewhere in Traherne's prose—and especially in the *Centuries of Meditations*—we find plentiful use of the periodic sentence, the quotation, the proverb, the aphorism, the fragment. We find, too, increasingly mannered syntactic structures, a wide variety of prose techniques, all used with a mind toward restatement: above all, repetition is the primary stylistic underpinning of Traherne's art. Passages like this approach the resonance of the best prose in the *Centuries*. For in *Christian Ethicks* Traherne has found the mode of composition most congenial to his talent. More than a treatise on behavior, *Christian Ethicks* resembles a meditative handbook in its hortatory fervor. In its direct personal testimony it has some relation to the spiritual autobiographies of the time. It is a work in which Traherne begins to show that syntactic flexibility which is the hallmark of his anthologized style. *Christian Ethicks* is of interest not only as the most complete expression of Traherne's philosophical and religious views, nor only as a gloss on the *Centuries* and *Poems* (though it is immensely valuable to the interpretation of both), but also because of what the work reveals about Traherne's philosophy and prose style.

TRAHERNE
AND THE
MEDITATIVE
MODE

IV

The heavens declare the glory of God; and the firmament sheweth his handywork.
—Psalms 19:1

O that I were as David, the sweet Singer of Israel! In meeter Psalms to set forth thy Praises.
—Thanksgivings

In *The Metaphoric Structure of Paradise Lost* (1962), Jackson Cope relates conceptions of space and time to criticism of Milton and the metaphysical poets.[1] His aim is to place modern criticism historically, to see it as an expression of a coherent intellectual development. It is no accident that Louis L. Martz's *The Poetry of Meditation* (1954) was the last book to deal effectively with the metaphysical revival; as Cope sees it, Martz's success and the downgrading of Donne are expressions of the same phenomenon (pp. 2-11). Meditative poems are amalgams of temporal associations, attempts to join all temporal events into one still moment. Of necessity, such attempts tend to fragment the past by using the past for commentary on the present. The purpose of such structures is to internalize the truths of Christian doctrine: but if, as with St. Ignatius Loyola, a persistent emphasis on visual imagery is employed, making affective vividness the medium of internalization, the rhetorical "reality" in meditative structure (and what Martz is most concerned with) becomes the movement from time T to time T_1. The repetitive pattern is the inner process by which the meditant arrives at new insight, enters into colloquy, resolves doubt, subdues his will. Yet in every case, change presupposes the existence of time. The desired still moment of the eternal present ("union betwixt the soul and her beloved Spouse") "is dissipated, as the corporal act of the past becomes mere history" (p. 11). The poem's structure is left as a formal trace of the act of memory, understanding, will. Cope's

74

argument, then, is that the abiding material of the best meta-physical poetry is process, the psychological act of meditation.

It seems to me that Cope touches on a stylistic point of considerable importance for this study. Surely the most successful devotional works are the longer ones: Herbert's *The Temple*, Donne's *Devotions upon Emergent Occasions*, Vaughan's *Silex Scintillans*, Traherne's *Centuries of Meditations*. In the more extended works the discrete meditation cannot be read as an unrelated point in time, with its structure of mental process starkly visible in the poem's brevity. Instead, each situation makes use of memory, intellect, and will in its own way, hinting at past developments or others to come; the contours of the larger sequence are rendered less obvious and more compelling by the intensity of the movement in a given part. Threads of memory become separated and intertwined again, and relations between figures and events are elucidated. But as we move into later sections of, say, *The Temple*, we become less sure of the exact temporal relation obtaining among particular objects or events. We know that "The Altar" precedes "The Sacrifice," but how do "Church Windows," "The Crosse," and "The Bag" relate in time?

The answer may be that they do not, at least not in the same sense as do poems like "The Church-porch" and "Superliminare." In a long novel, certain events are less important than others in the cumulative development of character and plot. But as in the long novel, so in the devotional sequence, guidelines are present. Cumulative images and events in *The Temple* hint at the passage of the Christian year. And as the latter half of "The Church" unfolds, poems of inner conflict diminish in number and emphasis.[2]

There is, then, it seems to me, a relationship between the way certain seventeenth-century poets handle the themes of time and place (especially as they affect formal structure) and at least one aspect of Traherne's sense of literary form: the impossibility of predicting where chapters not included in the preliminary outline will appear in *Christian Ethicks*.[3] The sequence of chapters represents not a logical argument but a flow of ideas, a meditative unfolding, which in turn has its effect on the speaker's plan. The book changes as it is being written; Traherne does not correct, he exploits the inconsistency between chapters 3 and 22. In a provocative study of seventeenth-century prose style, Joan Webber links this strategy with a statement made by Montaigne about his own method: "I have no more made my booke, then my booke hath made me."[4]

As temporal progress diminishes in importance—and it certainly does in Traherne's work—the principle of organization changes radically. We find few examples of the rigorously defined meditation described by Martz: composition, analysis, colloquy; in Traherne's mature work the form tends to be "open." Colloquy is likely to appear at the beginning or in the middle as frequently as at the end; at any moment the speaker may burst forth in prayer. Similarly, we get the sense that a "new" meditation, an additional sequence of rumination, resolve, and prayer, may be initiated and run its course at any moment, even after the work has been "finished." Not only can "new" chapters be added any time before *Christian Ethicks* is bound, but the characteristic pattern of association which holds the chapters and paragraphs together is inclusive or additive rather than logical or developmental.

Nevertheless, in *Christian Ethicks* this open element of Traherne's prose style is not dominant. On the face of it, the work remains discursive, and even the explanations which accompany certain lapses suggest the underlying norms of rational discourse, a "regulated" train of thoughts. Not so with the better-known works, which are characteristically alogical, and which cohere by a principle other than—and even antagonistic to—logical or historical categories. In contrast to the structural features of *The Temple*, little evidence of change appears in the *Centuries of Meditations*. Instead, whatever coherence the work possesses derives from the appropriate juxtaposition of ideas and images, not by any sense of logical or mensual order. Development is a conception from logic: beginning, middle, end; major premise, minor premise, deduction. With this in mind it is not very helpful to talk about the development of the *Centuries*. For what develops? Plot? Character? Tone? What we see are collocations of images and abstractions followed only by other collocations of images and abstractions, these frequently analogous or synonymous or both. Evidences of this repetitive technique appear even in the marginalia of *Christian Ethicks*, where clusters of scriptural references identify italicized quotations in the text, which then are followed by paraphrase. Whether one or many, the scriptural verses are used not only as illustrations of Traherne's theme but as the point of departure for paraphrase:

IT is not to be denied, that every Being in all Worlds is an Object of the Understanding: nor can that of the Psalmist be doubted, *In his Presence there is fulness of Joy, and at his right hand there are Pleasures for evermore*: that is, his Omnipresence is full of Joys, and his Eternity of Riches and Pleasures: nor is it to be denied, that the Soul is by its Creation intended for the *Throne of* GOD. For it is made capable of his Omnipresence and Eternity, and, as the Apostle speaketh, *may be filled with all the fulness of* GOD.[5]

And this sentence, which could easily appear without shift of word or tone in *Meditations on the Six Days of the Creation*, continues.

A pattern of association between biblical text and image cluster is deeply ingrained in Traherne's prose manner. The method derives largely from biblical exegesis, in particular from the "testimonies," or marginal glosses linking one scripture with another or with numerous others in both testaments.[6] Other sources were available too; the method received impetus from verse paraphrase of Scripture and from iconography, including such contemporary sources as Francis Quarles's *Emblemes* (1635), a work which exercised considerable influence in the seventeenth century. Translated from a Latin handbook, these emblems are verse paraphrases of biblical texts. In much the same manner each meditation in Traherne's hexameron focuses on a verse or passage from Scripture. For example, "Meditations on the First Days Creation" is a collocation of prayers and paraphrases based on eighteen separate verses from twelve books of the Bible, including Genesis, Psalms, Isaiah, Job, Matthew, Luke, John, and Revelation, all of which emerge as "dilation" on the text:

IN *the Beginning God created the Heavens, and the Earth; and the Earth was void and without Form, and Darkness covered the Face of the Waters.* [Gen. 1:1-2][7]

In colloquy the speaker paraphrases the text and then quotes again, this time from Isaiah: "Thou hast measured the Waters in the Hollow of thine Hand" (40:12). Creation, God's power, water—imagery connects the two passages. And after this quotation, Traherne returns to the "Beginning," to the "very first Word God spake," and thus "light" and apposite images ("Darkness," "Joy," "Bliss") unfold.

In the seventeenth century, biblical commentary is closely related to formal meditation. Indeed, in some cases it is hard to differentiate the two genres. The *Contemplations* of Joseph Hall are made up of rather free ruminations, but each one presupposes a text of Scripture. This passage from "The Creation" resembles Traherne's commentary on the text "Let there be light":

But whence, O God, was that first light? the Sunne was not made till the fourth day; light the first. If man had been, he might have seene all lightsome; but whence it comme he could not have seene .... Thou madest the Sunne, madest the Light, without the Sunne, before the Sunne, that so Light might depend upon thee, and not upon thy Creature. Thy power will not be limited to meanes. It was easie to thee to make an Heaven without Sunne, Light without an Heaven, Day without a Sunne, Time without a day.... One day we shall have Light againe, without the Sunne. Thou shalt be our Sunne; thy presence shall be our light; Light is soun for the righteous. ... That light which thou shalt once give us, shall make us shine like the Sunne in glory.[8]

The method here and throughout the more than six hundred pages of Hall's *Contemplations* is strikingly close to biblical commentary. Consider, for example, Henry Ainsworth's commentary on Genesis 1:3 ("And God said, Let there be light: and there was light"):

Vers. 3. *God said*:] This sheweth God created things by his *word*; saying, and it was; commanding, and it was created, Psal. 33.6.9. and 148.5. *light*] The first ornament of the world, wherewith the Lord decked it as with a garment, Psal. 104.2. This glorious worke, *Paul* applieth to our regeneration, thus, *God who said that out of darknesse light should shine, he hath shined in our hearts*, & c. 2. Cor. 4.6. that wee which *were once darknesse, are now light in the*

Lord, Ephes.5.8. yea, God himselfe, and Christ, is called *Light*: for the brightnesse of his glory and graces given unto us. I Joh.1.5.7. Joh.1.4.5. Psal.27.1. and 118.27. And as God made *light* in the first day; so Christ rose from death in the same day, the first of the weeke, Mark.16.1, 2. & he is the true light, which lighteth every man that commeth into the world, Joh.1.9. No man perfectly knoweth the nature of this excellent creature, as Job 38.19. *where is the way where light dwelleth?* & c.[9]

And he adds yet another quotation from 1 Timothy. The text, the simple word, has been the source for a new creation: a flood of apposite texts, as if the mind of the exegete were a veritable concordance of words and images and situations.

Apparently the human act of commentary, by attempting to see the meaning of the "Word" and by understanding how it conveys revelation, faintly resembles the original act of creation. The speaker sees the Old and New Testaments fused by the truth of the Resurrection. And finally, he perceives man's present existence in relation to the eternal processes of God. Commentary and meditation meet as the individual reiterates the sustaining truths of the Church's corporate body. Thus the structure of the hexameron, the division of the work into six parts, functions emblematically. Traherne may have known of the Pythagorean conception, expropriated by biblical exegetes, according to which the number six approximated the measure of earthly perfection. In creating the world in six days God established in the very beginning the totality of human and temporal limits. Hence, the seventh day was the shadow of eternity.[10] In this way the six days represent both the life of man on earth and the life of the earth itself; macrocosmic man would know his limits of six ages. Notice how the number six functions in so important a meditative handbook as St. Bonaventure's *Itinerarium mentis in Deum*. His threefold pathway to mystical union is actually divided into six stages, a division bearing elaborate parallels between Old Testament scenes and the six days of Christ preceding transfiguration:

Hence it is necessary that these three principal stages become six-fold, so that as God made the world in six days and rested on the seventh, so the microcosm by six successive stages of illumination is

79

led in the most orderly fashion to the repose of contemplation. As a symbol of this we have the six steps to the throne of Solomon [II Kings, 10, 19]; the Seraphim whom Isaiah saw have six wings; after six days the Lord called Moses out of the midst of the cloud [Ex., 24, 16]; and Christ after six days, as it is said in Matthew [17, 1], brought His disciples up into a mountain and was transfigured before them.[11]

Three honorable forms combine here, the hexameron, meditation, and biblical commentary. All of them are, by Traherne's time, emblematic and deeply imbued with the allegorical method.

I am aware that not all critics will agree with me here. Some critics deny that the fourfold interpretation of Scripture existed as late as the seventeenth century, or at least that it had much impact on literature. It seems to me, though, that several facts support the fourfold view: first, many seventeenth-century scholars and theologians clung to the practice; second, although inconsistencies in its use may be noted (as if in other periods none occur), the tendency is for the fourfold interpretation to merge into a tripartite or dual system.[12] But in addition to these considerations, and whether or not Traherne gave any thought to the various levels of application in his associational method, the practice of textual association was ingrained with allegory. Herbert, the poet whom Traherne most tried to emulate, wrote:

> OH that I know how all thy lights combine,
>   And the configurations of their glorie!
>   Seeing not onely how each verse doth shine,
> But all the constellations of the storie.
> This verse marks that, and both do make a motion
>   Unto a third, that ten leaves off doth lie:
>   Then as dispersed herbs do watch a potion,
> These three make up some Christians destinie.[13]

The implication here is that the life story of each reader is in the text: just as the spatial parts of Scripture cohere by their movements toward each other, the discrete moments of one's biography are embraced by a pattern, however difficult it may be to see. Herbert's diction suggests great spatial movements, celestial lines and arcs, for which the separation of verse from verse in Scripture is the emblem. Herbert understands Scripture as the total canon of human history, both as the cosmic movement of mankind ("Church Militant") and as the life progress of the soul.

I think a careful look at Traherne's hexameron will show that this is how he understood the sacred text also. Though the language of *Six Days* is quite frequently like that of the *Thanksgivings* and the *Centuries*, still the work differs little in technique from the plethora of commentaries, paraphrases, and poems based on Genesis available as models: Sir Walter Raleigh's *A History of the World*, Guillaume du Bartas' *Divine Weeks and Works* (1578-1603), Thomas Peyton's *The Glasse of Time* (1622), Milton's *Paradise Lost*, Sir Allen Apsley's *Order and Disorder* (1659). The roots of these works are in the rich alluvium of biblical commentary. As a learned divine, Traherne was as widely read in biblical exegesis as he was in philosophy. An admirer of Henry More, he had probably read *Conjectura Cabbalistica* (1653), a work which explicitly states that the first book of the Bible should be read by "a Threefold Cabbala" (title page), and that the meaning of Scripture should be understood according to "a triple Interpretation." Beyond the shock value of the term "Cabbala," More aimed at a species of mysticism, which he fused with a fashionable neo-Platonic philosophy. Though he thought of "the Jewish Cabbala . . . [as] a Traditional Doctrine or Exposition of the Pentateuch which *Moses* received from the mouth of God, while he was on the Mount with him" (sig. A6ᵛ), More dedicates one third of his attention to the "mystical" and "philosophical" (the hermetic) aspects of biblical meaning.

In certain other respects *Meditations on the Six Days* more nearly resembles Sir Allen Apsley's hexameron entitled *Order and Disorder* (1679). Naturally, since Traherne's work was not published until the second decade of the next century, no influence in either direction was likely or even possible. Nevertheless, Sir Allen's aim in selecting his subject, carefully explained, shows an attitude toward language which Traherne shared. In his work the reader was to find "nothing of fancy . . ., no elevations of stile, no charms of language." In a remark reminiscent of Traherne's pious claim in *Roman Forgeries*, Apsley delineates the poet's purpose as spiritual service based on the immediate recognition of creation's wonder: "I have not studied to utter any thing that I have not really taken in. And I acknowledge all the language I have, is much too narrow to express the least of those wonders my soul hath been ravisht with in the contemplation of God and his Works."[14]

In the preface to his long poem, Sir Allen Apsley harks back to a persistent theme of men like Gervase Markham and Jude Smith a century earlier. Christian poets of the Elizabethan age thought of themselves as participating in a literary competition with the satanic lyrists of a secular and corrupt world. They considered their paraphrases of the Psalms and the Song of Songs in direct competition with courtly love lyrics.[15] In a similar way, Sir Allen thinks of his hexameron as part of a conflict of ideas; heathen poetry on the same subject (he may have been thinking of Lucretius' *De rerum natura*) depicted creation blasphemously. The act of publishing the work ("not at first design'd for publick view" [sig. *1]) is part of the rhetoric of competition, aimed at exculpating "foolish, atheistical Poesie" (sig. *1ᵛ).

Sir Allen's hexameron is singularly unoriginal, but then, as we have seen, he thought of stylistic limitation as a virtue. The striking figure or conceit would not fit his pious intention. Many of the ideas and images found in this work may be found also in *Meditations on the Six Days*. For example, Apsley writes:

> Of the great God, Immense, and Infinite
> Containing all things in himself alone,
> Being at once in all, contain'd in none.
> Yet as a hidden spring appears in streams,
> The Sun is seen in its reflected beams,
> Whose high embodied Glory is too bright,
> Too strong an object for weak mortal sight;
> So in Gods visible productions, we
> What is invisible, in some sort see.
> [P. 3]

And in Traherne, too, the creation of corporeal light is not only emblematic of God's glory but of spiritual illumination, which informs the soul of things invisible:

If this corporal Light then be so beneficial and delightful, how much, O my Soul, is that spiritual Light which God hath given our Souls, more delightful and beneficial? ...
   Blessed be thy name, O Lord, for that corporal Light, by which I see all visible Things, but much more blessed be thy Mercy for this spiritual Light, by which I see Things Invisible. [Pp. 13-14]

Although their diction is frequently similar, the works themselves are quite different in shape and tone. Like Milton, Apsley depicts creation as part of a chain of events culminating in the Fall; his theme is the heavy load of guilt imposed on mankind from that moment:

> So were our parents fill'd with guilt and fear,
> When in the groves they Gods approaches hear,
> And from the terrour of his presence fled;
> Whether their own convictions caus'd their dread,
> For inward guilt of conscience might suffice
> To chace vile sinners from his purer eyes;
> Or nature felt an angry God descent,
> Which shook the earth, and tore the firmament,
> We are not told, nor will too far enquire.
> Lightnings and tempests might speak forth his ire.
> For at the day of universal doom
> The great Judge shall in flaming vengeance come;
> And all-consuming fire shall go before.
>
> [P. 54]

The remainder of the poem is a lugubrious treatment of the terrors and regrets which befall the originals, and is interrupted only by the speaker's scornful recriminations on the enormity of their act:

> There is no end, no intermitted woe,
> No more return from the accursed place,
> No hope, no possibility of grace,
> No sleepy intervals, no pleasant dreams,
> No mitigations of those sad extreams,

83

No gentle mixtures, no soft changes there,
Perpetual tortures, heightned with despair,
Eternal horror, and eternal night,
Eternal burnings, with no glance of light,
Eternal pain. O 'tis a thought too great,
Too terrible, for any to repeat,
Who have not scap'd the dread.

[P. 71]

The unsubtle use of anaphora leaves no doubt about the equation of negative values and eternity. Here the long day of Fall
is not allowed to die but is prolonged by torture. No passage
could provide a sharper contrast to Traherne's own interest in
the hexameral tradition. Whereas Sir Allen stresses the "Making and Unmaking" of the world, Traherne makes God's cre-
ative power his theme:

O my God, thou art a sovereign Lord of infinite Power! Was it
therefore to shew thy absolute Dominion, that they [the fallen
angels] were made and destroyed? Or else, since thou art a God of
infinite Justice, was it for the Declaration of thy Justice, that they
were permitted to apostatize? Almighty Lord! Thou art as great in
Mercy as in Power, and couldst never use thy sovereign Dominion
against either Justice or Mercy; it was not therefore to shew thy
sovereign Dominion that they were permitted to fall, nor yet to
declare thy Justice; for thy Dominion is exercised in doing Good,
and thy Justice glorified by administring Rewards, as well as Pun-
ishments. Was it then to manifest thy Power in tormenting as well
as in making happy? O Lord, not so! Thou art all Bowels of com-
passion, all Love and Goodness, and delightest not in the Misery of
any Creatures, much less in the Torments of those glorious Spirits
that were fitted to be Friends and Co-heirs of thine eternal Glory.
[P. 5]

For Traherne, the Fall is not associated with a sense of guilt or
sorrow; it is an occasion for joy in the recognition of justice,
love, and goodness: "It is my Joy, that I am exalted to see thy
Goodness in the Land of the Living."

Implicit in Traherne's choice of subject and his treatment of
it is a philosophy of language, as well as a program for devotion.
In the Old Testament story of creation Traherne found a con-

venient metaphoric situation, one which thematically joined eternity and time. Though in Scripture each day heralds a new creation, and although the passing of a single day is frequent synecdoche for the passage of life itself, in his meditations on the first week Traherne emphasizes no change whatsoever: one may easily interpolate apostrophes to light in the first and the fourth meditations. In this connection, comparison between *Six Days* and Donne's *Devotions upon Emergent Occasions* is revealing. Joan Webber points out that in Donne's work the passage of time is important to the meaning of the work. Illness comes and goes; each occasion differs, and with the ebb and flow of sickness we follow Donne's speaker through the twists of time.[16] Yet the motto preceding each devotion is drawn, seriatim, from the Latin poem prefixed to the sequence. Hence, the entire round of meditations is bound—like a commentary— to the introductory poem: "In the beginning was the word...."

A strikingly similar structural feature appears in *Meditations on the Six Days of Creation*. Prefixed to all but one of the six rounds is this verse, taken from the Psalms:

> Let the Words of my Mouth, and the Meditations of my
> Heart, be always acceptable in thy Sight, O Lord,
> my Strength and my Redeemer.
>
> [19: 14]

As we reread the *Meditations* we can see how they are organized around this passage and the fuller context it implies. The psalmist had always been the Christian archetype of the poet, the Christian Orpheus whose harp could still the raging passions of the greatest of men. But in particular the substance of the nineteenth psalm concerned the wonder of creation and the utterance of man and nature in praise of God's glory:

> The Heavens declare the glory of God; and the firmament sheweth his handywork.
> Day unto day uttereth speech, and night unto night sheweth knowledge.
> There is no speech nor language, where their voice is not heard.
>
> [19: 1-3]

On the other hand, the physical splendor of God's workmanship as evidenced in the world, and David's gratitude for it, were signs of a more magnificent wonder. As the appointment of Psalm 19 to be read at Morning Prayer on Christmas Day suggests,[17] David's prayer was believed to foreshadow the Incarnation:

Their line is gone out through all the earth, and their words to the end of the world. In them hath he set a tabernacle for the sun.

Which is as a bridegroom coming out of his chamber, and rejoyceth as a strong man to run a race.

His going forth is from the end of the heaven, and his circuit unto the ends of it.

[19:4-6]

Thematically, the temporal associations of the full context provide a variety of "Occasions" for thanksgiving.

In the Church's Year-Book Traherne explores the meditative possibilities of temporal order much more obviously, and this work provides a good perspective in which to appreciate *Meditations on the Six Days*. The Year-Book, which Dobell has called "a very valuable relic of the author,"[18] is based entirely on the feasts and holidays of the Christian calendar as Traherne knew them in the Anglican communion. Beginning with several lines on the Resurrection ("Hee is not heer, for he is risen . . .") and followed by a lengthy entry entitled "Meditations & Devotions upon the Resurrection of Our Savior," the sequence runs from Easter through All Saints' Day. In other words, what we have of the Year-Book covers the last half of the Christian year. But it is enough to shed further light on Traherne's meditative style.

The Church's Year-Book shares with the Commonplace Book Traherne's rather typical lack of originality.[19] For Traherne, originality is of little consequence, as we can see from his casual handling of ascription: "A Prayer Most of which was taken out of Dr. Featley for Acention Day." Similarly, without any comment at all, he lifts collects from the *Book of Common Prayer*. We must understand this easy expropriation of language as an important and functioning part of Traherne's style. His borrowing is a technique of characterization, a means by which he particularizes the speaker, demonstrating the way in which he worships God: "A good man out of the good treasure of his heart bringeth forth that which is good . . . for of the abundance of the heart his mouth speaketh" (Luke 6:45). The meditant makes no invidious distinction between the goodness and truth as he would express it and the expression of these virtues in the words of another man. His sharing is a form of adding to, and, as we shall see, it reveals something of his own humility and love.

Carol Marks's intensive study of the manuscript and sources of the Church's Year-Book has shed much light on Traherne's attitudes and practice as a literary artist. Thanks to Miss Marks, we can say with considerable assurance that the work was written between April and November of 1670, and that at least three people were closely involved in composition and copying of materials for the manuscript. Then, too, Miss Marks has painstakingly established numerous sources and analogues of various passages, ranging in length from single lines to entire sections. Traherne borrows openly or without comment from (among others) John Donne, George Herbert, Lancelot Andrewes, Edward Sparke, pseudo-Augustine, Daniel Featley, the Bible, and the *Book of Common Prayer*. What does this mean? Miss Marks provides us with a valuable observation:

[The Churchs' Year-Book] may have been meant only for Traherne's use as a private chaplain (but then why all the care for revision?), or for his private daily observation of the Church's "publick Offices, as one part of his devotion," or for the private use of some other devout member of the Church of England such as Mrs. Hopton (but certain parts smack of the sermon). It seems in fact to embody something of all these possibilities, a composite production of Traherne as vicar, chaplain, private Christian, friend. [P. 35]

Careful reading of the Year-Book corroborates this view: Traherne's speaker shifts from the hortatory and public to the earnest and private, and from the thankful meditant to the pious observer of man and creation. He is not consistently Traherne, but Traherne's creation, his metaphor, his literary representative.

Miss Marks herself hints strongly in this direction when she comments on Traherne's almost ubiquitous borrowing from other authors, which is so extensive that even she considers "the hunt for sources . . . a matter largely of luck" (p. 44). She suggests that perhaps Traherne may have written "with various relevant books open beside him or abstracted in a commonplace book, using the other works when it suited his aims, and helped in a minor way by C, who evidently had license to make modifications in Traherne's work" (p. 37). The arguments presented by Miss Marks for the complicity of C, and of Philip Traherne too, are not only persuasive but from a critical viewpoint highly suggestive.

Traherne's many strikeovers and revisions make clear that he considered the work a serious literary effort. Perhaps, as others have thought, he was preparing the Year-Book for publication. Be that as it may, the program followed tells us something about Traherne's conception of authorship in a devotional work. Traherne delegates authority to create his work to others, to C, to his brother, at the same time that he is engaged in "borrowing," say, from a commonplace book. But why not state this in another way? He and the others work together in composing a commonplace book, namely, the Church's Year-Book. Many of the same composite techniques found here are observable also in Traherne's Commonplace Book. Moreover, the act of borrowing from other authors is like the act of delegating to others the power to alter, expand, or add to a work.

Thus, originality is of no concern to the devotional sequence. Traherne borrows the writing of Edward Sparke, for instance, but as he borrows he alters. In employing and changing Sparke's language, however, Traherne does no violence to devotion or to truth. One need not consider a spontaneous alteration in a church hymn as indicative of Puritanical zeal. Indeed, the very composite nature of the Year-Book, the fact of multiple authorship, suggests the representative nature of Traherne's speaker. He is the creation of God, of course, but he is also the literary creation of many men; just as the *Book of Common Prayer*, sung by the individual Christian in the pew, is the passing through his mouth of the prayers of many, so the language of the Church's Year-Book is "common," that is, representative, not idiosyncratic.

Literary examples like the Year-Book are only one manifestation of the almost ubiquitous Renaissance and Jacobean interest in time, a concern which permeated many areas of life. The sun dial (and the "art of dialling" generally) enjoyed a vogue amounting to a fad. Sun dials, sometimes literally hundreds of them, occupied strategic spots in the formal Stuart garden. Almost uniformly, they bore inscriptions reminiscent of the *danse macabre*: "I tell men hourlie how the shadowes fly, / For men are shadowes and a shadow I."[20] It is a theme and tone to which Traherne gives way occasionally, as in "*Memento mori*": "Life is the Shadow of a Dreame."[21] But a more important development of this theme is structural. Donne, Vaughan, and especially Herbert experiment with the structural possibilities of the pilgrimage metaphor. John Bunyan's *The Pilgrim's Progress* employs this figure as the central focus of experience. It appears that the novel developed one important possibility of the metaphor: the changes in the individual between youth and age. But if we look at Herbert's "The Pilgrimage," we are closer to metaphor or allegory than to history. Poems like "Time," "Life," and "Sunday" remind the reader of the constant passing of time. In "Sunday," the passage of the days of the week represents the cycle of life and all of time. And throughout "The Church," Herbert metaphorically analogizes the life of man with the passage of the Christian year.

In comparison with the Year-Book, Herbert's *The Temple* shows slim use of the Christian calendar. Herbert omits many important holidays, and though he places those included in their proper order, he leaves the calendar structure more or less obscured. In contrast, Traherne scrupulously adheres to the order of the Christian year, and his meditations relate to this and only this main focus: Easter, St. Mark's Day, the Festival of St. Phillip and St. James, Ascension Day, Whitsunday, and so on through All Saints' Day. Whereas Herbert subtly alludes to the calendar, Traherne commemorates each major date. Yet it is Traherne, not Herbert, who fails to make the metaphor of the calendar work. Allowing for the fact that only the last half remains (the opposite is true of the *Faerie Queene*), the structure has no apparent function in the work.

Consider the impact of Herbert's structure: "The Church" ends, not with All Saints' Day, but with the death and transfiguration of the soul. Herbert makes the comparison between the year's passage and the cycle of man's life work by emphasizing the spiritual and autobiographical aspect of the analogy. In short, he departs from the liturgical so that the emphasis may be on life, for which the Christian calendar (like the flower) is only one legitimate metaphoric expression. As the second portion of *The Temple* unfolds—as death nears—the intense conflict of such poems as "The Thanksgiving" and "The Reprisall" diminish; the emphasis is on death and ultimately on reconciliation. The closing poems trace the progress of the soul beyond the time of life: "Death," "Doomsday," "Judgement," "Heaven," and then (a tour de force) "Love" (III) depicts that feast-day beyond time promised in the Apocalypse. In contrast, the Church's Year-Book provides no such perspective, no glimpse of the future, no death, no change. In other words, in Traherne's work the passage of time does not function; thus, the effectiveness of the calendar figure seems diminished. The Year-Book is not in the tradition of spiritual autobiography, and the pilgrimage metaphor does not operate; though time passes, Traherne's speaker remains the same. Significantly, Traherne ends his celebration of All Saints' Day by rehearsing a poem from *The Temple*, and by punctuating this quotation and his work, not with a "Church Militant," not with any shift of temporal or emotional point of view, but with (almost as afterthoughts) two antiphons:

The Glorious Virgin Mother with all the holy Angels & Blessed Saints Fall down on their faces & Adore him that Liveth for Ever Singing Halaluiahs unto him: Giving Glory, Honour, Wisdom power & praise to him that sits on the Throne & to the Lamb forever more. Alleluia, Alleluia, Alleluia.[22]

It seems to me clear that these lines—paraphrasing Revelation 5:13—differ very little or not at all from many interspersed throughout the work. Traherne's theme in Antiphon is like that of all angels and saints described in the Apocalypse: "Holy, holy, holy, Lord God Almighty, which was, and is, and is to come" (4:8).

Though Traherne employs the Christian calendar, this linear arrangement has little to do with his thematic material or the way it is organized. Temporal progression is not a serious issue in the work. Quite the opposite, Traherne's style amplifies his thematic interest in the eternal or timeless—from a syntactic form of stasis. Hence, the almost monotonous use of repetition. The marked lack of originality in the Year-Book is actually more significant than its temporal structure. The focus is on the singer, not the song. One may always add another word or prayer because, in eternity, the song is endless: "As it was in the beginning, is now, and ever shall be. . . ." The underlying literary model of the Year-Book is the *Book of Common Prayer*. But unlike Herbert, who also draws heavily on the prayer book, Traherne shows little interest in the eucharistic possibilities of his material. He copies the prayer book's design, its "common" quality. For just as the psalms and canticles of ancient composers cross the Christian's lips at Morning Prayer, just as the angels make no show of originality in their eternal hymn, so too Traherne's easy use of the Bible, the prayer book, and other authors serves to characterize his speaker. In his repetition of another's poem or prayer the speaker manifests Christian humility. He returns to God one part only of what God (maker of both the singer and the song) has given him.

The extraneous structural use of the calendar indicates at least one reason why the Church's Year-Book does not succeed as a work of art. Thematically, time is unimportant in the work; yet the dominant figure is the calendar. Traherne handles the same problem with greater tact in *Meditations on the Six Days of the Creation*. As the title indicates, the meditations are "on" the creation of the world. But they are on the "six days" of creation. That is, temporality is implied, at least partially, in the very title; and this theme is carried through in that each series of meditations treats of a different day. But the meditations do not form a complete round; the week remains unfinished. No meditation on the seventh and last day appears, and this omission must be seen as part of Traherne's strategy. Associations of days and weeks work against the sense of incompletion. And the creation itself places time in a perspective of the cosmos: "And on the seventh day . . . he rested." Structure and subject matter work contrapuntally, for (like the end) the beginning brings to mind all that is not diurnal and subject to limits. Traherne does not use the week to suggest time's passage; he sees in these six days an emblem of divinity in man, who differs from the beasts in his capacity to contemplate creation.

Here is a crucial difference between Traherne and the poet he most admired, George Herbert (and it probably explains why Herbert more than Traherne is attracted to the eucharistic aspects of the liturgy). Herbert is constantly returning to his theme of anxiety, of struggle between man and God (p. xxxvii). He emphasizes the monumental gulf between human and divine. For Herbert, time exists so that man may learn his limits:

> These are thy wonders, Lord of love,
> To make us see we are but flowers that glide:
> Which when we once can finde and prove,
> Thou hast a garden for us, where to bide.
> Who would be more,
> Swelling through store,
> Forfeit their Paradise by their pride.
> [P. 167, "The Flower"]

Here and in "Church-monuments" Herbert sounds the tone of the *danse macabre*, one seldom heard in Traherne. For Traherne time is not the destroyer of the Dance of Death but a temporal expanse in which creation takes place. Traherne emphasizes man's potentiality for creation, which he regards as infinite in magnitude. Hence, he sees man's knowledge of time from the expansive view quite like Pico della Mirandola's: animals, creatures of sense, are limited because they cannot conceptualize the past or the future:

But man can see, and know, and love any object, in any Age or Kingdom in the World. He can look into any Region, tho it be never so far removed and be as familiar[l]y conversant with any Person or Transaction there, when represented once in a clear

Light, as with any Object in his own country. He can look into *Eden* consider *Adams* Dust in its first Creation, survey the Procedure of God in his Six Dayes Works, pass out of Time into Eternity it self, run up to the Original and fountain Head of all existence, ponder the nature of GOD, search in his Bosom for his Eternal Counsels, pierce into the Centre of the Earth, and survey the Circumference of all Immensity.[23]

In *Christian Ethicks*, Traherne depicts what is in effect the point of view of his speaker in *Meditations on the Six Days*. In transcending the "now" of instinct, man is supremely human; he has passed "out of Time into Eternity it self," viewing creation from a timeless "Circumference of all Immensity."

If this analysis is correct, the structure of *Six Days* functions more effectively than the calendar form of the Year-Book. Attention to the first week of time mythologizes the past, removing the reader's focus from human occupations, from the quotidian associations of daily life. Ironically, the week of creation becomes a metaphor of timelessness. God took six days to create the universe, six days to bring order out of chaos and so to fuse time and eternity, flesh and spirit. On the seventh day he rested; Sunday, the day omitted from the sequence (the miniature eternity of Herbert's poem) seems just beyond the speaker's concern. The dominant epigraph of the work ("Let the words of my mouth, and the meditation of my heart, be acceptable in thy sight") refers both to prayer and to the imagined act of speaking. Like the Deity, the meditant and poet generates words; and the spiritual industry of his week of meditation is a microcosmic reflection of divine creativity.

Verses from Genesis are the verbal evidences of time: they function as Occasion in Traherne's meditations, which are made up largely of biblical passages or paraphrases, followed by "rumination."[24] The pattern is associative, with the meditations following the texts (and each other) in much the same manner as "dilation" upon Scripture. In Hobbes's nomenclature, the method has "unguided" and "regulated" elements: the movement from text to text, from image to image, is the basic, ruminative pattern of the work. Though one may be struck by the inevitable repetition, the images generated are not always predictable. First we have the text ("And God said, Let there be light") and then the unfolding of its meaning through paraphrase and association, leading often to colloquy with God, in which the speaker renders his petition:

O Lord, our Governour, how excellent is thy Name in all the World! There are yet greater things than these, for we have seen but few of his Works. For the Lord hath made all things, and to the Godly hath he given Wisdom. Lord make me holy, religious, devout and godly, that I may understandingly praise thee for thy Works. [P. 38]

And the round ends with a poem of praise:

> The Hills and Dales, the Lawns and Woods around,
> God's Wisdom, Goodness, and his Pow'r resound.
> Both far and near his Wonders they proclaim.
> How vilely then is wretched Man to blame,
> If he forget to praise that liberal Hand,
> Out-spread from Sea to Sea, from Land to Land?
> [P. 39]

The open and unpredictable quality of this method allows for a paradoxical turn. By looking back to the beginning, to Genesis and to the creation, Traherne also directs attention to the end: the hexameron as apocalypse. The final lines of the work are intended to evoke associations of the eternal city, of the endless Sabbath described in Revelation:

> That thankful, holy, happy I may be,
> May please thee here, and to Eternity
>   May bless thee with a cheerful Voice,
>   And with the Saints, who all rejoice
> To warble forth thy Praises, may
> Enjoy thee in an everlasting Day.
> [P. 91]

Something of the same idea seems to permeate Traherne's play on the word "end." Given his conception of time, the beginning ended with man: "A third Reason why Man was created last, was to shew that he, and only he, was the end of all the Creation,

94

for his Soul had no need of Corporal Beings or material things" (p. 71). Before time actually began it came to an end in man. Traherne's apocalypse points toward the moment of meditation, to the "now" of time. Mythological time—duration preceding the first Sabbath—ends in the eternal Sabbath of the meditative process. This is what is meant by God's breathing into man:

So that the Soul is a Power inspired into the Body of Man by Almighty God, whereby he is able to see Eternity, to enjoy Infinity, to contain his Omnipresence, to apprehend his Omniscience, to behold his Omnipotence, and to be his Temple. For he who breathed in the Soul first, himself follow'd after, and there will he dwell for evermore in his Power. For the Truth is, by his entring in, he breathed in the Soul, that is, by manifesting himself within the Body; for by the in-dwelling of his Omnipresence do we conceive him. Hence comes it to pass, that all Ages and Kingdoms, Heaven and Earth, Time and Eternity, Angels and Seraphins, the infinite Heights and Excellencies of God, are, after a sort, in the Soul of Man. [Pp. 80-81]

Toward the end of the meditative sequence Traherne sees in the "last" act—the creation of man—the "end" of time. The figure of the partial week functions powerfully to amplify this paradox. *Meditations on the Six Days of the Creation* is an apocalypse without time and without prophecy.[25]

But these remarks concern only structural and thematic aspects of style. Just as important to an understanding of Traherne is a grasp of his syntactic characteristics. It seems to me that above all other works the dominant model is the Psalms. In each of the six "Meditations" Traherne refers to, echoes, or quotes from the Psalms, often from several in sequence. Ironically, the same cannot be said of Genesis, reference to which he omits in "Meditations on the Fourth Day's Creation." Frequently Traherne will quote long passages from the Psalms:

Every Day will I give Thanks unto thee, and praise thy Name for ever and ever.

All thy Works praise thee, O Lord, and thy Saints give Thanks unto thee.

They shew forth the Glory of thy Kingdom, and talk of all thy wondrous Works.

The Earth is filled with the Fruits of thy Works, thou bringest forth Grass for the Cattel, and Herb for the Use of Man.

He bringeth forth Food out of the Earth, and Wine that maketh glad the Heart of Man, and Oil to make him a chearful Countenance.

He prepareth Rain for the Earth, and maketh the Grass to grow upon the Mountains.

[P. 35]

And when he has finished with the 104th ("The Song of Creation"), he turns without comment to Psalm 65. It would be hard to overestimate the impact of the Psalms on Traherne's meditative style. Especially striking is his fondness for anaphora, one of the central rhetorical figures of the Psalms:

> Consider, O my Soul, ...
>
> O how beautiful and admirable . . . .
>
> O the Joy of all Joys . . . .
>
> Oh! the heavenly Songs . . . .
>
> See here the Mutability . . . .
>
> See here, and tremble . . . .
>
> Behold the miserable Effects . . . .
>
> But, O the Wonder!
>
> It is wonderful, O Lord, it is wonderful to consider . . . .

Similarly, eighteen paragraphs of "Meditations on the Sixth Day's Creation" begin with "I praise thee." We think also of the Order of Morning Prayer, of the Canticles, with their incantatory emphasis on praise, and their recurrent rhythms: "I will praise thee," "I will praise thy name forever." All but one of the verses of the last chapter of the Psalms begin with "Praise": "Praise ye the Lord. Praise God . . . praise him. . . . Let every thing that hath breath praise the Lord."

The Psalms play an important role in other Traherne works, for example, the lovely volume known as the *Thanksgivings*. Published posthumously in 1699 under the title *A Serious and Pathetical Contemplation of the Mercies of God, in Several*

Most Devout and Sublime Thanksgivings for the Same, this marvelous little work is in many respects an open imitation—or as Bishop Hall might have called it, "an open paraphrase"—of the Psalms. The pattern of the work is made clear from the beginning. The opening lines of "Thanksgivings for the Body" are drawn nearly verbatim from Psalm 103:

Bless the Lord, O my Soul: and all that is within me bless his holy name.

Bless the Lord, O my Soul: and forget not all his benefits.

Who forgiveth all thine Iniquities: who healeth all thy Diseases:

Who redeemeth thy life from destruction. Who crowneth thee with loving kindness and tender mercies.

Who satisfieth thy mouth with good things, so that thy youth is renewed as the Eagles.

The next ten lines are paraphrastic.

> O Lord who art clothed with Majesty,
>   My desire is, to praise thee.
>   With the holy Angels and Archangels
>   To glorifie thee.
> And with all thy Saints in the Church triumphant.
>   For the eternal brightness
>   Of thine infinite bounty,
>   The freedom of thy love
> Wherein thou excellest the beams of the Sun
>   To celebrate thee.
>
> [II, 214]

This passage represents the speaker's response to David's opening lines. Unlike the responsive readings at Morning Prayer, the language here and the length of line are freer (or as George Hickes put it, "of the *freer* sort")[26] than either the patterns of their prose model or of the stanzas found in contemporary lyrics.

Yet the stylistic implications seem clear enough. The response is a spontaneous "contemplation" on the text; its formal characteristics reveal the speaker's desire to imitate the psalmist as a poet, a desire coinciding with a deeply-felt conviction of God's bounty toward the poet as a Christian. Like David, the speaker recalls God's benefits. Thus, the two passages are strikingly parallel in meaning, and this parallelism is meant to indicate a significant relation between model and imitator: the speaker's act of devotion no less than his words claim the heritage of the Psalms.

As I have already suggested, comparison between the sacred and profane poets was part of an honorable tradition. In the sixteenth and seventeenth centuries, by far the most widely published lyrics were metrical paraphrases of the Psalms.[27] Of course, the Psalter occupied a special place in the life of the Church, described by Anthony Sparrow in this way: ". . . the Church appoints [the Psalms] to be read over every moneth, that her children may be thoroughly acquainted with this rich treasure of Prayers and Praises, and by a frequent exercise of holy *Davids* devotions, may come to holy *Davids* temper, who was a man after God's own heart."[28] As we might expect, the versifiers of the Psalms tried to capture something of David's ethos. We get some idea of the rhetorical power of this aim in works like Thomas Becon's *Pomaunder of Prayers* (1560). A concatenation of verses from Psalms 103, 104, and 107, these entries are called "prayers" in which *"The godley geveth thanks for the great benefites, which God hath bestowed upon them"* (fol. 75). Men like Becon, Jude Smith, Gervase Markham, and others looked upon their paraphrases as natural competitors to courtly love lyrics. The psalms were love songs but they were also a "Mirrour of Devotions." Francesco Giovanni Loredano, who dedicated his metrical paraphrase of the fifteen psalms of degree to the Holy Virgin, considered his literary effort to be "Piety . . . exemplary like *David's*."[29]

Traherne may have known Becon's little work; *The Pomaunder of Prayers* is deeply imbued with the spirit as well as the diction of the *Book of Common Prayer*. In this lovely volume we find prayers for morning, prayers for evening, "The Letany" (including the "Agnus Dei"), "Generall Collects," and (even more important for our purpose) several "Thanksgivings." The language and method of these thanksgivings strongly resemble Traherne's. For example, in "A thanksgiving unto God for all his benefits" we read:

Thy benefits towarde me (O most loving father) are so great and infinite, whether I have respect unto my body, or unto my soule, that I find not in myselfe how to recompence any part of thine unspekable goodnesse toward me.[30]

In this thanksgiving for the body and the soul we see that Becon and Loredano agree: choice of the Psalms as material for poetry reaffirms the truth that "the two chief Duties of Religion [are] *Prayer* and *Thanksgiving*" (sig. b.1).

The title of Loredano's work, *The Ascents of the Soul* (1681), suggests further literary implications of the Psalms. It may seem strange initially that, like Richard Baxter (who praised Gerson for teaching Protestants how to meditate), Loredano's English translator, Henry Lord Coleraine, chose to translate the work of a professed Roman Catholic. Indeed, he apologizes for the fact that the work was written by a Catholic, and protests that Loredano has omitted doctrinaire and super-stitious evidences of Rome. It is clear to the reader from the prefatory remarks, however, that Lord Coleraine's choice of material is part of his open repudiation of those men who made it their purpose to alter the beauty of the liturgy. He sar-donically remarks that perhaps the Psalms of David will soon be banished from the church. But happily that time has not yet come: "We are not yet sunk down into that utter darkness of the days of *Antichrist*, when the saying, or singing of Psalms, will be rejected with the Church. But we [still] have the liberty to go up, with *David*, into *God's House*" (sig. b.2). Paraphrase of the Psalms, and imitation of the psalmist, imply the opposite of Milton's "unmeditated" prayer. Though Traherne puts the Psalms to his own use, his habit of paraphrase and direct quota-tion similarly exemplifies his high-church sympathies.

Then, too, Lord Coleraine makes clear that, beyond the lyric and devotional aspects of Loredano's work, he finds a mystical sense:

I have fancied the whole Piece to be a Sketch of *Jacob's* Vision, and *David's* Psalter, like *Israel's* Scale, reaching to the Divine Throne, whereon devout Spirits have scope to run descant up and down, and by the various Motions of their Piety, (as by the several Degrees of their Understandings) they make better Music than the imagin'd Spheres could ever be supposed to do: For surely, thereupon is grounded the best Harmony of Heaven and Earth.   [Sigs. b1-b1^v]

Prefixed to Coleraine's own *La Scala Santa: Or, A Scale of Devotions,* a marvelous engraving serves as a visual link between the two works.[31] In the foreground, King David performs on the harp; before him on a table the Bible lies open to 1 Chronicles 16. Behind an entrance in a marble balustrade, an altar supports a flaming heart. Further still, fifteen steps, each inscribed with texts from the Psalms, lead to the *Sancta Sanctorum* of the Temple. To the right, we see three angels ascending Jacob's Ladder (Colossians 3:16, 17), carrying with them a scroll, both sides of which the reader may see. On one side we read *"Psalmodia"* and on the other the title of Loredano's book, *The Ascents of the Soul.* At the very top we see the word "Assents," with the obvious *double-entendre.* Moreover, both words rhyme with "DESCANTS," seen directly opposite, on the title page of Coleraine's *La Scala.* Thus, verbal associations from music, poetry, and doctrine converge to amplify a central theme: the mystical meaning of the Psalms. The mind assents, the soul ascends. In his "DESCANTS," his *"Contemplations and Collects,"* Coleraine imitates Loredano, and both men imitate David: musician, poet, seer over creation—all these things, but preeminently a man who communed with God.

This is an important point for our understanding of how Traherne uses language. For him, meaning is an interior, spiritual quality. He imitates the psalmist by his attitude, his thought. In "The Inference" Traherne writes, "well-guided *Thoughts* within possess / The Treasures of all Blessedness" (II, 139). And David was treasured by the Deity for his thoughts:

> *David* a Temple in his Mind conceiv'd;
> And that Intention was so well receiv'd
> By God, that all the Sacred Palaces
> That ever were did less His Glory pleas.

> [II, 141]

Again, in "Thoughts. II," we read:

> That Temple David did intend,
>   Was but a Thought, and yet it did transcend
>   King Solomons.

[II, 173]

This idea is widespread in the seventeenth century, sometimes (as in the case of Anne Collins) being the sole justification for rather inept verse. The same belief persists today in such critical norms as "authenticity" and in the whole notion that the value of a work resides in the "thought" or attitude of the author.

With Traherne, this critical understanding has all the force of a metaphysical certainty; it is an expression of his particular brand of Platonism, which allows him to paraphrase the "meaning" but not the diction of Psalm 103. It explains also why Traherne returns so frequently throughout his meditative prose and poetry to the Psalms. To copy is to imitate the thought: the poet is like the worshiper at Morning Prayer—repeating the words of the Psalms in the effort to recapitulate the spirit of the psalmist, and so, of Christ. Traherne makes this explicit comment on his intention:

> O that I were as *David*, the sweet Singer of *Israel!*
>   In meeter Psalms to set forth thy Praises.
> Thy Raptures ravish me, and turn my soul all into melody.

[II, 223]

In this prayerful outburst, Traherne's speaker expresses both the wish and the fulfillment of it.

The imagery of the preceding several examples suggests that Traherne is using Scripture in much the same way as Bonaventure used the world. Traherne's method mythologizes time; the reader gets little sense of narrative. Events are practically nonexistent. As Cope suggests, the longer sequences of meditations seem to escape the stark, skeletal quality of the Ignatian pattern. I think this is true of Traherne. The past is not used for present analysis in order to guide the meditant in the future. The past is not really used for anything. Traherne replaces temporal progression with the word, with verbal associations. Of course, verbal associations transpire in time. But Traherne emphasizes thematic and structural techniques which tend to subvert the purely historical or biographical conceptions of time. And this remark applies a fortiori to *Centuries of Meditations*, to which we now turn.

"A MYSTERIOUS ABSENCE OF TIMES": THE CENTURIES

V

There is within the Earth,
so many Treasures,
Such glorious honors
& delightfull pleasures,
That who enjoys
all these felicities
Enjoys indeed,
an earthly Paradise.
—Robert Crofts,
The Terrestriall Paradise

. . . Thoughts can come
to Things, and view,
What Bodies cant
approach unto.
They know no Bar,
Denial, Limit, Wall:
But have a Liberty
to look on all.
—"Thoughts. I"

The quatrain prefixed to the *Centuries of Meditations* makes several claims about the form and content of the work:

This book unto the friend of my best friend
As of the Wisest Love a Mark I send
That she may write my Makers prais therin
And make her self therby a Cherubin.[1]

Most striking of these is the claim that completion of the "Book" of *Centuries* will require the efforts of a second hand. We notice also that by filling the blank pages of the manuscript the recipient of the "Book," who is also its original donor, will be given a chance to complete "her self," to "make her self" into an angelic being. As the receiver of her own now altered gift, this reader is not to remain detached from the work but to become a part of it by adding something of herself: by adding to the *Centuries* she will add to "her self." Meanwhile, the present state of the work is a "Mark" or token of a gift. The shared origin of that "Mark" and of the manuscript itself is "Wisest Love."

As we learn in the first meditation, the author is returning his notebook to the friend (presumably Mrs. Susanna Hopton) who gave it to him in the first place. His benefactress made a gift of the "Book" in just the way that his "best friend" bestowed the gift of life: "An Empty Book is like an Infants Soul, in which any Thing may be Written. It is Capable of all Things, but containeth Nothing" (I.1). The empty page is a *tabula rasa* —like the soul at the moment of birth: blank space and time, void of impression, void of "Act." By analogy, human life is a universe of possibility; the notebook is an emblem of the infinite possibilities of the soul. The motive or "Essence" behind the gift and behind the author's nativity will now be the guiding force behind each entry: "I hav a Mind to fill this with Profitable Wonders. And since Love made you put it into my Hands I will fill it with those Truths you Love, without Knowing them." Here the speaker directs attention to three discrete acts: the gift of the notebook, the author's birth, and his first inscription in the "Empty Book." When he reveals his "Mind to fill this [Book]," he draws his reader's attention to the act of filling the page, which was accomplished in the past, but he also keeps the figure of the empty or only partially filled page in "Mind." Just as the "Empty Book'" is the moment of inception before the advent of the written word (or Century), so birth is the beginning of human time. The blank page is an operative figure, emblematic of the abyss of space, which was the "Book." But the figures of empty space are soon qualified by language suggesting generative processes. We find a pronounced repetition of plural nouns: "Beauties," "Truths," "Things," "Hands," "Wonders." Emulating both Creator and created (the latter in the form of Susanna Hopton), the author "fills" the eternity of empty pages with the discrete acts of time: the word.

The mediation between past and present inheres in this act of "filling." The friend is to remember the blank pages as they were when she gave the notebook, and to recognize the quality of those acts now represented on the page. For Traherne, the act of composition is the reduction of "Essence" into "Act," love manifest. God gives the time of life; Susanna Hopton provides the literary analogue, occasion. In his turn, in imitation of his friends and benefactors, the speaker and meditant gives verbal birth to the *Centuries*. Of course, there is an element of flattery here: the final test of the spiritual guide will be in the performance of his pupil. But metaphorically more important, the expectation of her completing the *Centuries* is the presence of the future in the word on the page. The intimacy between speaker and audience is the rhetorical means by which Traherne mediates also between present and future. This collaboration involves an interchanging of roles between giver and receiver, between guide and guided, one which represents a fusing of times present, past, and future.

For the moment I wish to consider this collaboration as more than a hyperbole for the speaker's affection and trust. From a rhetorical standpoint it is also an expression of the speaker's character. In earlier chapters we examined the strong indications of shared authorship in Traherne's work, especially in the Church's Year-Book and the Commonplace Book. It seems to me that many of the observations made earlier apply also to discussion of the *Centuries*. Almost the first thing we learn about the speaker is his wish that he not have the last word in his creation. And here even the ambiguity of the word "creation" suggests the way in which Traherne's audience is expected to help in making him by completing composition of his work. Mrs. Hopton will change "her self" in adding to the *Centuries*, but in so doing she shapes the speaker's being too. In his willingness to share authorship we see his openness to the shaping influence of a friend. His attitude on this issue is profoundly Christian, and, as we shall see, it is also deeply imbued in the style of the work: "Hath not the potter power over the clay?" The strategy of shared authorship, which expresses itself in a number of ways throughout the *Centuries* in Traherne's persistent use of literary allusion as well as unannounced direct lifting, illustrates the speaker's comprehensiveness no less than his humility.

Nowhere is this strategy of self-revelation more evident than in the Third Century. Often described by critics as an autobiographical account, the Third Century has become the sole basis for most commentary and surmise on the poet's life.[2] I have no way of knowing if the Third Century is "Traherne's own history,"[3] but if we are to think of it as such, we ought to keep certain other examples of autobiography in mind. The aim of most explicitly autobiographical writing seems to be the delineation of the exact qualities of a particular individual, in some cases down even to his ancestry: "My Father's Name was *Richard* (the son of *Richard*) *Baxter*";[4] "I was born in the month called July in the year 1624, at Drayton-in-the-Clay, in Leicestershire. My father's name was Christopher Fox."[5] It is not too much to tell the reader of one's father's occupation and even his nickname. The author's birthplace must be located exactly with respect to certain named hills a specified number of miles from the Severn. Dates, places, people, settings whether of room or landscape, meteorological data: such details are the stock in trade of the autobiography. John Evelyn's *Diary* begins: "I was borne about 20 minutes past two in the morning, [on Tuesday] being the xxxi, and last of October Anno 1620, after my Father had been married about 7 yeares, and that my Mother had borne him 3 Children viz. Two Daugters and one sonn, about the 33rd Yeare of his age, and the 23d of my Mothers."[6] After specifying the exact moments of the births of everyone in his family, Evelyn tells his reader that his "Father, named Richard, was of a sanguine complexion, mix'd with a dash of Choler," and he adds selected notes on the history of his father's hair, which had turned gray by the time he was "30 yeares of age."

The autobiographer's proliferation of details presupposes the value of detail in elucidating the qualities of the self. Evelyn describes his father's complexion on the assumption that this quantum of experience is relevant to an understanding of the diarist presently speaking. Implicitly, man in the here and now is the equivalent of his memory, a being radically composed of the events accreted in his life. Regardless of what philosophical disagreements with Hobbes he may have pretended to have, the diarist conceives of human experience and character as an accretion of the atoms of discrete experiences. In this sense, it is interesting to note that even in the Third Century Traherne explicitly rejects the defining and limiting claim of events. In order to be free, man must transcend the pressures of the particular and eccentric. Instead of rehearsing the history of his birth or relating details of his lineage, Traherne looks further backward in time: "Certainly Adam in Paradice had not more sweet and Curious Apprehensions of the World, then I when I was a child" (III.1). By naming his generic rather than individual father Traherne suggests that infancy in the personal sense is not the subject of this meditation. By depersonalizing the associations of infancy, he heightens the emphasis on "the Infancy of [a] sublime and celestial Greatness." Yet in this, the opening sentence of the Century, Traherne uses the demonstrative adjective ("this sublime") to indicate a link with the preceding Century in the form of the antecedent of "celestial Greatness."

A glance at the close of the Second Century will show, unsurprisingly, a concentration of themes of "Felicity," time, and self. The speaker invites his audience to recognize that all things ("GOD, THE WORLD, YOUR SELF") are gifts from God: "*All Things* in Time and Eternity being the Objects of your Felicity GOD the Giver, and you the Receiver." Paradoxically, time and eternity are objects subordinated to the self in that they are means or objects prior to their common end in the self: Felicity. This would seem to suggest a form of egoism. But the opposite is true. Century III begins with an intimate, earnest appeal: "Will you see the Infancy of this sublime and celestial Greatness?" The relation of speaker to audience continues to be important in the *Centuries*. As in *Christian Ethicks*, the speaker insinuates his distance from the audience by supposing himself as leader. Even so, the "you" is not provided an autobiographical rehearsal of facts as in Fox or Evelyn. Rather than facts, the speaker presents the qualities of perception associated with "Infancy." And as meditation unfolds he reminds the audience of his status as spiritual guide. In short, he returns to the substantive material of the beginning (I.1). Rather than the date and time of birth, the speaker relates the quality of his seeing, of his "Apprehensions." Rhetorically, the first few meditations in the Third Century destroy the boundaries between the objects, time and eternity, with the aim of leaving only their residue: "All Time was Eternity, and a Perpetual Sabbath. Is it not Strange, that an Infant should be Heir of the World, and see those Mysteries which the Books of the Learned never unfold?" (III. 2).

In delineating this relationship between speaker and audience Traherne seeks a quite similar dissolution of boundaries. The apparent egoism of the speaker's professed role as guide is temporary and therefore illusory. By initiating those committed to his charge, the guide destroys the boundary between them. I have suggested that the opening lines of the Third Century hark back to the beginning of the First, where the speaker makes a similar assertion of his function as guide. Now in the context of the dedicatory quatrain we learn that the work, so far as the speaker's hand is concerned, is finished. Traherne develops his theme of collaboration in the following meditations, first, by restating the momentary distance between teacher and pupil: "I have found, that Things unknown have a Secret Influence on the Soul." The initiated one has "found" and is willing to reveal certain esoteric truths:

I will open my Mouth in Parables: I will utter Things that have been Kept Secret from the foundation of the World. Things Strange yet Common; Incredible, yet Known; Most High, yet Plain; infinitly Profitable, but not Esteemed. Is it not a Great Thing, that you should be Heir of the World? Is it not a very Enriching Veritie? In which the Fellowship of the Mystery, which from the beginning of the World hath been hid in GOD, lies concealed! [I.3]

From the hortatory tone of *Centuries* I.2, the speaker turns to the vatic tone of the prophet. He is more than a spiritual guide, hence even further distanced from his audience. Implicitly he declares his literary and spiritual relation to Matthew and to Christ, and hence to the unction of the Holy Ghost. The speaker sees himself as the lineal artistic descendant of Christ as he addressed the multitude. Like Christ, he becomes simultaneously both prophet and the fulfillment of prophecy. All of time's secrets are fulfilled in him, just as all of time was redeemed in Christ. Through the poet-prophet-speaker of the *Centuries*, all the hidden "Truths" of existence will be made known.

Christ delivered the Word to the multitude just as he would soon surrender his body for man's sake, to restore communion between God and man. Though the speaker's gift to his friend is merely verbal, it is also mysterious. The "Mystery" unfolding in the pages of the *Centuries* existed "from the beginning of the World." Traherne emphasizes this idea: "The Thing hath been from the Creation of the World. The fellowship of the Mystery

hath been hid in God, since the Creation." Implicitly, communication between guide and guided in the *Centuries* takes on
sacramental overtones; the author will "communicate" the hidden, mystical "Truths" which exist apart from time. In a position to reveal that which "hath been hid in God" (I.3 and 5),
the speaker arrogates a species of divinity to himself.

The passage is even more complicated than I have suggested.
In commenting on the quoted verse from Matthew, Calvin
writes: "Matthew does not mean, that the psalm, which he
quotes, is a prediction which relates peculiarly to Christ, but
that, as the majesty of the Spirit was displayed in the discourse
of the Prophet, in the same manner was his power manifested in
the discourse of Christ."[7] This passage is almost a gloss on
Traherne's use of Matthew 13:35. For Christ, the quotation
from the Psalms served a double purpose. On the one hand it
directed attention to David as prophet, thus heightening the
sense of dignity in the language; on the other, it reminded his
audience that he was the fulfillment of David's prophecy. Traherne claims a double heritage, casting himself as the poetic
representative of the joined Law and Gospel, first and foremost
the imitator of Christ: "And I after his Similitude will lead you
into Paths Plain and Familiar" (I.4). Soon he will be quoting
from Thomas a Kempis, invoking the associations of the *Imi-
tatio Christi* but submerging his ego in an authorship widened
by yet another being. Just as Traherne's personal history begins
to be absorbed early in the Third Century in the speaker's
devotional and pedagogic functions, so, as the decades proceed,
the historic individual is blotted out by the most powerful of
literary influences.

Like the speaker of the Church's Year-Book, the speaker of
the *Centuries* is a literary composite; his synthetic character is
the most powerful shaping metaphor in the work and the major
hint as to the structure and method of Traherne's prose style.
The "Centuries" are the work of many men; the speaker is the
product of experience greater than the single autobiography.
Similarly, the work itself is additive rather than linear in structure. The speaker does not live or learn in the ordinary sense of
autobiography; he is put together by a process of addition. Not
only does the speaker bring all parts of his own memory to bear,

he draws on the memory of others: friends, philosophers, prophets, the church. This explains why we find such a sharp distinction between the conception of youth found in Traherne and that found in such other figures as Baxter or Bunyan. Here is a typical treatment of an event from Baxter's youth:

About Seventeen years of Age, being at *Ludlow* Castle, where many idle Gentlemen had little else to do, I had a mind to learn to play at Tables, and the best Gamester in the House undertook to teach me! As I remember, the first or second Game, when he had so much the better that it was an hundred to one, besides the difference of our skills, the standers by laugh'd at me, as well as he, for not giving it up, and told me the Game was lost: I knew no more but that it was not lost till all my Table-men were lost, and would not give it over till then. He told me, that he would lay me an hundred to one on it, and in good earnest laid me down ten shillings to my sixpence.[8]

The game proceeds to its predictable outcome, which is accompanied by the hero's recognition of the evils of dice. What is most striking about this prose passage is its narrative precision. Even the fact that the memory is not a perfect instrument is recorded by Baxter's qualifications regarding time: "About seventeen years of age," "As I remember, the first or second game," and so on. The strategy serves not to suggest the ragged fringes of the memory, but to assure the reader's attentive credulity. This is exactly what happened to Richard Baxter, this very event in just this way. Of course such a precise narrative strategy necessarily sharpens the distinction between past and future. The autobiographer is not living his childhood over (except perhaps in the timeless, Augustinian realm of the psychoanalyst). He is recalling and also reifying the past.

The only passage in all of Traherne that comes close to such a strict narrative line is found not in the Third Century but in the front matter of *Roman Forgeries*. I am speaking, of course, of that vivid reminiscence of Traherne's meeting on the steps of the Bodleian with a friend and the subsequent confrontation with the friend's Roman Catholic cousin. Certainly everything points to the authentic quality of this reminiscence, down even to the curt, polemical portraiture of Traherne's attitude toward his opponent:

> You met me this Evening at the *Library door*; if you please to meet me there tomorrow morning at eight of the Clock, I will take you in; and we will go from Class to Class, from Book to Book, and there I will first shew in *your own Authors*, that you publish such Instruments [forgeries] for good *Records*.[9]

The precision of this passage is aimed at defining the exact boundaries between Traherne and the other characters in the action. Implicitly, since the truth resides with Traherne and the Church of England, careful discrimination among the various individuals has an important relation to truth. Separation between Traherne and the not-Traherne is therefore an important feature of the prose. Is it not so in all autobiography? The defining features of a character are only those which separate him from the other inhabitants of his spatio-temporal world.

At one point at least Traherne seems to have toyed with the idea of fictionalizing his speaker completely. He began his Fourth Century with this suggestion:

> Since the Author in the last centurie hath spoken so much concerning his Enterance and Progress into the Study of Felicity, and all He hath there said pertaineth only to the Contemplativ Part of it I will in this Centurie supply his Place and Speak of the Principles with which he endued Himself to enjoy it. [Margoliouth, I, 284]

Why Traherne entertained this strategy may be, as Margoliouth thinks, "difficult to understand." Nevertheless, the proposed strategy points again to Traherne's effort to distance himself from the speaker of either the Third or Fourth Century, and to distinguish in some measure each of them. If this fiction would have been "transparent," it is nonetheless informative. Throughout the *Centuries* we find the speaker shifting from one perspective to another, openly or somewhat covertly changing identities but gathering his being from his very anonymity. As Miss Webber has pointed out, Traherne will sometimes even suffer a grammatical lapse in his handling of pronouns, with the rhetorical effect, again, being a lack of precision as to who is speaking.[10]

Even in the first half of the Third Century, reminiscences of childhood are imbued with something other than history: the rhetorical victim of Traherne's prose is the event. General postulates take the place of such appurtenances as description and dialogue. The speaker recalls not what he did but what attitudes he possessed: "It was a Difficult matter to persuade me that the Tinsild Ware upon a Hobby hors was a fine thing"; "The Glass of Imagination was the only Mirror, wherin any thing was represented or appeared to me. All Things were Absent which they talkt not of" (III.9, 10). He remembers "Being Swallowed up . . . in idle . . . talk" rather than a single conversation (III.14). As the reader has been instructed, the memory of this being is subject to the modulations of an inventive spirit. Experience in the diarist's sense of the word is transformed into dream; autobiography becomes allegory:

I lived among Shadows, like a Prodigal Son feeding upon Husks with Swine. A Comfortless Wilderness full of Thorns and Troubles the World was, or wors: a Waste Place covered with Idleness and Play, and Shops and Markets and Taverns. [III.14]

It is up to the reader to infer particular buildings and people from the existence of unadorned and general nouns: Troubles, Idleness, Shops, Markets, Taverns. Further, the parable of the prodigal son bears a good part of the narrative burden. Instead of personal history Traherne conveys a sense of alienation between father and son. This dreamlike landscape composed of allegorical associations as well as abstract nouns emphasizes a theme of separation between the child and his rightful inheritance.

The dreamlike quality of reminiscence elicits a gathering sense of the child's insulation from the humdrum world of everyday life. He seems never to have responded to the raw materials of experience, but only to their implied motives. Accordingly, raw experience seems never to penetrate the meditation either. Even the experience of thinking is subject to the fuzzying effects of reverie: "Once I remember (I think I was about 4 yeer old, when) I thus reasoned with my self. sitting in a little Obscure Room in my Fathers poor House. If there be a God, certainly He must be infinit in Goodness" (III.16). That is the last we hear of either house or room. The diction swiftly widens in scope to include earth and sky—infinity—from which the child feels alienated. The comparison is clear enough: the speaker was like the Prodigal Son not in any physical separation from his historical father. History in the ordinary sense makes up no part of the author's theme. The child was apart from the treasures given him by the Father of all. Of course the strategy here may be looked upon as autobiographical, in the sense that Traherne is characterizing the speaker of the *Centuries*; but this speaker occupied a landscape of the total "World," in a season coeval with "Creation."

I think that both the diction and structure of such passages attempt to fuse landscape with literary creation. The voice merges with the vision; Traherne tries to construct a metaphor which will equate human capacity and infinity. Hence, the emphasis on the movement of the speaker's thoughts to the uttermost regions of space and time. Ideas of this kind were widespread, as we might expect in a period attracted to both Plato and mysticism. In the age of the Stuarts no more common commonplace exists than the view of man as microcosm. But it is one thing to lend one's voice to a cliché and quite another to explore its metaphoric possibilities with respect to place and time. In *The Differences of the Ages of Mans Life* (1607), Henry Cuff sees in the various epochs of each biography the temporal impress of the ages; and like Traherne he puts special emphasis on the expansive aspects of the springtime of youth. Similarly, he takes the spatial possibilities of the microcosm image seriously: man is justly called an "*Analogicall World*" because of his cosmic reach:

MAN the *Epitome* of the whole *world*, Lord of the *Creatures*, in regard of that perfect analogie and resemblance between him & the great worlds frame, is not unfitly by the Learned, both *Divines* and *Philosophers*, termed the *Lesser* world: for there is nothing in the vaste compasse of this universall circumference, whose likeness and lively representation we have not summarily compressed in man, as in a most perfect compendium and abridgement.[11]

Just as the single life encompasses all of time, so it compresses total space. Here Cuff's diction, especially his use of adjectives, sharpens the emphasis on the expansive qualities of the metaphor of man as microcosmic sphere. Man is like the "great worlds frame" in his wholeness, greatness, vastness, in his universality. In a mysterious way he shares the world's qualities of extension.

When Traherne juxtaposes speaker, Matthew, Christ, and David, besides invoking a set of literary associations, he attempts radically to destroy the exact boundaries defining this microcosm of man. His speaker cannot be isolated in time, reduced to the impoverished moment. By invoking the language of others the speaker internalizes a part of them, losing, in the general expansion of being that follows, whatever "Defects of lonelinesse" existed previously. As in "The Extasie," "(All which before was poore, and scant,) / Redoubles still, and multiplies." Similarly, in the Third Century the speaker's narrative is one of spatial and temporal expansion: "I was enlarged," the speaker says. A sojourner in other kingdoms and other ages, he enters other places and other times in his imagination, and they become part of him, just as does the Word of the prophet or poet. In order to understand the nature of this expansion, the reader must relinquish all ideas of limitation:

No man will believ besides the Space from the Centre of the Earth to the utmost bounds of the Everlasting Hills, there should be any more. Beyond those Bounds perhaps there may, but besides all that Space that is illimited and present before us, and absolutly endles evry Way, where can there be any Room for more? This is the Space that is at this Moment only present before our Ey, the only Space that was, or that will be, from Everlasting to Everlasting. This Moment Exhibits infinit Space, but there is a Space also wherin all Moments are infinitly Exhibited, and the Everlasting Duration of infinit Space is another Region and Room of Joys. Wherin all Ages appear together, all Occurrences stand up at once, and the innumerable and Endless Myriads of yeers that were before the Creation, and will be after the World is ended are Objected as a Clear and Stable Object, whose several Parts extended out at length, giv an inward Infinity to this Moment, and compose an Eternitie that is seen by all Comprehensors and Enjoyers. [V.6]

As the spiritual guide of the *Centuries*, Traherne's speaker is just such an enlarged being of enjoyment and comprehension.

114

The Fifth Century (actually only a decade of meditations) represents the final annihilation of history. It is largely a sequence of abstract nouns which attempt to render final definitions of infinity and eternity. We are not surprised to read that "Infinity of Space is like" the empty pages before the speaker at the beginning of things, like "a Painters Table" prepared for the "Ground and feild of those Colors that are to be laid theron" (V.5). Eternity and time exist in God for man's enjoyment; but only the creatures able to transcend the commonsense limits of the quotidian world are able to do so:

Creatures that are able to dart their Thoughts into all Spaces, can brook no Limit or Restraint, they are infinitly endebted to this illimited Extent, becaus were there no such Infinitie, there would be no Room for their Imaginations; their Desires and Affections would be coopd up, and their Souls imprisoned. [V.3]

According to Thomas Jackson, whose *Treatise of the Divine Essence* (1628) Traherne had read,[12] absolute extension is a necessary attribute of God. Jackson recognized that unless one believed in God's infinite extension he must perforce accept the notion of Divinity's movement from one place to another. Mutability and omnipotence are logical contraries; of necessity, God's essence transcends every space, real or imagined: "He is every where, because no body, no space, or spirituall substance can exclude his presence, or avoid penetration of his Essence."[13] Although "penetration" implies movement, Jackson is firm in his belief that God occupies all space from the beginning. This is so because, for Him, discrete moments do not exist. Time is an illusory concomitant of existence whose perception fallen man shares with the animals. Conceptions of time have always moved between static and dynamic poles.[14] The former Aristotelian view of time recognizes the integrity of the particular moment. This is the way of classification, and (in the literary sense of this discussion) it ends with a nominalist attention to details and events. The temporal universe of Samuel Pepys is one of shifting events, a veritable kaleidoscope of evanescent scenes and times and faces. The diarist proliferates details out of a strong persuasion that meaning and classification inhere in differences: "By their fruits ye shall know them" is the rule of one for whom appearances provide boundaries. Ledgers are only important when past, present, and future retain their boundaries. This is why autobiography is so full of the sense of keeping on top of things. The tide of history is always about to overwhelm one in an apocalyptic turn of events. Without change we can have no autobiography, much less the novel.

In the *Centuries* the linear progress of events is less evident than Traherne's stylistic means of undermining personal history. The speaker loves the Bible because its pages add to him (III.24), increasing the purview of his soul's eye by "10000 Ages," which are to him eternally present. "On News," the poem which makes up the whole of *Centuries* III.26, explores the relation between experience and words; in the speaker's opening awareness of Scripture, it seems "As if the Tidings were the Things" themselves. Made possessor of the words, he is enlarged by them. For him, change is a process of spatial expansion. The apparent identity of word and object reveals a profound truth which only the paradoxical nature of human life momentarily obscures. The child sees things properly, but he cannot press beyond appearances; he is the "Crown of all," but he does not yet know it.

Though the child may be unaware, the speaker is not: "I will open my Mouth in Parables: I will utter Things that have been Kept Secret from the foundation of the World." Surely the spheral imagery of "On News" is more than ornament. Its use reminds the reader that man is "Crown of all" because he is truly a little world:

> Yet thus it was. The Gem,
> The Diadem,
> The Ring Enclosing all
> That Stood upon this Earthy Ball;
> The Heavenly Ey,
> Much Wider then the Skie,
> Wher in they all included were
> The Glorious Soul that was the King
> Made to possess them, did appear
> A Small and little thing!

Then, too, that imagery distances the speaker from his own past. Since his soul embraces all time and space, all moments of his life are before him. We must understand this in order to properly assess the emerging theme of education in the Third Century. *Centuries* III.36 reads more like a catalog of course offerings than a record of college experiences. Like the Bible, these studies serve not to inform the reader of personal happenings but to provide additional times and spaces to the speaker's expanding ego:

There I saw into the Nature of the Sea, the Heavens, the Sun, the Moon and Stars, the Elements, Minerals and Vegetables All which appeared like the Kings Daughter, All Glorious within, and those Things which my Nurses and Parents should hav talkt of, there were taught unto Me.

The single fault in the curriculum extends not from what is taught, but from what is not taught. Unlike Agrippa, Montaigne, Descartes, and Greville, Traherne believes that every study adds to the self of man, who is a priori educable.[15] Traherne's only objection to the university is its omission of the proper study of "Felicity." To men like Greville and Montaigne the various disciplines (III.41) bore testimony to man's pretense only, a protestation of knowledge based on a grossly inaccurate estimate of both reason and sense. In contrast, Traherne values even the "bounded" perspective of "Natural Philosophy," "for it Openeth the Riches of Gods Kingdom and the Natures of His Territories Works and Creatures in a Wonderfull Maner, Clearing and preparing the Ey of the Enjoyer" (III.44). As a phenomenon of a particular and isolated moment in time, the apparent defect in the educational process does not exist. The speaker has himself filled the vacuum: he is in truth the absent "Tutor that did professly Teach Felicity" (III.37).

Beginning with Meditation 46, the Third Century gives the appearance of becoming more personal: "When I came into the Country, and being seated among silent Trees, had all my Time in mine own Hands, I resolved to Spend it all, whatever it cost me, in Search of Happiness." This appearance proves to be misleading, for what follows is not narrative at all. Meditation 52 begins:

When I came into the Country, and saw that I had all time in my own hands, having devoted it wholy to the study of Felicitie, I knew not where to begin or End; nor what Objects to chuse, upon which most Profitably I might fix my Contemplation.

The speaker's thoughts immediately return to the question of limits, limits of time, limits of space. In a setting notable for its lack of background, Traherne places his motionless speaker. Now the only movement is that of mind, in the speaker's fantasy of travel:

I saw my self like som Traveller . . . resolved to spend his Days in visiting Strange Places. . . . What then I should do? Even imitat a Traveller, who becaus He cannot visit all Coasts, Wildernesses, Sandy Deserts, Seas, Hills, Springs and Mountains, chuseth the most Populous and flourishing Cities, where he might see the fairest Prospects, Wonders, and Rarities, and be entertained with greatest Courtesie: and where indeed he might most Benefit himself with Knowledg Profit and Delight: leaving the rest, even the naked and Empty Places unseen. For which caus I made it my Prayer to GOD Almighty, that He, whose Eys are open upon all Things, would guid me to the fairest and Divinest.

If we look back at what has transpired between Meditations 46 and 52, we find three poems and two prose pieces on sin. The entire round is an elaboration of elements in Meditation 46—in particular, themes of time and Felicity. *Centuries* III.46 ends with a comparison between the Edenic "World" of the "Study of Felicity" and the destructive qualities of "Care and Labor," themes treated in a manner reminiscent of Marvell's "The Garden." "A Life of Sabbaths" (Meditation 47) elaborates on the same thematic contrast. This poem carries out the timeless associations of the figurative opening. Some variant of the copula occurs nine times in the poem, and the past tense is used only once. For that matter, the preterit is notably muted throughout the sequence. It appears that in Meditation 51 the speaker provides his own explanation for the organization of the interlude. The thought of sin has disordered and disturbed his "Proceeding." What occurs is a "long Parenthesis," a hiatus.

And so we return to the opening utterance of Meditation 46, which is also the opening utterance of Meditation 52. The sequence, entirely lacking in any narrative line, serves to polarize the speaker's thoughts and the temporal world.

The same point might easily be made about the succeeding section, which leads up to Meditation 66: "Little did I imagine that, while I was thinking these Things, I was Conversing with GOD." This portion is likewise void of depicted events. While such syntactic devices as the relative pronoun or the conjunction lend a sense of logical development to Meditations 54, 56, 62, and 64, such ligatures cannot obscure the tenuous divisions between the meditations themselves. I think it is quite clear that we may often move the numbers about within the flow of thoughts, lengthening or shortening various entries without materially altering either meaning or mood. We would not dampen any development or progress, because neither can be said to correspond to the organizational principle of the work. Traherne might have put the 64 between "Imperfect" and the last sentence of Meditation 63, which clearly dramatists or novelists can seldom do. Not only are the boundaries of discrete meditations quite tenuous, but their order under broad thematic sequences is also alogical. The "Possible" of Meditation 64 could just as easily precede as follow the "Impossible" of Meditation 63. One could interpolate Meditations 60 and 61 and only a photographic memory would cause a reader to stop on a second reading. Of course we cannot do this with all or even most of the parts of this work. *Centuries* IV.1 cannot be interpolated with *Centuries* III.100 without producing an undecorous *non sequitur*. But in the sequence we are discussing, no logic—certainly not the logic of temporal development—governs the speaker's dilation on his century figure: Felicity as represented in the objects about and within man.

It seems to me that these tenuous divisions and the undermining of temporal setting work together as part of the larger metaphoric principle of organization in the work. The Fifth Century is only a decade, and it ends with two digits, the same as are prefixed to *Centuries* I.1. Perhaps Traherne had in mind one or another of the many devotional works of his time which make use of the century form. In its four centuries Thomas

Wilson's *Theologicall Rules* (1615) was thought to embody mystical truths.[16] Traherne may have known Alexander Ross's *Three Decads of Divine Meditations* [1630] or his later work, *A Centurie of Divine Meditations* (1646).[17] Be that as it may, in Traherne's work the figure of the "Century" is operative in many ways. It may mean simply one hundred (in which case it conflicts with the final Century, which has only a decade and two digits, plus blank sheets). Like all other categories, Traherne erects them only to obliterate them later by subsuming them under ever finer and more encompassing ones. The final decade points back to the beginning, suggesting the illusory quality of time. Or the figure of the "Century" might also imply lifetime, saeculum;[18] and here the metaphor is also self-destructive. For this lifetime of meditation is not constructed of the paltry happenings—or even the slender thoughts—of one rectilinear life's motion.[19] The powerful operation of spheral imagery in the *Centuries* intricately relates to Traherne's rhetoric of destroying boundaries. The sphere of the speaker's being is always expanding, as times and places are swallowed up by eternity and the infinite.

At the center of all is the ego, the present. But by valuing the world's present objects properly, the seer quickens all objects, near and far, past and present. Simultaneously, he is enlarged by their being added to his parts. Man's "Endless Intellect" is that expanding "Ey"[20] which recognizes no limits. Thus, in the closing decade of the *Centuries* the speaker describes himself:

Creatures that are able to dart their Thoughts into all Spaces, can brook no Limit or Restraint, they are infinitly endebted to this illimited Extent, becaus were there no such Infinitie, there would be no Room for their Imaginations; their Desires and Affections would be coopd up, and their Souls imprisoned. We see the Heavens with our Eys. [V.3]

But true "Joy" is in the recognition of "Capacitie":

Nothing is in vain, much less Infinity. Evry Man is alone the Centre and Circumference of it. It is all his own, and so Glorious, that it is the Eternal and Incomprehensible Essence of the Deitie. [V.3]

"Evry Man is alone the Centre and Circumference of it." Typically, Traherne attributes the same immensity to both God and man:

Tho the Sprit of an Angel be limited and Circumscribed in it self, yet the Supreme Spirit, which is GOD, is uncircumscribed. He is evry where and wholy evry where: which makes their Knowledg to be Dilated evry where. for being wholy evry where They are immediatly present with his Omnipresence in evry place and wholy. It filleth them for ever. [III.98]

Utterances like these are common in the *Centuries*—and throughout the Traherne canon, for that matter. His fondness for the microcosm image and his love of the Psalms go hand in hand and are frequently present in the same meditation (as, for example, in *Centuries* IV.74). Traherne's apostrophe to man claims the heritage of David, and of Pico and Hermes as well. But just as the speaker expands to include even these august identities, he also transcends them. He considers man as "A seeming Intervall between Time and Eternity, . . . the Golden link or Tie of the World, yea the Hymenaeus Marrying the Creator and his Creatures together." But the divine Essence, and hence the speaker's self, transcends even these: "All these things are Great, but they are not the Principal." Man cannot be limited to any spot, not even one equidistant between earth and the Empyrean.

For this expansive quality man deserves praise above the angelic hosts, a being raised not only "abov the Beasts but abov the Stars, and . . . envied even of the Supra Celestial Spirits" (IV.74). With this view in mind, it is interesting to consider Traherne's use of Pico's *Oratio*, quotation from which makes up the following three meditations (IV.75-77). Traherne draws on perhaps the most memorable passage, but he emphasizes not its microcosmic aspects in the contemplation to follow; instead, he focuses on the center of the cosmos: on man's will. In "Select Meditations" we read that "every Soul is an Infinite Centre" (I.83).[21] Likewise, in *Centuries of Meditations* man is a being capable of infinite "Capacitie"; as that circle whose center is everywhere, and whose circumference is nowhere, man is in exact spatial "Correspondence" to God (IV.70):

A sand in your conception conformeth your soul, and reduceth it to the Cize and Similtud of a sand. A Tree apprehended is a Tree in your Mind, the whole Hemisphere and the Heavens magnifie your soul in the Wideness of the Heavens. All the Spaces abov the Heavens enlarg it Wider to their own Dimensions. And what is without Limit maketh your Conception illimited and Endless. The infinity of GOD is infinitly Profitable as well as Great: as Glorious as Incomprehensible: so far from streightening that it magnifieth all Things. And must be seen in you, or GOD will be Absent. Nothing less then infinit is GOD, and as finit he cannot be Enjoyed. [IV.73]

No message is clearer in the *Centuries* than the speaker's claim to such enjoyment, a declaration of the pleasures of infinity. By returning to "Him self, in the centre of his own Unity," paradoxically, man expands; this is "the Greatest Miracle" of creation. In the infinite swell of this unity, the speaker apprehends the Form or Idea only dimly approximated by the concrete image, locked in one small part of time and space. As if in defense of the literature of abstraction, Traherne writes:

Yet is this Greatest of all Miracles unknown becaus Men are addicted only to Sensible and Visible Things. So Great a World in the Explication of its Parts is easy: but here the Dimensions of Innumerable Worlds are shut up in a Centre. [IV.81]

Examples like this explain, I think, Traherne's great interest in the spatial aspects of Pico's cosmogony. If all space was filled before man's creation, it follows that man as a being cannot be said to exist in space: in order for a new creature to be made, different from all others, a dimension transcending space was required. Two words describe this new dimension: infinity and will. In Traherne, the concept of infinity governs major stylistic features of his art. He presents an image, a comparison, a description of man or object, only to undercut the category which that being or object appears to fill. His aim is to teach the concept of infinity, which he believes "Few will believ the Soul to be" (II.81). This skepticism on man's part is full of irony, for "Infinit is the first Thing which is naturaly Known." In a most interesting passage Traherne discusses what we now think of as the psychology of perception, pointing out that the idea of limitation is learned through the opposition to the senses. In the infant's mind no such boundaries exist. Freud would later make a similar point in declaring the existence of "oceanic" feelings in the child before the synapses of the nervous system provide the means of distinguishing his body from any other.[22] Thus, only the senses are acquainted with limits. The soul knows only "That first of Properties infinit Space."

We see the stylistic implications of this idea in Traherne's treatment of such microcosmic figures as the mirror image. In "Select Meditations" we read:

Shadows in the water are Like their substances. And so reall. that no painter can againe Express them. even here beneath the sun is seen, and the face of Heaven. [II.72]

Just as the sun shines on the water mirror, reflecting itself to itself, so love touches, enflames, and returns without being spent: "The Soul beneath is Like that abov . . ." (II.73). And in the *Centuries* we read that "the World serveth you as it is a Mirror wherin you Contemplat the Blessed Trinity. for it Plainly sheweth that GOD is Lov" (II.45). Again, "Man is made in the Image of GOD, and therfore is a Mirror and Representativ of Him" (II.23). But like all other categories, as the *Centuries* unfolds, this comparison is subject to adjustment and qualification. In the Second Century, friendship turns the world of experience into multiple mirrors, in which man lives "again in other Persons" (II.70). In the Fourth, the mirror image undergoes a radical adjustment of planes and, finally, of nature. A flat surface is too limited in space to represent the soul's love of God:

And were they Mirrors only that return his Lov, one would think it impossible, while he shines upon them, to forbear to shine. but they are like the Ey, Mirrors with Lids, and the Lid of Ignorance or Inconsideration interposing, they are often Ecclypsed, or shine only through som Cranies; so that here upon Earth having free Power to hold open or shut their Lids, to send, or turn away their Beams; they may lov me, or forbear. [IV.86]

The metamorphosis which the figure undergoes expresses Traherne's abiding voluntarism. At the center of the cosmos is a unity of essence (love) and act (will). By adjusting the reception of light, Traherne asserts the importance of will: "I hav placed Thee in the Middle of the World, that from thence thou mayest behold . . . the whole World . . . that . . . thou mayst shape thy self into what Nature thy self pleaseth" (IV.76). But the shift both alters and expands the spatial quality of the perception; the reflected image assumes a spheral form.

In this voluntarism Traherne most clearly declares himself heir to the neo-Platonism of men like Ficino and Pico, in whose expansive view man's freedom of will and cognitive capacity were other sides of the same coin: potentiality. Implicit in the mystical humanism of the *Oratio* is a denial that knowledge can be limited to either sense or reason. Where reason and the senses end, the instructive devices of Contemplation and Felicity begin. It was in just such optimism that the skeptics Greville, Montaigne, and others perceived an elemental *hybris*. Since the recognitions of the mystical pathway do not lend themselves to common-sense formulations, the language of neo-Platonism is often that of paradox. We see this point clearly in Traherne's treatment of self-love. On the one hand, self-love is a basic fact of nature in that all animals love themselves. To transcend a vegetable existence, one must love one's self. Nevertheless, though "self Lov is the Basis of all Love," in an equally forceful sense "It is true that Self Lov is Dishonorable" (IV.55). What, then, was God's purpose in creating the world and in making man in his own image? The answer is in order that he might enjoy himself, love himself, *in* his own creation. Similarly, man in loving the objects of creation, especially in loving other men, transmits his love to them, which returns, allowing himself to bask in the radiance of his own love of himself in others. In the Church's Year-Book we read:

. . . by Communicating our selves we are united to others, give others the Benefit of our selvs, & Enjoy our selvs in being Enjoyed. . . . Becaus Narcissus like, none can Enjoy Himself in Himself, unless he hath a fountain. Nor can any Enjoy themselvs in a fountain; tho they see the Reflexion of themselvs.[23]

Similarly, in Peter Sterry's *Discourse on the Freedome of the Will* (1649), a work known by Traherne, Sterry writes of the soul communicating itself to itself. The figure is a Christian analogue of the Gnostic doctrine of emanations, and the neo-Platonists of the seventeenth century are fond of it. For Traherne, the idea of communication implies spatial and temporal enlargement. Love is a means by which man "Expandest and Enlargest [his] self" (I.73). Traherne, the priest, may have in mind the prayer following the General Confession:

Grant us therefore (Gracious lorde) so to eate the fleshe of thy dere sonne Jesus Christ, and to drynke his bloud in these holy Misteries, that we may continuallye dwell in hym, and he in us, that oure synfull bodyes may bee made cleane by his body, and our soules washed through hys most precious bloud. Amen. [*The Booke of the Common Prayer* (1549)]

In lines reminiscent of Herbert's "The Thanksgiving," the speaker in *Centuries* I.75 offers his soul and body in return for the Sacrifice; and in the following meditation he interprets the effect of Christ's "Precious Blood" as an enlargement of his own capacity to love.

Expansion is only one spatial aspect of self-love. The paradoxical quality of this idea requires also that we recognize its implosive character. In "Select Meditations" the meditant asserts: "When I retire first I seem to com in my Selfe to a Centre" (I.81). This center is the same image of love described in *Centuries* I.56, the "Journeys of the Soul" being a concentration on the Sacrifice. Later in "Select Meditations" the speaker describes the "Eternitie" of this center as "An omnipresent Sphere within our Sphere" (II.66). In the same manner the speaker in the *Centuries* recounts how, when alone "and without Employment," his "Soul would return to it self" (III.17); the motif in the Second Century depicting the self alone at the center of the cosmos suggests the same spatial collapse: man as the invisibly small point in the infinite abyss of the universe, with the theme of service as the palliative. Even more typical of Traherne, however, is the use of the miniature. Like Blake, Traherne makes rich use of synecdoche. In *Christian Ethicks*, in one of many passages that would go unnoticed in the *Cen-*

125

turies for any diminution of tone or quality, the speaker expatiates on the sun's virtues: "THE Sun is a glorious Creature, and its Beams extend to the utmost Stars, by shining on them it cloaths them." The emphasis seems to be on the expansive benefits of the sun. But as the passage unfolds, the focus shifts to the particular and small in such a way as to suggest an implosion from macrocosm to microcosm:

It enlightens the Eyes of all the Creatures: It shineth on forty Kingdomes at the same time, on Seas and Continents in a general manner; yet so particularly regardeth all, that every Mote in the Air, every Grain of Dust, every Sand, every Spire of Grass is wholly illuminated thereby, as if it did entirely shine upon that alone.[24]

This passage might serve as a gloss on the Blakean meditation beginning "You never Enjoy the World aright, till you see how a Sand Exhibiteth the Wisdom and Power of God" (I.27), where the emphasis is on "how" the speaker perceives and understands and values the smallest object, a view reinforced in the Second Century: "O what a Treasure is evry Sand when truly understood!" (II.67).

Traherne uses synecdoche in such a way as to subvert the distinction between part and whole. He will suddenly shift from abstract category, from the whole or universal, to particular instance, and back again. The rapidity of the shift, which is frequently accomplished without a tensed verb, functions as an implied copula; the reader can see by such juxtaposition that the particular is the act (or emanation) of an essence, which transcends and includes a myriad of such instances. Moreover, the symmetry of nature requires the perfect agreement of all respective planes and surfaces, whether of larger or smaller spheres. A major device for obliterating the boundaries between part and whole is the temporal shift, the speaker's recognition that apparent differences are only illusory aspects of fragmented time. For example, in *Centuries* II.96 the seed seems to be only part of the pomegranate (Cant. 6:7), and common sense, in turn, would seem to argue against the proposition that "The World is a Pomgranat indeed." But to one initiated in those mysteries held sacred "from the foundation of the

World," this equation is eminently just. The pomegranate contains the world because of what it is, because of the occult resemblance between part and whole, time and eternity. Within the pomegranate lie "Seeds of Grace and the Seeds of Glory." Just as Solomon foreshadowed the "true Solomon," so the seed is (*in utero*) the full-grown plant. But the inscription in the seed bears a truth transcending past or passing; its ultimate truth is of things to come. Like the typological implications of the Solomonic tradition, which looks beyond the Passion to the final epithalamion and Wedding Supper, the seed encloses triune time. When man understands the principle in seeds, the marvel of their growth, their wisdom in knowing when and how to flourish and reproduce, he must acknowledge that the seed is quite literally more than meets the eye of the moment. Traherne's meaning is similar to that in Vaughan's "Cock-crowing," but with a significant difference. Vaughan's poem is full of longing and nostalgia; the seed of the soul's light "Dreams" but dreams only "Of Paradise and Light." In Traherne, the seed of man's soul in the pomegranate of the world already dwells in the timeless, roomy enjoyments of both: "*All Things* in Time and Eternity being Objects of your Felicity GOD the Giver, and you the Receiver" (II.100).

We notice the same bifurcated thrust of imagery in the First Century, where the contour of thematic material stresses the Passion sequence (I.56-91). The diction of the preceding meditations recurrently suggests the spatial qualities of God: movement, filling, communication, expansion. But the language is strikingly general, reminding the reader that the speaker views his material from the prospect of eternity: "He overfloweth Eternaly"; "Did you not from all Eternity Want som one . . .?"; "The Contemplation of Eternity maketh the Soul Immortal" (I.42,45,55). Simultaneously, the way is prepared for the total collapse of this perspective by the redefinition of the ligatures binding man to God. "Bands and Cements," "Ligatures" and "Sinews" are static figures, meaningful only to the supratemporal vision. But these figures are radically qualified in the section on the Passion in which the verbs suggest movement, especially contractive movement. The Cross as the "Centre of Eternity": "When I am lifted up saith the Son of man I will

Draw all Men unto me" (I.56). In Meditations 56 and 57, one or another form of "draw" occurs. Bands securing have turned to cords, used to draw man to his center. From the abstract prospect of eternity the speaker thrusts the reader into an intense and vivid experience of one moment: "O Thou that Hangest upon this Cross before mine Eys, Whose face is Bleeding, and covered over with Tears and filth and Blows!" (I.64). Throughout the sequence Old Testament analogues witness to the preparation made by time for this moment, to the way in which the face or image of this act existed "from all Eternitie" (I.62). Again we grasp a vision of the Trinity: for in this act inheres the static ligature, the cement bond holding all means and times in constant place. And yet this same act is also the collapse of history, the movement along the radius of time to the still point in the center. Finally, the Sacrifice is like a monumental outward extension of this center, enclosing every sphere of time.

In this vision, one act resolves the riddle of time, reducing past, present, and future to One.[25] In accordance with a perfectly symmetrical scheme of things, man emulates the Trinity in his own self-immolating act of love. Just as Christ was raised ("When I am lifted up") drawing all men under the shadow of his substance, so toward the end of the Century the speaker describes himself as "raised out of Nothing" to embrace other beings. Like the object of his love, he becomes a cosmos, "lately raised out of dust," but raised and extended interminably in time and space: "Interminable Temple, out of which nothing can be, from which Nothing is removed, to which nothing is afar off; but all things immediatly near." This intellectual paragon is one whom "20 Millions of Ages" cannot circumscribe; his "Endless Life . . . can at once extend to all Eternity" (I.92). By the merging of his will with God's, man's soul is equally extended (I.93). Evidence of this identity is seen in the fecundity of the new Soul: "By Loving a Soul does Propagat . . . it self" (II.48); "By loving a Soul Does Propagat and beget it self" (II.56). God takes great pleasure in the "Voluntary Act of an Obedient Soul" because through such acts He is united with His own essence. Since every act of that essence is generative, the appropriate imagery depicting love is that of multiplication and fecundity. Heaven's geometry is Euclidian: things equal to the same things are equal to each other. Hence, the figure of expanding center is richly meaningful, for man's will is truly the center and end of all things. God may only love Creation through His intellectual act, which is man. In Traherne's cosmogony, man is both end and means of the essence emanating as the universe, and in man's love of God flowing back to its source:

For GOD hath made you able to Creat Worlds in your own mind, which are more Precious unto Him then those which he Created: And to Give and offer up the World unto Him, which is very Delightfull in flowing from Him, but much more in Returning to Him. [II.90]

In his conception of love, Traherne fuses his orthodox Anglicanism with the mystical neo-Platonism. For him, love is intrinsically paradoxical, and therefore justly compared to the Trinity. To the Platonist, the common-sense world seems radically dyadic: form-being, body-soul, material-immaterial, time-eternity, light-dark, and so on. There is something Manichean about the division in the universe between mind and body, good and evil (and, today, conscious and subconscious). Cartesian philosophy is only one expression of dyadic codification: the Idea and the Appearance can never meet in such a system except by a plenary act of metaphor. In *The Divine Pymander* of Hermes, Traherne read that all things could be reduced to "but Two things, *That which maketh, and that which is made*; and the One of them cannot depart, or be divided from the other."[26] Similarly, in Ficino the soul of the lover does not exist in itself, but only in the one loved. If the lover is not directed outwards, he cannot be said to exist; he is dead. In the generative sense, the opposite of propagation is death: so Traherne answers, "the Soul without Extending, and living in its Object, is Dead with in it self" (II.56). Further, this exchange of identities is one of the world's great mysteries (or metaphors). It is the underlying spatial metaphor of all mysticism: the recognition that to reconcile the dyad, one must posit a paradoxical triad, namely, a third element which accounts for movement, interchange. To destroy the principle of identity, one must also destroy space.

So it is that Traherne undertakes to undermine the principle of identity; personal identity is only one of the many instances of apparent boundary which he rhetorically destroys. He recognizes that in the love of God man expresses his wish to be divine.[27] But such a recognition implies a distinction between human and divine. Further difficulties arise: If a man lays claim to divinity, how does he avoid the *hybris* sensed by men like Greville and Montaigne? The answer is, again, paradoxical. In self-love man loves both himself and the world, and yet simultaneously limits and even withdraws that love in order to achieve a perfect union with God. It was commonly observed that love unites lover to beloved.[28] But man could not enjoy the love of God and love of self at the same time: "The love of God enters not into the soul, unless self-love and the love of the world first go forth."[29] This seems to be Traherne's theme in *Centuries* I. But in *Christian Ethicks,* he insists that the love of God stems from the fact that "we love our selves and delight in our own Happiness."[30]

The paradox of self-love and its seeming arrogance resolve upon the imitation of the Godhead, with its implicit spatial destruction of the principle of identity. Love reveals the same triune nature:

Where Lov is the Lover, Lov streaming from the Lover, is the Lover; the Lover streaming from Himself: and Existing in another Person. [II.42]

So that in all Love the Trinity is Clear. [II.40]

In language with strong eucharistic overtones the speaker delineates each of the three entities or elements of love: "The Lov that lieth in the Bosom of the Lover, being the Lov that is perceived in the Spirit of the Beloved: that is, the same in substance . . . . Lov in the Bosom is the Parent of Lov, Lov in the Stream is the Effect of Lov, Lov seen, or Dwelling in the Object proceedeth from both" (II.40). Traherne is at pains to make sure that the exactness of the metaphor be made clear to his reader. Love as the speaker knows it exactly corresponds to the Godhead (II.40-46):

In all Lov there is some Producer, som Means, and som End: all these being Internal in the Thing it self. Lov Loving is the Pro-

ducer, and that is the father; Lov Produced is the Means, and that is
the Son: for Lov is the Means by which a Lover loveth. The End
of these Means is Lov: for it is Lov, by loving: and that is the H.
Ghost. [II.46]

Thus, love issues, proceeds, and ends at the same point, as if in
the Trinity a perfect circle had been drawn through the points
of an equilateral triangle. In Pythagorean number symbolism,
the triad and the circle mystically referred to the same Unity.[31]
Plotinus insists on the triune nature of the soul's form.[32] For
Traherne, the Trinity was the perfect figure of self-love, which
is nothing less than the mystery of God in man. Isolated self-
love is destructive in that it constricts the soul's proper expansion. As Peter Sterry writes, "true knowledge of the self is never
limited to any One Particular Thing."[33] If a man would know
himself, he must reach out, look around him as well as within.
One of the major themes of *Christian Ethicks* proclaims the
diminution of the self when any object is deprived of its full
attention and value.[34]

Extend, expand, flow, stream: those elements of diction
which erode the idea of set position in a frame of space tend
also to undermine the integrity of isolated moments and of
particular biographies. God created the world and man because
"He wanted the Communication of His Divine Essence, and
Persons to Enjoy it" (I.41). Ever reflecting the divine image, in
the "Glass of Imagination," man creates worlds peopled by
multitudes. In the verbal cosmos of the *Centuries* biographies
shade into one another, as if the host of echoed authors, the
inspired prophets of Scripture, Mrs. Susanna Hopton, and the
author himself were one pulsating Being, whose life occupies
the whole expanse of time. In "The Extasie" the lovers' souls go
out in order "to advance their state," and in that movement they
procreate and multiply.[35] At the same time, though achieving an
increase of members, the souls simultaneously merge as one
"refined" or "abler soule." In the single, isolated soul lies limitation and eccentricity: "All which before was poore, and scant,
/ Redoubles still, and multiplies."[36] Similarly, toward the close
of the Fourth Century, Traherne begins a theme which dominates the final decade. Like Donne's "abler soule," "Infinity,"

the room of his speaker's soul, "is but one Object" (IV.98). Many voices of many ages exist now as objects on a painter's canvas.

As we can see, in the Trinity the contrarieties of expansion, stasis, and contraction are reconciled and souls' mysteries "unperplexed." What the ecstatic point of view seems to insist upon, however, is the basic incompleteness of the particular individual. Understanding depends upon spatial and temporal accretions to the soul's sphere: self-love as growth. At the beginning of this chapter we distinguished the perspective of the Third Century from "autobiography." Autobiography in the seventeenth century tends to be univocal; the speaker's voice is that of the diarist, closely concerned with the details of a single life. But in Traherne personal identity, like any other object, must be permeated, extended, brought to its infinite center. We see this throughout the *Centuries*, but especially in the emerging dominance of the psalmic voice in the Third Century. The speaker's personality as well as his voice becomes absorbed in the being of another. And this is a major addition, for as we read in the poem introducing the psalmic sequence, David's voice from the past was eminently one of a comprehensive soul:

> A Shepherd, Soldier, and Divine,
> A Judge, a Courtier, and a King,
> Priest, Angel, Prophet, Oracle did shine
>   At once; when he did sing.
> Philosopher and Poet too
> Did in his Melodie appear;
>   All these in Him did pleas the View
> Of Those that did his Heavenly musick hear
> And evry Drop that from his flowing Quill
> Came down, did all the World with Nectar fill.
>
> [III.69.5]

Early in the First Century, the juxtaposition of speaker and Matthew implied a disintegration of temporal and physical boundaries, finally identifying speaker, David, Christ, and Matthew in one sweeping denial of the univocal voice. In the Third Century we find a variation on this theme. In a manner reminiscent of the *Thanksgivings* (see chapter 4) the speaker (more and more resembling Donne's imagined reader of the Psalms translated by Sir Philip Sidney and his sister) falls in with the Psalms, to sing his part. He recognizes that in his thoughts he was like David, "Conversing with GOD," and that in his understanding of the Psalms lay the seed of total recognition: "Me thoughts a New Light Darted in into all his Psalmes, and finaly spread abroad over the whole Bible" (III.66). This Meditation, in turn, is a prelude to the visionary *Centuries* III.67-68: "There I saw Moses . . ."; "I saw moreover. . . ." Old Testament scenes appear before the speaker, as he enjoys a temporal and spatial freedom from the restrictions of the present. As he had at the beginning of the *Centuries*, the speaker now returns to the creation: "There I saw Adam in Paradice." Toward the end of the sequence, the meditant reasserts the theme of David's extended Being in his own voice; his was a comprehensive soul, "like an infinit Ocean," whose lyric praise exceeded "10000 vents" (III.94). Again, the geometric equation applies. Since the speaker's voice has merged with David's, so has his Being. By a process of inclusion, distinctions between past and present —all vestiges of the personal and limited—are destroyed. Like David, the speaker has transcended time:

His Soul recovered its Pristine Liberty and saw thorow the Mud Walls of flesh and Blood. Being alive, he was in the Spirit all his Days, while his Body therfore was inclosed in this World his Soul was in the Temple of Eternity and clearly beholds the infinit Life and Omnipresence of God. having Conversation with Invisible Spiritual and Immaterial Things. . . . Kingdoms and Ages did surround him, as clearly as the Hills and Mountins: and therfore the Kingdom of God was ever round about Him. [III.95]

As George Kubler observes, the concept of duration presupposes a systematic, serial arrangement. Successive occurrences in a series necessarily reduce the number of possibilities remaining in that series: "No duration . . . can be discussed save in respect to its beginning, middle, end, or to its early and its late moments."[37] In a work like *The Temple*, in which temporal arrangement is an important structural feature, the serial arrangement of the included Christian holidays follows the same logic as that obtaining between "Death" and "Judgement." The same is true of the parts of "Church Militant." Once the cyclic figure of the sun's passage west begins to function, the parts of the poem become difficult to move without producing confusion. Evening follows afternoon; one reaches the nearer areas of European west before America. The Christian year is the structural substratum of *The Temple* as it is the sole linear feature of the Church's Year-Book. In Traherne's hexameron, "Meditations on the First Day" appropriately precedes those on the second. But what is the serial order of the *Centuries of Meditations*? Here moments, hours, years, decades, eons—all are present to the speaker's view, as if all objects exist *sub specie aeternitatis*.

This perspective, the point of view of "Endless Intellect," is the subject of the speaker's rapt contemplation in the Fifth Century. In a work which eludes biographical construction, we find this literary portrait of the speaker/artist as seer:

Creatures that are able to dart their Thoughts into all Spaces, can brook no Limit or Restraint, they are infinitly endebted to this illimited Extent, becaus were there no such Infinitie, there would be no Room for their Imaginations. . . . Nothing is in vain, much less Infinity. Evry Man is alone the Centre and Circumference of it. [V.3]

In the speaker's purview, all boundaries are destroyed by the recognition that the given category is subsumed within a more capacious sphere. Ultimately, the distinction between time and space must dissolve:

This Moment Exhibits infinit Space, but there is a Space also wherin all Moments are infinitly Exhibited, and the Everlasting Duration of infinit Space is another Region and Room of Joys. Wherin all Ages appear together, all Occurrences stand up at once, and the innumerable and Endless Myriads of yeers that were before the Creation, and will be after the World is ended are Objected as a Clear and Stable Object, whose several Parts extended out at length, giv an inward Infinity to this Moment, and compose an Eternitie that is seen by all Comprehensors and Enjoyers. [V.6]

It seems to me that here we have a major rhetorical device of the *Centuries*; Traherne will erect a category (a person, object, event, or point of view) and proceed to expatiate on its expansive qualities. But this expatiation is like a search, a rumination through frequently synonymous utterances, one which often isolates an implied limit in the concreteness of the language as originally formulated.[38] The transition from mirror to "Ey" was one example. The rhetorical drift of Traherne's method is always toward more general locutions: the abstract noun as a metaphor of quantity. This explains Traherne's obfuscation of events, which, if particularized, represent a too constricted point of view. In order to convey a properly capacious point of view, one must defy the most basic fact of human existence, namely the sense of duration. The means of such denial is paradox: intervals both are and are not. Even God was, though he was not.[39] Human life seems necessarily tensed; and yet this tensed quality of language, the distinction between present and preterit, is only one more boundary to demolish. If a man in a carriage passes through a forest, the trees "Seem to run Backward." But this illusion is the affective residue of a limited point of view. In reality, "The moments stand, we mov by." The speaker distances himself from the human prospect when he recognizes the wider view within which it exists: "Tis we are Successiv / Eternity is not so."

In an apt phrase John Wall speaks of "the congruity of times."[40] The alternative to serial arrangement is spatial reduction to a plane surface. This fictionalizing process "doth unperplex" the ultimate mystery, the meshing of eternity and time.

Eternity is a Mysterious Absence of Times and Ages: an Endless Length of Ages always Present. . . . For as there is an immovable Space wherin all finit Spaces are enclosed, and all Motions carried on, and performed: so is there an Immovable Duration, that contains and measures all moving Durations. [V.7]

By spatializing time, Traherne renders yet another boundary permeable to the point of tenuousness. We may detect a similar erosive pattern in the structure of the work itself. Divisions between parts are often quite tenuous. It is not only events or objects which give way before the erosive quality of this rhetoric; the logic of progression does also: the syllogism is only one more emblem of serial order.

The more one reads Traherne the more uncomfortable he becomes with the critical view of Traherne's prose style as "simple and straightforward."[41] Traherne is not, as one critic thinks, merely an educated Bunyan. Modern readers are often unresponsive to literary experiences not based on novelistic assumptions about beginning, middle, and end. And like the novel, the syllogism has taken its toll on our ability to respond to certain literary values. Many critics identify repetition with monotony; if a work does not develop, it must lack tension. If it lacks tension, how can it be good?

It is true that Traherne depends heavily on repetition. But as Bach and Breughel, not to mention Donne and Milton, demonstrated, repetition and monotony are hardly the same thing. Traherne can and does use repetition very effectively, as in this example, following a discussion about self-love and the Christian injunction to love others "as" one loves himself:

The more you lov men, the more Delightfull you will be to God, and the more Delight you will take in God, and the more you will enjoy Him. So that the more like you are to Him in Goodness, the more abundantly you will enjoy his Goodness. [IV.57]

In this passage, all six members are linked by occurrence of the item "more" within each. The result is a sense of overflowing or fullness of quantity. Each new member appears to develop an aspect of category introduced in the preceding clause: the quantity of God's delight is increased, the quantity of man's delight in God multiplied, and so on. One notices, however, that the meditation could easily end with the first quoted sentence. For although each member adds to the effect, each also in a sense restates what has already been said. Earlier in the meditation the speaker observes that the love of men is the love of self. The concluding sentence reiterates: "By loving others you live in others to receive it." Thus, the syntax of each sentence and repetitive diction reinforce the single emphasis on addition, on the generative qualities of love. Traherne had not been taught the fallacy of imitative form; to him, an increase of instances might suggest an increase of capacity, enclosing a myriad of objects and beings in a more intensely perceived unity.

Traherne is victimized by other preconceptions. We train our students to look for logical or organic form in a work, as if literature must never organize itself except on logical norms— or (worse) as if a poem were really like a plant, alive in the perfect interrelation of its parts. As critics we may become the victims of our own vocabulary. Certainly, *Centuries of Meditations* resists the imposition of either the logical or the organic metaphors. One finds discontinuity as well as continuity in this work. To be complete, the alogical inclusion must be made as well as the more predictable. Thus, one senses throughout the *Centuries* a pervasive undermining of logic as well as of time.

When at its best, Traherne's prose conveys a sense of onrush, as if the speaker is inundated by a tide of thoughts, which overflow the restraints of the English period. That is why so many periods occur where no sentence ends; and why so many sentences end where either an inappropriate sign or no sign at all appears—or, as in this case, the parenthesis seems to suggest a strand of thought lost in the motion of ideas:

By this we may Discern what Strange Power GOD hath given to us by loving us infinitly. [Who more Prizeth our Naked Lov then Temples full of Gold: Whose Naked Lov is more Delightfull to us then all Worlds: And Whose Greatest Gifts and Treasures are Living Souls and Friends, and Lovers. Who as He hath Manifested His Lov by giving us His Son, hath Manifested it also by giving us all His Sons and Servants. Commanding them to lov us with that Precious Lov wherwith they do them selvs. but most] He giveth us a Power more to pleas him, then if we were able to Creat Worlds and present them unto Him. [II.60]

Here the parenthesis seems appropriate at the beginning but suggests a disrupted line of thought at the close. The period and the opening parenthesis sweep away the sense of apposition, which lends parallelism to the clauses. Similarly, this technique may be used along with allusion as if to suggest that the memory is flooded with literary experiences directly related:

It [Love] seems it will break in evry where, as that without which the World could not be Enjoyed. Nay as that without which it would not be Worthy to be Enjoyed. for it was Beautified by Lov, and commandeth the Lov of a Donor to us. Lov is a Phoenix that will revive in its own Ashes, inherit Death, and smell sweetly in the Grave. [IV.61]

Margoliouth has noticed the echo of Shirley's brilliant lyric, "The Glories of our blood and State,"[42] and certainly the affirmation of the closing couplet in Shirley's poem resembles the exultant tone of this passage; and love, like the "actions of the Just" smells "sweetly."[43] But Traherne may also have remembered the marvelous shift in tone in *Hydriotaphia: Urn-Buriall* occasioned by this line: "But man is a Noble Animal, splendid in ashes, and pompous in the grave."[44] In any case, Traherne emphasizes the theme of resurrection with one of its most powerful emblems. To the Donne of the *First Anniversarie*, the phoenix was a symbol of the disintegrating features of unbridled egoism. In Traherne, allusion and emblem merge in a single affirmation: Love as the resurrecting Deity in man.

Traherne's diction and syntax are not like Donne's, and to the casual reader his language will be less excitingly urbane. Traherne's is an artistry of abstraction: abstract nouns in great numbers, apocopated conjunctions, intransitive verbs. In language Traherne attempts something like the aim of the "action" painters of the 1950's. He bases his entire strategy on the idea that one cannot think of the whole as apart from its smallest segment. The whole painting will not stay put as the mind settles focus on the part; one wall of Monet's "Lilies in a Pond" is always behind the viewer, and he is engaged and excited by only parts of the panel before him. How does one relate the parts of Jackson Pollack's "Opus 11" to the whole? Does it matter? Similarly, suppose the relevance to the *Centuries* of the *itinerarium mentis* theme, with its tripartite path neatly divided into a sixfold way. Certainly the speaker sees himself as a guide along such a path. But then again he need not lead one—or move himself—toward the place where he is already. The speaker's shifts inside and outside of time are part of a rhetoric of erosion functioning in the work, isolating parts, connecting others, but discontinuity is almost as important as continuity. Even the figure of the "century" is compromised and finally destroyed.

"INFINITE CENTER": THE LYRIC VOICE

VI

*No curling Metaphors
that gild the Sence,
Nor Pictures here,
nor painted Eloquence;
No florid Streams
of Superficial Gems,
But real Crowns
and Thrones and Diadems!
That Gold on Gold
should hiding shining ly
May well be reckon'd
baser Heraldry.
—"The Author to
the Critical Peruser"*

Traherne's poetry has never quite caught on, not even with the admirers of so-called "metaphysical poets," with whom his name is often linked. Critical disinterest in Traherne as a poet seems to me symptomatic of certain critical biases, in particular the concern, almost obsessive in some circles, for what is called "organic unity." This concern goes hand in hand with the assumption that good poetry relies on concrete diction. As the most cursory reading shows, Traherne makes copious use of such abstractions as "Joy," "Light," "Treasure," and "Infinity"; indeed, they are the main staple of his vocabulary. Unlike Marvell, Traherne never attempts to imitate "A Valediction Forbidding Mourning," and his poetry lacks the wit of the Herbert he so much admired.

No good purpose will be served by suggesting that the Donne and Marvell revivals will now be followed by a commensurate surge of interest in Traherne's lyrics. I should think that for those who seek the values of Donne's wit Traherne will likely remain a poet who is "mostly a bore."[1] A colleague of mine once said that perhaps when we say "metaphysical poetry" we mean merely to refer to certain aspects of certain parts of certain poems written by Donne. Certainly the fashionable statements on what is and what is not "metaphysical" poetry inevitably resort to Donne for illustration: "If they be two they be two so / As stiff twin compasses are two...." But if Donne is one of the major talents in the English language, insistence on the particular merits of his verse as the single standard of excellence does little more than nail a narrow scale of values to the mast, thus eliminating from consideration most of the poetry written in the seventeenth century and since.

Traherne has been victimized by a similar assumption that his real gifts were those of the prose writer. Thus (in an interesting *non sequitur*) his poetry is somehow little more than a short-hand version of the prose; and since that prose is excellent, the poetry must be poor. Such a view seems to suggest that the distinction between poetry and prose is self-evident, and, further, that in the Traherne canon the two are in competition. Not only are these assumptions unwarranted, but they are patently at odds with the facts. We have the poetry and the prose; further, as linguists have shown, in many cases an absolute distinction between them cannot be made (without resorting to prescriptive categories). In a work like *Meditations on the Six Days of the Creation*, where we have clear examples of both "forms," we find that poetry and prose may be used in such a way that the success of either depends on the success of both.

The same is true of "Select Meditations" and *Centuries of Meditations*, where Traherne intersperses poetry throughout the sequences of largely prose meditations. Meditation 69 of the Third Century is a good example. Several preceding entries are linked syntactically:

> This Spectacle once seen....
>
> With this we are Delighted....
>
> Little did I imagine that, while I was thinking these Things....[2]

and so on. The material has been Traherne's recurrent theme of God as Act, with the speaker recalling how he came to recognize the affinity between his thoughts and communion. Like David, he found his understanding and appreciation of God in the workmanship of the world. Simultaneously, the truth of Scripture and of events far removed in time appeared to him. This understanding and the affections which accompany it are called Felicity. Now Meditation 69, which treats the prototype of human felicity, King David, is in verse. As we see the poem in relation to its immediate context, we recognize how it re-capitulates themes developed throughout the *Centuries,* but especially amplified in this particular section: "Enflamed with Lov it was his [David's] great Desire, / To Sing Contemplat Ponder and Admire." Above all, David was one who "Enjoyed Himself": he enjoyed the world, "the Beauty of Heaven and Earth" which God intended as man's "Treasure." For Tra-herne, David is a comprehensive figure, the ultimate man:

> A Shepherd, Soldier, and Divine,
> A Judge, a Courtier, and a King,
> Priest, Angel, Prophet, Oracle did shine
>   At once; when He did sing.

[III.69]

Traherne draws the analogy clearly: in the Psalms we have a compendium of human understanding—not just the best that has been thought and said in the world, but the best that has been done. Within himself ("Philosopher and Poet too") King David performs many functions of society. He is like a micro-cosmic commonwealth at perfect harmony, a miniature anti-Leviathan. But in what exactly did the psalmist excel? A "Deep and perfect Sence" of God's glory, "hid" from most, invested David's life and song with majesty and "made him seem [to be] in Gods Celestial Quire." The seventh stanza of the poem re-capitulates the statement of stanza 6. Now it is not David's "Sence" that is "Deep," but the "Things" surrounding him. Traherne shifts the sides of the subject-object equivalence, only to restate that equivalence. Then he returns, as if to reassert the close relation between speaker and subject, to remind the reader of the way in which the chosen people loved the music of the Psalms. If we look carefully at the final stanza, and beyond at following meditations, we see something of Traherne's method in using the lyric throughout the piece. This meditation in verse allows for an emphatic repetition of a dominant theme: the speaker as the literary heir and imitator of the psalmist.

As a technique of emphasis and repetition in the prose works, Traherne's use of the lyric is often very effective. Along with the repeated epigraphs from Scripture, the verse finales seem especially to lend a sense of order to his hexameron. But Tra-herne's poetic achievement cannot be limited to an emphatic use of verse interludes; his reach is broader also than the anthology set pieces indicate.

Traherne wrote meditative poetry, verse paraphrases, apothegms, epigrams, hymns, long poems in heroic couplets, epitaphs. Apropos of the last of these, in a period very fond of that minor genre, Traherne wrote some of the finest epitaphs of the seventeenth century. "In Obitum," on one John Chomeley, compares favorably with poems by Jonson, Donne, and others, which employ virtually the same metaphors. But it seems to me that Traherne gets beyond the conventional figures of "precious Dust" lying beneath the sod, beyond the typical allusions to the Resurrection, and beyond the typical expressions of personal grief. The final quatrain is reminiscent of the fifth chapter of *Hydriotaphia*:

> Tis not this Stone which after Death,
>   Doth make his Name to live;
> It was his Life which so much breath,
>   To this dumbe Stone did give.[3]

Here, as in Browne's reflective passages, the themes of fame and immortality fuse. But here (if I may be permitted a spatial analogy) the poet turns his figure inside out. The stones do not simply tell of a life well spent; that would suggest the value of fame. Instead, the stones live, as if quickened by the godlike spirit of John Chomeley.[4] Like the Creator, Chomeley breathes life into inert matter.

"Memento mori" is even more impressive. Also from the Early Notebook, this poem is an intense variation on a common theme: "Beneath that Stone, lies buried One, / Confin'd in narrow roome." While alive, he moved about the world as if restrained: the world as prison. As in the similar "Epitaphium," all of this seems quite predictable, but soon Traherne extends the metaphor:

> Not all the Treasures, nor the Pleasures,
>   Where with the Earth is fill'd;
> Can meat afford, fitt for the Board,
>   where Soules are to bee still'd.

Typically "Life is the Shadow of a Dreame," but in "Memento mori" Traherne delineates a sense of desperation, of longing, implying that anxiety impinges on all consciousness. Only momentarily does the communion table quiet the tumult; earth and time are "fill'd" with the objects of anxiety.

This sense of longing Traherne now treats under the figure of sleep. In life, man "never truely was awake." The metaphor (which may conjure thoughts of spiritual torpor) is a powerful development of the figure of life's prison. Limitation, restraint —these features apply to perception, to sense. As in Donne's fourteenth *Devotion*, the closing of the physical eyes on earth becomes the opening of the spiritual eyes in that more spacious room beyond time:

> But now mine Eies, (above the Skies)
>   are open; and I see
> Things in the Light, not in the Night,
>   but cleerly shewne to Mee.
> Yea Lord! though here my body lies
>   confus'd with other Earth;
> At thy Command my Crummes shal rise,
>   The same as at my Birth.
>
> [P. 162]

This is more than a casual working of the Resurrection motif. The shift from third person to first heightens the intensity of the poem. It is not that the speaker suddenly identifies with the dead man, undertaking to speak with his voice. Rather, he apprehends the affinity between his present condition and the physical remains of the departed soul. "Now" he sees momentarily what he will one day see forever, when his body no longer "lies / confus'd with other Earth." The ambiguity of the figure suggests that whether alive or dead, in this life earth mixes with earth, rendering all things into confusion. The Resurrection of the "Crummes" of the body is like the coming of sudden sight, a rebirth.

In a similar way, Traherne's talents show in his efforts at another popular pastime of the Jacobean poet: verse paraphrase. We have discussed the best examples of this mode in connection with the *Thanksgivings*. One lyric, however, has gone all but unnoticed. Crossed out in the manuscript,[5] "Rise noble soule and come away" (pp. 159-160) is one of the most graceful examples of paraphrase based on the celebrated passage from the Canticles (2:10-13). Unlike most of his contemporaries who worked with this form, Traherne takes great liberties with the text:

> Come lett us goe: and doe not fear
> the hardest way, while I am neer.
> My heart with thine shall mingled bee;
> Thy sorrowes mine, my Joyes with Thee.
>   And all our Labours as wee goe
>   True Love shall sweeten still.
>   and strew our way with Flowers too,
>   whilest wee ascend the Hill.

It is not unusual for Traherne to invite comparison between the Song of Songs and lyrics in the *carpe diem* mode. But he also heightens the sensual aspects of his invitational passage by juxtaposing the imagery of related (or thought to be related) sections from the Song of Songs. Harking back to a favorite theme of poets and artists throughout the Middle Ages and the Renaissance, Traherne invites the visual associations of the lovers' rose-strewn retreat. He construes the luxuriousness of that scene in the manner of the mystic, with the heraldry of spiritual union:

> Come letts unite; and wee'l aspire
> like brighter Flames of heavenly fire;
> That with sweet Incense do ascend,
> still purer to their Journeys End.
>   Two—rising Flames—in one weel bee,
>   And with each other twining play,
>   And How, twill be a joy to see,
>   weel fold and mingle all the way.

Traherne's poetry is full of figures suggesting a "mingling" or "twining" of man with objects outside him. He is fond of the mirror image, which not only fits his interest in the mutual identity of things but also his preoccupation with the cognitive reversal involved in perceiving that identity. Man must come to see—and he will do so only if he learns properly to value his eyes—that the fulness of God's glory inheres in the discrete objects of creation: "You never Enjoy the World aright, till you see how a Sand Exhibiteth the Wisdom and Power of God...." Here is the significance for Traherne of the biblical text: Man must become as a little child in his capacity to perceive and to respond to objects of nature, and this transformation is a prior condition of entry into the kingdom.

We can examine the workings of this theme in its complexity in one of Traherne's finest poems, "Shadows in the Water" (pp. 116-118). First reading suggests that the water mirror is the controlling figure in the poem:

> Thus did I by the Water's brink
> Another World beneath me think;
> And while the lofty spacious Skies
> Reversed there abus'd mine Eys,
>   I fancy'd other Feet
>   Came mine to touch and meet;
> As by som Puddle I did play
> Another World within it lay.
>
> [Stanza 2]

But more careful examination will show that Traherne invites a tactile response beyond that implied by the reflected image. The "Shadows" are "in" the water, just as the other world lies "within" the "Puddle." Moreover, Traherne's diction reveals the poem's interest in time: We see that the dominant image is actually a *Gestalt* of the water mirror *and* the child viewing. In the past, the speaker's "thought" of a "Reversed" world revolving beneath his feet "abus'd [his] Eys," the eyes being part of the child's response. It seems to me clear that Traherne is talking about more than the infant's spontaneity; the child is notable for his "fancy," for his imagination. This quality of mind opens the door to the possibilities of other worlds, to ideas which will not brook the stringent application of the adult's judgment. Finally, in its capacity to fuse perception and imagination, the child's fancy includes the tactile sense, for "... other Feet / Come [his] to touch and meet."

It would be a mistake to think of Traherne's use of the figure here as quaint or naïve. As a poet, Traherne is no less "scholastic" than Donne, but he uses his learning in a different way. At this point in the poem he is not just asserting the Christian cliché about becoming as a little child. He is suggesting how one's memory preserves a sense of the child "knowing" intuitively an experiential truth that blurs as he grows older:

> In unexperienc'd Infancy
> Many a sweet Mistake doth ly:
> Mistake tho false, intending tru;
> A *Seeming* somwhat more than *View*;
>   That doth instruct the Mind
>   In Things that ly behind,
> And many Secrets to us show
> Which afterwards we com to know.
>
>   [Stanza 1]

Traherne is saying not merely that the child's intuition functions effectively but that it directly contradicts common-sense experience. The "sweet Mistake" lies in the perception of "unexperienc'd Infancy." Though the mistake is "sweet," it is nonetheless a mistake. On both quantitative and qualitative grounds, however, this particular mistake is superior to the experienced view because of its intention. Hence, though mistaken, the "Seeming" of the child "instructs the Mind" in the canon of that "somwhat more than View."

The final couplet of the first stanza poignantly suggests that the perceptions of the child are destroyed by experience: the fall from grace and innocence is an inescapable fact of human biography. But the fall is not irrevocable. For Traherne life is cyclic, and accordingly man is able to recapture the intuitive life: "And many Secrets to us show / Which afterwards we com to know." In this way, in the child's confusion between appearance and reality lies a spiritual cue for the adult. The judgment which accompanies experience corrects the child's error, but it may introduce a "Mistake" of its own. Experience is the breeding ground of potential *hybris*; for the adult is tempted to identify the limits of his perceptions with the boundaries of the universe. The great reductionist, Thomas Hobbes, erected a system on this *hybris*—an atomistic world view repugnant to Traherne's neo-Platonism and anathema to his relatively expansive view of human capacity.

Of course, the child's notion that another world converges with his own where his feet touch the water is mistaken in the physical sense. But the adult persuasion that the perception of his senses is the final arbiter of truth overlooks the fact that truth transcends the numerous "accidents" of personal observation. Hence, the speaker stresses the spatial range of the child's thoughts:

> Beneath the Water Peeple drown'd.
> Yet with another Hev'n crown'd,
> In spacious Regions seem'd to go
> Freely moving to and fro:
>   In bright and open Space
>   I saw their very face;
> Eys, Hands, and Feet they had like mine;
> Another Sun did with them shine.
>
> [Stanza 3]

With their heads beneath the water, the creatures in the other world are in the child's mind doomed to death by water. Yet this is not the point primarily occupying the speaker: again, it is the "seeming," the seeing, the visual *Gestalt* which determines experience. The child observes that the others are "crown'd" by "another Hev'n." They are in some way not quite understood to be true royalty, but they are "crown'd," nevertheless. In this stanza the speaker stresses the physical movement in the expansive regions of the other world; it is as if the child's concentration has magnified the chink into a cosmos. The other world is a mirror image of his own: the miniature water mirror as macrocosm.

We know from our reading of Traherne's other works what an important place the idea of self-love occupies in his thinking. The workings of this idea emerge in this poem, with its evident echolalia from Book III of the *Metamorphoses*. The infant viewer is a countertype of the arch self-lover, the beautiful Narcissus. Actually, the beginnings of Narcissus' fall lay not in any inordinate fondness for his own appearance (presumably he has not seen his image until the fateful glance into the pool). Rather, Narcissus betrays his ignorance in his hostile treatment of his admirers and pursuers, whose dilemma he is to share with a vengeance. Once smitten by the reflection of his own face,

Narcissus exchanges roles with his pursuers, becoming not the
loved but the loving. The difference is that he must love an
"insubstantial hope" ("spem sine corpore amat").[6] In the epigraph affixed to the title page of one moralized version, the
author construes the metamorphosis as evidence that "God
resysteth the proud in every place." The lesson was explicit;
the water mirror was an emblem of self-love: "Now in thys
welle the apperaunce of theyr state / Doth them [the proud] so
please" that they place themselves "above the rest" of
humanity.[7]

Traherne's employment of this figure, however, is not quite
conventional; he alters it to fit his purpose. His aim is not to
denigrate but to applaud self-love; and death is not the punishment for the viewer's pride but an imagined release from the
restraints of time, which separate the higher from the lower
worlds. In Hades, Narcissus continues staring into the Stygian
pool; in contrast, death will endow Traherne's speaker with a
capacity for wider movements and with a larger circle of
friends. John Denham thought of the water mirror as an emblem of deceit, and so preferred the rushing waters of the
Thames:

> O could I flow like thee, and make thy stream
> My great example, as it is my theme!
> Though deep, yet clear, though gentle yet not dull,
> Strong without rage, without ore-flowing full.

The reflection of the face is, as in Ovid's poem, untrue, and
therefore destructive:

> The stream is so transparent, pure, and clear,
> That had the self-enamour'd youth gaz'd here,
> So fatally deceiv'd he had not been,
> While he the bottom, not his face had seen.[8]

The river's virtue inheres in its depth and clarity; the Thames
deceives no man. Denham's poem considers the proper moral
and political limits between the self and others, and in so doing
it thematically approximates its Ovidian model. Denham suggests that narcissistic love in its debilitating form derives from

illusion. The speaker admires the Thames as a norm between extremes, as an emblem of the wise man's truthful estimate of his place in the scheme of things. In sharp contrast, Traherne explores the opposite possibilities of the reflected image. The water mirror misleads; it invites its viewer's affections to a heightened love which cannot fully be consummated. But its illusory aspect is not fatal; it is "a sweet mistake"—in some Orphic way, true.

Structurally, this illusion, the child's "mistake," is the "occasion" of the poem. The child misunderstands; he is confused, yet filled with a sense of wonder. Peering at the water mirror he becomes absorbed by his sense perceptions in such a way that seeing and believing (and therefore knowing) fuse as act. Traherne seems to be describing what we now call "eidetic imagery,"[9] which many children possess. Whatever else this sense may be, it is part of the wholeness of the child, whom experience has not yet fragmented. The child may be confused, but only by the sense of restraint implicit in the experience:

> 'Twas strange that Peeple there should walk,
> And yet I could not hear them talk:
> That throu a little watry Chink,
> Which one dry Ox or Horse might drink,
>   We other Worlds should see,
>   Yet not admitted be;
> And other Confines there behold
> Of Light and Darkness, Heat and Cold.
>
> [Stanza 4]

The situation strikes the child with wonder: a "little watry Chink," easily annihilated by a thirsty animal, embraces an entire world (or rather "Worlds"—"far other Worlds and other Seas," as Marvell put the same idea). Traherne is concerned here partly with the power of the imagination. The child's imaginative sense of wonder coincides with an attitude of confusion or doubt. Tension between the two worlds is puzzling; it makes no sense that he cannot communicate from one world to the other. The impasse contradicts the seeming immediacy of the world beneath.

Like Narcissus, the child loves what he sees in the water

mirror; but unlike Narcissus, he does not perceive his own reflection. The other world is populated by many "Peeple," all of whom he loves: "I call'd them oft, but call'd in vain," and so the theme of unrequited love. The cosmos begins to change, as if in response to the reversed images in the mirror: "I plainly saw by these / A new *Antipodes*." Everything in the other world is strange, and yet somehow familiar too. The people seem to be alive; bodies, attached to the feet, appear to meet, but they point in opposite directions. This vivid description of the infant's sense perception suggests the alienation from each other of the separate worlds, which are held apart by a most tenuous partition: "Whom, tho they were so plainly seen, / A Film kept off that stood between."

The texture of the image depends upon a complex set of feelings and associations. The mirror does not simply reflect what *is*, it reverses and enriches it. The mirror multiplies the world. But we must not overlook the important tactile dimension of the figure: the mirror is the marvelously thin meeting place of the two worlds. Moreover, because it is thin, it is susceptible to the impinging or pressing of one world upon the other:

> By walking Men's reversed Feet
> I chanc'd another World to meet;
> Tho it did not to View exceed
> A Phantasm, 'tis a World indeed,
>   Where Skies beneath us shine,
>   And Earth by Art divine
> Another face presents below,
> Where Peeple's feet against Ours go.
>   [Stanza 6]

More than merely reiterating his theme of appearance and reality, the speaker now invests the image of the water mirror with a tactile quality ("Shadows *in* the Water"). We not only grasp the speaker's sense that the other world does in fact live and move and have its being, but also that the child feels the other world pressing upon his own: "Another face presents below, / Where Peeple's feet against Ours go." Now it is as if the "Film" were like the skin of the seer's own body, thin as the water's surface, but capable of feeling the press of foot on foot.

This stanza has an almost surreal quality. As the child peers into the puddle, a single face appears, but the feet of many press against his own and those of others. The image possesses the quality of dream-rightness. We get the feeling of a discontinuity between face and feet. In the following stanza Traherne shifts the point of view, widening the spatial perspective. The speaker grasps a sense of the limitless spaces of the other world, inhabited (we learn) by the speaker's "yet unknown Friends"; visual sensation has been the springing place of love, and from love grows faith. At this point, and for the first time in the poem, the speaker shifts from narrative:

> O ye that stand upon the Brink,
> Whom I so near me, throu the Chink,
> With Wonder see: What Faces there,
> Whose Feet, whose Bodies, do ye wear?
>   I my Companions see
>   In You, another Me.
> They seemed Others, but are We;
> Our second Selvs those Shadows be.
>
>   [Stanza 8]

The "Shadows" in the water are more than literal sense data dredged up from the memory of a visual experience. Just as one face and one body become many, so occasion generates meanings greater than the literal, historical sense. The spiritual sense of the experience is like the thinness of the water's surface: tenuous, delicate, but true. The child sees that the water mirror is an imitation of the "real" world, but this recognition is not enough. The occasion has its anagogic meaning: somewhere in the "shadows" of the water lurks a "second" self. Now, the discontinuity between image and world is emblematic of the discontinuity between youth and age. As he reaches for the regions of the other world, the speaker wonders if in some way he is not reaching for buried lives:

> Look how far off those lower Skies
> Extend themselvs! scarce with mine Eys
> I can them reach. O ye my Friends,

What *Secret* borders on those Ends?
Are lofty Hevens hurl'd
'Bout your inferior World?
Are ye the Representatives
Of other Peopl's distant Lives.

[Stanza 9]

The speaker's address to his "Friends" and the hint of their
proximity (standing on "the Brink") join with diction and
tense shifts to indicate an intimate quality. As he had as a child,
so now as an adult the speaker calls out to the citizens of the
other world. As feet press against feet, as the meditant considers
the nearness of his "Friends," the speaker feels as if the "Film"
separating the two worlds has momentarily given way. In an
almost cinematic manner, Traherne suggests the impingement
and even the intrusion of the worlds upon each other:

Within the Regions of the Air,
Compass'd about with Hev'ns fair,
Great Tracts of Land there may be found
Enricht with Fields and fertil Ground;
    Where many num'rous Hosts,
    In those far distant Coasts,
For other great and glorious Ends,
Inhabit, my yet unknown Friends.

[Stanza 7]

All at once the speaker's "unknown Friends" are his "Companions." More than "Companions," they are multiple expressions of himself. In a daring maneuver, Traherne extends the
identity of the speaker to include the reader too: "I" becomes
"We":

I my Companions see
In You, another Me.
They seemed Others, but are We;
Our second Selvs those Shadows be.

The shifts in tense and person are evidences of a strategy of
erosion with which the author undermines the boundaries he
himself has imposed. Comparison becomes contrast, as Tra-

herne delineates his speaker as a counter-Narcissus, not as one who does not love himself, but as one who does. Narcissus erred in not truly loving himself; true self-love cannot remain solely focused on the narrow sense of ego; it is impelled outward, toward other manifestations of God's love. In a godlike manner, the child's affections populate the other world with creatures to be loved. A relevant gloss from the Second Century reads: "By Loving a Soul does Propagat and beget it self. By Loving it does Dilate and Magnify it self. By Loving it does Enlarge and Delight it self" (II.48). The effect is similar to that of Donne's "Extasie," where pictures in the lovers' eyes "get" and "propagate" in the same way that the transplanted violet "multiplies." In "Shadows in the Water" a tiny point in space becomes a mirror of all creation. The world provides the company of saints and of the Deity Himself as one of its services. Accordingly, Traherne's "Infant-Ey" gazes into the mirror only to glimpse another's face. Again in the Second Century, in cataloging the manifold pleasures offered by the world, Traherne expresses the same idea:

Besides these immediat Pleasures here beneath, there are many Sublime and Celestial Services which the World doth do. It is a Glorious Mirror wherin you may see the verity of all Religion: Enjoy the Remainders of Paradice and Talk with the Dietie. Apply yourself Vigorously to the Enjoyment of it. For in it you shall see the face of God: and by Enjoying it, be wholy Converted to Him. [II.17]

Finally, Traherne's handling of the mirror image contrasts sharply with the Ovidian model. It is instead reminiscent of the *Spiritual Canticle* (1584) of St. John of the Cross:

> O crystal brook, if on
> the silver surface of the water
> you instantly might form
> the eyes I most desire
> I feel them in me like a scar.[10]

In Traherne as in St. John, the face of the beloved is not the impoverished literal reflection; instead, the contours of the love-object are more richly shaped by the imaginative effects of longing and hope.

Structurally, Traherne's poem moves from memory to understanding.[11] The speaker recognizes the "truth" inherent in the child's error. A proper understanding of the world and the imitation of divine self-love are one and the same thing. The truth emanating from the world is that love annihilates the boundaries between the self and the other: "Love is uniting affection." In his meditation upon Pentecost in the Church's Year-Book, Traherne interprets the descending flames as representative of spiritual union; and he is led to make this remark of the spiritual meaning of Narcissus:

But flame cannot so mingle with flame, as Light with Light in its perfect Effusion. Yet those are but Shadows in Comparison of the Union of Souls. Which are made to See & Feel & Admire each other, & Enflame each other. For all the Joy even of Living in Heaven, is the Twofold Joy of Communicating & Receiving. Without which the most Excellent Creature might pine away. Becaus Narcissus like, none can Enjoy Himself in Himself, unless He hath a fountain. Nor can any Enjoy themselvs in a fountain; tho they see the Reflexion of themselvs, but in a Shady manner; Compared to that wherby Solid Objects, & Diviner Creatures enjoy each other. These more Real Flames Amorously folding enjoy each other in another Manner; being, as the Apostle speaketh, Rooted and Grounded in Lov.[12]

Similarly, the child is in communication with himself and the other; without learning and without effort, he is able to transcend the narrow conception of himself by multiplying worlds and by loving the worlds he has created. In this spiritual reality lies the reconciliation between the child's mistake and the adult conception of the world; intuition and intellect merge in a more commodious overview of the soul's place in creation:

> Of all the Play-mates which I knew
> That here I do the Image view
> In other Selvs; what can it mean?
> But that below the purling Stream
>   Som unknown Joys there be
>   Laid up in Store for me;

> To which I shall, when that thin Skin
> Is broken, be admitted in.
>
> [Stanza 10]

Now the speaker recognizes the truth *in* his childhood experience. He responds in the here and now to his immediate sense perception with the child's love and wonder. The adult "correction" of the child's mistaken view of the water mirror may now be seen as in one sense trivial, since it merely states what is later known to be obvious. But that "correction" is actually an overcorrection, and therefore wrongheaded. The child sees what often the adult stubbornly refuses to see—that the wonders of creation and its true aims transcend the immediate and personal perceptions of any man. For they are only the evanescent tracings of nerve and fiber, the stirrings of instincts known to the lowliest beast. Man's being is invested with a capacity to love in different measure, and with a different quality, than do animals.[13]

True self-love fuses past with present, the child and the man, forming from the two partitioned and once alienated perceptions a more adequate and unified vision. Interestingly, the poem ends with the fully articulated figure only hinted at earlier in the text with the touching of feet. Now, the film separating the speaker from his friends in the other world is a "thin Skin," the speaker's own. The pleasure of the company of his longed-for friends will be his only when that fragile skin of mortality finally breaks. Even now the worlds press upon each other; and the speaker's imagined intimacy with the spirit world is only a hint of the pleasures lying in store.

We have been discussing stylistic elements in one of Traherne's better poems. The full achievement of "Shadows in the Water" does not appear, however, until we see how the poem functions as part of *Poems of Felicity* (British Museum MS. Burney 392). Miss Ridler refers to this sequence as the poems from Philip Traherne's manuscript, and, except for her exclusion of "The Author to the Critical Peruser,"[14] I think her arrangement of the poems is entirely correct. Except for Philip Traherne's "The Dedication," "To the Critical Peruser" marks the beginning of a collection of poems, which Philip altered by

155

including versions of poems from the fair copy in Thomas' hand, now called the Dobell Folio.

John Wallace has persuasively shown that the Dobell *Poems* form a separate sequence.[15] I think the same point may be made of the poems in the Burney manuscript. If we excise those poems included also in the Dobell *Poems*, we are left with a sequence of poems in many ways parallel to that in the other volume. It is well to note that the *Poems of Felicity*, subtitled "Divine Reflections on the Native Objects of An Infant Ey," is marked "Vol. I." Evidence seems to point toward a missing manuscript, one containing enough poems, along with the fifteen remaining poems from the Dobell sequence not already used in the first, to complete a companion volume.[16] The new grouping would begin with "The Author to the Critical Peruser" as Traherne's verse Preface and end appropriately with the two poems entitled "The Review."

We have reason to believe that Philip was in possession of a fair copy of the sequence, now preserved only in Dobell. For one thing, Philip almost always includes a group of poems rather than a single poem, thus testifying to his suspicion, for example, that "The Salutation," "Wonder," "Eden," and "Innocence" belong together. Again, he splices in "The Preparative" and the following three poems together. He never separates poems in the Burney manuscript which clearly belong together ("Bells" I and II, "Churches" I and II, "The Inference" I and II, "Insatiableness" I and II, and the "Review" poems). On the other hand, he seems to have taken certain liberties; "The Apostasy" is begun before "The World," then crossed out and placed after it.[17] "Misapprehension" was, it appears, started before "Adam," and then included much later in the sequence.

Although it may be premature to attempt an evaluation of the Burney manuscript poems at this time, several tentative judgments may be in order. Philip must have had a transcript of Thomas Traherne's manuscript—perhaps the Dobell Folio itself —when he worked out his own arrangement of the *Poems of Felicity*, which he refers to as the "Sacred Relicks" which his brother "hath left behind."[18] Since the Dobell *Poems* are in Thomas Traherne's careful hand, we can be reasonably sure that the poems are to be read in that sequence. Further, as editor,

Philip intervenes only seven times to alter the sequence. It was he who attached "The Author to the Critical Peruser" to the sequence beginning with "The Salutation"; the poem belongs in the only place we actually find it in manuscript, as "The Preface" to the Burney poems. The first of Philip's major intrusions follows the verse "Preface"; he inserted here the opening four poems from the other manuscript. The appearance here of "The Salutation," "Wonder," "Eden," and "Innocence" obscures the thematic connection between "The Author to the Critical Peruser" and the second poem rightly belonging in this sequence, "An Infant-Ey"—which is, in effect, the title poem of the lyric suite.

"The Author to the Critical Peruser" is something of a commentary on the doctrine of poetic simplicity as a literary analogue of the "Simple Light" by which the soul perceives the "Divine Objects":

> No Curling Metaphors that gild the Sence,
> Nor Pictures here, nor painted Eloquence;
> No florid Streams of Superficial Gems,
> But real Crowns and Thrones and Diadems!
> That Gold on Gold should hiding shining ly
> May well be reckon'd baser Heraldry.
>
> [P. 3]

The "Preface" is Traherne's answer to the metaphysicals, who "Ransack all Nature's Rooms" to speak "In Meteors" or "blazing Prodigies": "Things that amaze, but will not make us wise." The alternative is the life and vision marked by "An easy Stile" and the "Engins" of the body and soul which properly see "God's Work." The theme of this "Preface" concerns the "open Eys" with which the soul perceives the simplicity of the "highest Mysteries." This "Ey" and its "simple Light" link the "Preface" with the first poem in the sequence proper, "An Infant-Ey":

> A simple Light from all Contagion free,
> A Beam that's purely Spiritual, an Ey
> That's altogether Virgin, Things doth see
> Ev'n like unto the Deity:

That is, it shineth in an hevenly Sence,
And round about (unmov'd) its Light dispence.
[P. 77]

Rhetorically, the speaker continues his comment on the two ways of viewing the world, but now replaces the "polisht Flesh" or "Shining Banks" of the secular poet that emit light with the beam uniting the inner "Ey" to the exterior "simple Light." By this elaborating on the earlier, rather more pointedly literary aspects of the image cluster, the speaker builds the "Infant-Ey" into the dominant figure of the Burney manuscript poems.

Of all of Philip's additions to what I shall call "Divine Reflections," all but one involve the inclusion of poems from the Dobell sequence in the exact order that we find them in Bodleian MS. Eng. poet c.42.[19] This may suggest that Philip was aware of his brother's structural intention; if so, he was, in effect, the first critic to recognize the structure of the lyrics as a group, which he attempts to be guided by and also to enhance. He includes the four opening (and often anthologized) poems from the Dobell sequence. Similarly, except for the addition following "Admiration," he never varies from his practice of preserving the order of the separate groupings from the Dobell sequence. And even his single departure from the pattern seems to indicate an awareness of the critical implications of his editorial decisions. Here he takes up in the Dobell sequence where he has left off by including "The Approach." Then, before "Dumnesse," which follows in the Dobell Folio, he places "Nature" and "Eas," contiguous poems from later in the group, and he keeps them in what I take to be the received order with respect to each other. After returning to include "Dumnesse," he interpolates "Silence" and "My Spirit" before including the group of six poems between "Admiration" and "Right Apprehension."

The next inclusion involves only the change in the title of the poem which Thomas inscribed as "The Design." Philip assumes that "The Apprehension" rightly follows "Right Apprehension," so he strikes the title and assumes the strategy of the numbered poems, and places a Roman numeral II before the

158

single stanza of "The Apprehension," proceeding to include the following four poems from the Dobell sequence. If this analysis is correct, all of the poems from the Dobell Folio should be excised from "Divine Reflections," and the "Preface" ("The Author to the Critical Peruser") ought to be returned to its rightful place before "An Infant-Ey." This grouping reveals an order which still may suffer from the contamination of Philip's editorial hand. But if he was as scrupulous with the manuscript of "Divine Reflections" as he was with his version of the Dobell sequence, then we may have a grouping quite like the one Thomas put together. "Divine Reflections" is an appropriate title for this group of poems, with its manifold workings of the reflected image and its thematic interest in the "Ey."

Repetition of spheral imagery provides a certain technical unity in the sequence, but, as in the *Centuries*, it also has a blurring effect on the linear development of the work. The first two poems cohere in much the same way as many of the meditations in the *Centuries*, with the last stanza of "An Infant-Ey" as the explicit precursor of "The Return":

> O dy! dy unto all that draws thine Ey
> From its first Objects: let not fading Pleasures
> Infect thy Mind; but see thou carefully
>   Bid them adieu. Return: Thy Treasures
> Abide thee still, and in their places stand
> Inviting yet, and waiting thy Command.
>
> [P. 78]

As the sequence unfolds the speaker returns again and again to spheral imagery, especially in relation to the "Infant-Ey." This repetition runs counter to the elements of history and of spiritual autobiography which constitute the larger contours of the work. The child is born, becomes aware of the other world ("News"), and in his expanding consciousness apprehends the truth of "Adam's Fall" in man's alienation from "uncorrupt Simplicity" (p. 82). But in these poems Traherne treats the Fall as an attenuation of vision. In the prelapsarian world, and in the cosmos of the child's consciousness, the universe was an orb of sight:

The hev'nly Ey,
Much wider than the Sky,
Wherein they All included were....

["News"]

Again:

No empty Space; it is all full of Sight,
All Soul and Life, an Ey most bright,
All Light and Lov....

["Felicity"]

and in "Adam":

The World its self was his next Theme,
Wherof himself was made Supream:
He had an Angel's Ey to see the Price
Of evry Creature....

Perhaps the stanza from "News" is the most revealing here:

But little did the Infant dream
That all the Treasures of the World were by,
And that himself was so the Cream
And Crown of all which round about did ly.
Yet thus it was! The Gem,
The Diadem,
The Ring enclosing all
That stood upon this Earthen Ball;
The hev'nly Ey,
Much wider than the Sky,
Wherein they All included were....

The repetition of the spheral image of the "Infant-orb" is reminiscent of a technique employed in the *Centuries*. Traherne piles up instances which reiterate a simple equation: Adam before the Fall—the child before the stirrings of conscience. The strategy tends once again to blur events. As in the *Centuries* and *Meditations on the Six Days of the Creation*, the speaker's temporal perspective transcends time. Hence, the stress on the orb as a great expanse: "Much wider than the Sky." "His Mind," we read in "Felicity," "is higher than the Space / Above the Spheres, / Surmounts all Place."

In "Divine Reflections" the speaker's thoughts "move" from

Creation to the New Jerusalem ("The City"), which is also a "Return" to infancy. The speaker emphasizes the "unspeakable" and "unknowable" qualities of the experience he is talking about:

> Did I grow, or did I stay?
> Did I prosper or decay?
>   When I so
> From *Things* to *Thoughts* did go?
>   ["The Review I," p. 138]

As in the early grouping, so in the concluding section, the spheral image dominates Traherne's thematic development. The speaker ("I the Center") apprehends the dissolution of all boundaries ("Consummation"):

> The Thoughts of Men appear
> Freely to mov within a Sphere
>   Of endless Reach; and run,
> Tho in the Soul, beyond the Sun.
> The Ground on which they acted be
> Is unobserv'd Infinity.
>   [P. 134]

In "Insatiableness" he sees (or rather in his insatiable desire and satisfaction feels) the spurious nature of such destructions as "beginning," "now," and "end":

> Till I what was before all Time descry,
> The World's Beginning seems but Vanity.
>   My Soul doth there long Thoughts extend;
>   No End
> Doth find, or Being comprehend:
>   Yet somwhat sees that is
>   The obscure shady face
>   Of endless Space. . . .
>   [P. 133]

In one way or another, the figure of the "Infant-Ey" appears in almost every poem in "Divine Reflections." In a poem like "Shadows in the Water," as we have seen, the concrete figure of the child viewing forms an emblem that is the lyric medium between the two worlds of sense and spirit. In succeeding poems we can trace this process of disintegration. For example, "On Leaping over the Moon" (pp. 118-120) takes for its subject the intellectual recognitions of "Shadows in the Water":

> I saw new Worlds beneath the Water ly,
> New Peeple; and another Sky,
> And Sun, which seen by Day
> Might things more clear display.
> Just such another
> Of late my Brother
> Did in his Travel see, and saw by Night
> A much more strange and wondrous Sight:
> Nor could the World exhibit such another,
> So Great a Sight, but in a Brother.
>
> [Stanza 1]

After reiterating material from the preceding poem the speaker suddenly shifts to a related topic, as if prompted by the memory, which presents a scene at once apposite and opposite. The scene depicted now was witnessed by another person, the Brother, who similarly viewed a mirror image. Conversely, however, the scene is set at night, and the "wondrous" quality of the "Sight" has something to do with innate properties of the "Brother." In "Shadows," the thematic movement was from speaker downward into the other world; in contrast, now the "Brother" flies, like Icarus, upward and outward.

The reflected image is presently the occasion for fantasy; the speaker suggests that faith and fantasy merge in this vision of spectacular flight. Whereas in "Shadows," the surface of the water, the reflected image, was the "thin Skin" dividing two worlds, now the ether, the element through which the "Body" of the brother flies, is "thin" and potentially dangerous: "He might hav dropt throu that thin Element / Into a fathomless Descent" (lines 31-32). The danger is overcome, and as a result the speaker can speak with authority about the wider circles of the spheres. Just as the two events have their likenesses ("Deeds all appear again / In higher Spheres"), so do visions alter with the shifting of lights. The "Ey" and the uttermost circumference of the universe correspond: "On hev'nly Ground within the Skies we walk, / And in this middle Center talk: / Did we but wisely mov, / On Earth in Hev'n abov, / We then should be / Exalted high / Abov the Sky" (lines 51-57). Still, the problem of the one and the many, of the correspondence between microcosm and microcosm, remains unsolved; after "Leaping over the Moon" the speaker returns "To the same purpos." How is it possible that the world in its splendor serves everyone? Would this not imply division and disunity?

The answer seems to come in "Sight" (pp. 121-123), which begins abruptly, as if to suggest a sudden apprehension of meaning:

> Mine Infant-Ey
> Abov the Sky
> Discerning endless Space,
> Did make me see
> Two *Sights* in me,
> Three Eys adorn'd my Face:
> Two Luminaries in my Flesh
> Did me refresh;
> But one did lurk within,
> Beneath my Skin,
> *That* was of greater Worth than both the other;
> For those were Twins; but this had ne'r a Brother.

The speaker now is like the lover of the sonnet cycle ("Two loves have I of comfort and despair"), restrained by the eye of sense, by the common-sense world around him. The *"that"* of line 11 means one dispensing beam "throu the Hevens" frees man from constraint and from longing. Even the number shift (from "Those Eys" to *that* "Ey"), left unexplained, fits the gathering sense of excitement in the climactic poems. The speaker's "Ey" is now on the "distant Coasts" (the figure is directly repeated from "Shadows in the Water"), as if he has passed into that once "inferior World." He does not understand what has happened (lines 37-48). This other eye has transformed the self from valuing objects to Essences:

> Life, Joy, Lov, Peace, appear'd: a Light
> Which to my Sight
> Did Objects represent
> So excellent;

> That I no more without the same can see
> Than Beasts that have no tru Felicity.
>
> [Stanza 5]

"Far distant Coasts" become "distant Coasts," the same objects
seen in the "Glass of Imagination," but seen now in their true
and "signal Worth," as the source of "Life, Joy, Lov, Peace."
These abstract nouns are piled up in such a way as to suggest the
speaker's attempt to articulate the unspeakable. And even as a
grouping they fail to summarize the sense; we return to "Light,"
yet another abstract noun.

In *The Arte of English Poesy* Puttenham describes the rhetorical device of *Sinathrismus*, "the *heaping figure*,"[20] as closely
related to "recapitation" (the frequent use of synonyms). This
"*heaping figure*" is used when the speaker is under the sway of
powerful emotions. Circumstances move the speaker "to be
earnest in [his] speach," and he is prompted by his feelings to
"lay on such load" as to "go to it by heapes as if [he] would winne
the game by multitude of words & speaches, not all of one but
of divers matter and sence. . . ." Puttenham's example is: "*I
deeme, I dreame, I do, I tast, I touch*." Similarly, Traherne's
speaker's deeply-felt desire for repose emerges in this fashion:
"I breathe, I long, I seek" ("Dissatisfaction," p. 96). And in
"Christendom," the stacking of nouns and phrases, and the
marked apocopation of verbs, help to depict the seeming tense-
less quality of the child's consciousness:

> Among ten thousand things,
> Gold, Silver, Cherub's Wings,
> Pearls, Rubies, Diamonds, a Church with Spires,
> Masks, Stages, Games and Plays,
> That then might suit my yong Desires,
> Fine Feathers, Farthings, Holidays,
> Cards, Musick, Dice,
> So much in price;
> A *City* did before mine Eys present
> Its self, wherin there reigned sweet Content.
>
> [P. 97]

Here is the "*City*" toward which the soul inevitably arches in

"Divine Reflections," the "City" in which the same church
bells play in the eternity of "*Christmas-Day*." In the companion
pieces, "*Christendom*" and "*On Christmas-Day*," the speaker
implicitly celebrates the completion of his pilgrimage; inherent
in the relation between child and Incarnation is the timeless
sphere of spiritual union between God and man.

In this way the spheral imagery functions contrapuntally to
the theme of spiritual pilgrimage. The movement from childhood to adulthood is the temporal development which the
"Reflections" rhetorically undermines. Even the tenuous lines
of demarcation between poems function to suggest the tentative
quality of various boundaries. As distinctions between line and
sphere and center and circumference disappear, so do boundaries between sense and intuition. Sense knows only "narrow"
limits, while intuition soars beyond times and regions:

> Those Eys of Sense
> That did dispense
> Their Beams to nat'ral things,
> I quickly found
> Of narrow Bound
> To know but earthly Springs.
>
> ["Sight," Stanza 2]

Man's spirit coincides with the more capacious universe: "My
better Sight / Was infinit." The speaker is in a position to adjust
his dominant figure to this awareness. Thus, in "Walking"
(pp. 123-124), this superior sight takes on preternatural power,
the power to move, equipped with "silent Feet": "To *walk*
abroad is, not with Eys, / But Thoughts, the Fields to see and
prize" (p. 123). Seeing is a spiritual act; wagons move, but cannot see the sun. In just the same way, men may have eyes, but,
"Like Statues dead," be unable to see "The Bliss in which they
mov." This is perhaps another way of stating the theme of
recognition, which in other poems we observed in detail:

> To *walk* is by a Thought to go;
> To mov in Spirit to and fro;
> To mind the Good we see;
> To taste the Sweet.

"Walking" is richly sensual in imagery: visual, tactile, olfactory, even auditory. But the theme of the poem is a reiteration of what has preceded in other poems. The intellect now grasps the intense capacity of the child to value, to delight in the world:

> A little Child these well perceivs,
> Who, tumbling among Grass and Leaves,
>   May Rich as Kings be thought,
>   But there's a Sight
> Which perfect Manhood may delight,
>   To which we shall be brought.

In a marvelous closing stanza, the speaker returns to the metaphor of perception as a kind of locomotion:

> While in those pleasant Paths we talk
> 'Tis *that* tow'rds which at last we walk;
>   But we may by degrees
>   Wisely proceed
> Pleasures of Lov and Prais to heed,
>   From viewing Herbs and Trees.

As in "Shadows in the Water," so in the larger suite of poems to which it belongs, the speaker's theme is the child's "hevenly Sence" of the glory inherent in the objects of creation. Traherne manipulates his material in such a way as to suggest the equation between "An Infant-Ey" and its "Native Objects." Hence, the traditional distinction between subject and object (and the disharmony between nominalist and realist) disappears. Throughout the sequence, Traherne returns to the strange disjunction between infancy and adulthood: " 'Tis strange that I should Wisest be, / When least I could an Error see" ("The Return"). The operative word here is, of course, "see"; the entire suite of poems is a lyric exploration of the figures, "Infant-Ey" and "Native Object," which the author treats more philosophically, *qua* theorist, in "To the Critical Peruser." Accordingly, the visual sense functions as a metonymy for the potentialities of the whole man. In "News" the "Ey" suggests the expansive nature of the child's vision. And in "Felicity" the speaker recalls how frequently his "Eys" sought to transcend "the Spheres":

> Prompted to seek my Bliss abov the Skies,
> How often did I lift mine Eys
> Beyond the Spheres!
>
> [P. 81]

Nature informs the speaker that limitless regions lie within his own soul. The poem develops about the spherical nature of the cosmos, which bears the shape of the infant-orb of sight: "Let man's soul be a sphere." This abyss of space is no vacuum, but "full of Sight." Now it is not the sun but the speaker's "Ey" that is "most bright." In this endless, brilliant sphere, time is enclosed by eternity: "A Scene abov / All Interludes."

The theme of time, introduced in the closing lines of "Felicity," is echoed in "Adam," "The World," and "The Apostacy," all three of which allude to the Garden of Eden, the Creation, and the Fall. Before the Fall, man's senses functioned properly, and Adam dwelt in pleasure, "Encircled in a Sphere of Light" (p. 83), surrounded by a heaven of all things. But even Adam's "Eys" never surpassed the splendor of the speaker's orb, whose sight was restored by the Incarnation. The speaker views and values all the wonders illumined by "that unsufferable piercing Ey," the sun. He has returned to man's rightful place in the center of the universe. He is the owner of what his eye beholds:

> No House nor Holder in this World did I
> Observ to be:
> What I did see
> Seem'd all *Mine Own*; wherin did ly
> A Mine, a Garden, of Delights.
>
> ["The World," Stanza 8]

Implicitly, the speaker's wealth is a return to Eden, the end of "Walking," the end in the beginning of childhood:

> A Royal Crown, inlaid with precious Stones
> Did less surprize
> The Infant Eys
> Of many other little Ones,
> Than the great Beauties of this Frame,
> Made for my sake,
> Mine Eys did take,

Which I Divine, and *Mine*, do name.
Surprizing Joys beyond all Price
Compos'd a Paradise,
Which did my Soul to lov my God enflame,
And ever will the same.

[Stanza 9]

The Fall has its biographical analogue. Man "falls" into a limited conception of the world, which he learns to see through "blemisht Eys." Dutifully, as if paying a debt to the human race, he becomes "A Stranger to the Shining Skies" ("The Apostacy"). The Fall happens after birth, following infancy in time (the speaker loved his "Cradle," knowing it as the time of wisdom: "My early Tutor is the Womb"). But infancy gives way to time; spontaneity vanishes with joy. As Traherne puts it, the universe of light has been "unmade": instead of seeing, "The Child being taught to look" (p. 88) has been spiritually destroyed.

The closing sequence of "Divine Reflections" juxtaposes the city of man and the New Jerusalem. Though the former is present for man's pleasure, its "walls" represent "bounds," "confines," the restraints of mortal existence. "Insatiableness" I and II (pp. 133-134) invoke the mystic's stance of intense longing for separation from the world:

No Walls confine! Can nothing hold my Mind?
Can I no Rest nor Satisfaction find?
Must I behold Eternity
And see
What Things abov the Hev'ns be?
Will nothing serv the Turn?
Nor Earth, nor Seas, nor Skies?
Till I what lies
In Time's beginning find;
Must I till then for ever burn?

"Consummation" and "Hosanna" (pp. 134-138) are filled with an expansive spirit. The eye of the soul is infinite, moving over earth into and through the heavens. All walls have been breached. God has given all, and the speaker sees all things. All obfuscations of the senses have disappeared. The speaker is

168

heir to all eternal (as distinct from "new-invented") wealth.
His ego has undergone an absolute expansion of time and space:

> Transcendent Objects doth my God provide,
> In such convenient Order all contriv'd,
>   That All things in their proper place
>   My Soul doth best embrace,
>   Extends its Arms beyond the Seas,
>   Abov the Hevens its self can pleas,
>   With God enthron'd may reign:
>   Like sprightly Streams
>   My Thoughts on Things remain;
>   Or els like vital Beams
>   They reach to, shine on, quicken Things, and make
>   Them truly Usefull; while I *All* partake.
>   ["Hosanna"]

In "The Review I," the speaker reminds the reader of his
progress "From *Things* to *Thoughts*" by asking a rhetorical
question about the value of his experience. He understands that
thoughts may be for good or ill. "The Review II" returns to the
figure of childhood. The speaker's thoughts are encompassed
by the sphere of childhood. He has relearned the child's art of
wonder and imagination:

> Which makes my Life a Circle of Delights;
> A hidden Sphere of obvious Benefits:
> An Earnest that the Actions of the Just
> Shall still revive, and flourish in the Dust.
>   [P. 139]

THE
EXPANDED
VOICE:
THE DOBELL
POEMS

VII

*A Strange Extended
Orb of Joy,
Proceeding from within,
Which did
on evry side convey
It self,
and being nigh of Kin
To God did evry Way
Dilate it self
even in an Instant, and
Like an Indivisible
Centre Stand.
—"My Spirit"*

In 1903 Bertram Dobell published the poems from the folio manuscript discovered in 1895 by William T. Brooke; but although Miss Wade's edition printed the manuscript sequences separately, in effect the Dobell Folio *Poems* have never been published as a separate and discrete group of poems. In an important article in 1958, John Malcolm Wallace applied the Jesuitical pattern of devotion to the Dobell *Poems*, describing what he believes to be "a complete five-part meditation"[1] and thus setting the stage for the disengagement of the Dobell sequence from the poems in the Burney manuscript. Placed in "the Catholic tradition in which [Traherne] worked," the structure of the Dobell *Poems* is seen by Wallace as follows: composition of place, a second prelude, and the analysis, divided into three parts corresponding to the memory, the understanding, and the will. Respectively, the parts include four poems (whose relation to each other Philip perceived), six, eight, ten, and nine, making up the full complement of the thirty-seven poems in the Dobell Folio.

Gladys Wade did not recognize the coherence of the Dobell poems, preferring Philip's arrangement in *Poems of Felicity*.[2] Wallace's essay is important in that it challenges this view and examines the sequence as a thematic whole. But we need not believe that the Dobell *Poems* neatly represent spiritual exercises in the manner of St. Ignatius in order to support Wallace's major argument that the sequence is a patterned work of art made up of individual poems, each with its own structural and thematic coherence as well as individual integrity. The memory operates in "The Salutation," and in the final portion of the sequence we find analytical observations: "Thoughts are the Angels which we send abroad, / To visit all the Parts of Gods Abode" ("Thoughts. III").[3] Further, many verbs throughout the sequence imply linear and spatial movement or expansion. As in *Divine Reflections*, the journey of the soul from birth to the New Jerusalem informs the structure of the sequence:

> The Soul is present by a Thought; and sees
> The New Jerusalem, the Palaces,
> The Thrones and feasts, the Regions of the Skie,
> The Joys and Treasures of the DEITIE.
> ["Thoughts. IV"]

By a "Thought," the distant is made near; the metaphor of the journey thus functions in being destructible. Similarly, the Dobell *Poems* are concerned with time, but as we have seen so often in Traherne's other works, if time exists as a poetic fiction, it exists to be the victim of the poet's presentation.

For instance, "The Salutation" (pp. 5-6) purports to be a poem about birth and the period shortly thereafter. But the poem actually deals with an anxiety similar to Augustine's: Where was the self before time?

> These little Limmes,
> These Eys and Hands which here I find,
> These rosie Cheeks wherwith my Life begins,
> Where have ye been? Behind
> What Curtain were ye from me hid so long!
> Where was? in what Abyss, my Speaking Tongue?

When Philip alters "Speaking" to "new-made Tongue" he shows that he misses his brother's point. Originally and rightly the language suggests a paradoxical state of affairs in which the speaker's tongue was owned but owned without his knowing it. The stanza has a surreal quality that tends to blur the distinction between the times before and after the moment of birth. Personal existence seems to precede cognition: "Rosie cheeks" are temporally prior to "Life." Implicit in these rhetorical questions is the assertion that for aeons the speaker lay, along with his "Speaking Tongue," in "Chaos." Malcolm Day has recently pointed out Traherne's belief in the doctrine of the preexistence of the soul.[4] In this stanza we find a hint of the preexistence also of the body. The opening poem is the speaker's salute to his bodily parts which for "So many thousand thousand yeers / Beneath the Dust did in a Chaos lie." In the infinite expanse of this eternity before time, the "I" remained silent because of the alienation of part from part. We encounter the striking notion of a tongue, "Speaking" in the void of eternity, without the willed participation of the self.

The speaker seems to suggest that the tongue speaks but is not heard. Various parts of the body appear from the speaker's vantage point in the present to have been hidden from each other, behind curtains or in vast reaches of physical space. If Philip's revision is therefore not completely wrong-headed, he did miss the fact that the "newness" hinted at in Stanza 1 belongs to the apprehensions of the speaker:

> I that so long
> Was Nothing from Eternitie,
> Did little think such Joys as Ear or Tongue,
> To Celebrat or See:
> Such Sounds to hear, such Hands to feel, such Feet,
> Beneath the Skies, on such a Ground to meet.

What is new is the organizing consciousness, the "I," composed from "Nothing." This disengaged ego could not "think" of the full satisfactions lying in store for his fragmented sense receptors. Stanza 4 is an apostrophe to the new sense of "Joy" which emerges coeval with the "Lims," the "Organized Joynts" of the child. Before time or organized consciousness or wholeness, the veins and limbs of the body possess this joy.

The opening poem is not a "composition of place" but rather a blurring of the sense of place and time; the moment of birth loses its temporality as it is pushed back into the timelessness of chaos. Indeed, it seems that the self was present as witness to the body's birth:

> From Dust I rise,
> And out of Nothing now awake,
> These Brighter Regions which salute mine Eys,
> A Gift from GOD I take.
> The Earth, the Seas, the Light, the Day, the Skies,
> The Sun and Stars are mine; if those I prize.

First a stranger to his parts, the speaker now presents himself as a stranger to the world. The heroic proportions of the ego (seen in the speaker's habitation of chaos) enable him to occupy the universe: "The Earth, the Seas, the Light, the Day." In the last stanza of "The Salutation," some variant of "strangeness" appears six times. What once appeared as merely new is now construed as awesome; the fragmented has been resurrected as the wonderful, a quality that provides coherence between the first two poems. "How like an Angel came I down," the speaker exclaims, only to repeat the theme of "The Salutation": again, the skies are bright, the body like a little world, the world full of treasure.

Just as in Chapter 5 above we have discussed Traherne's technique of mythologizing autobiographical material, so in this early section, generally, the focus is not on childhood in the autobiographical sense, but rather on infancy as a way of responding to the world: "The World resembled his *Eternitie,* / In which my Soul did Walk" (lines 5-6). "Wonder" (pp. 6-8) deals with this quickened awareness:

> A Native Health and Innocence
> Within my Bones did grow,
> And while my GOD did all his Glories shew,
> I felt a Vigour in my Sence
> That was all SPIRIT. I within did flow
> With Seas of Life, like Wine;
> I nothing in the World did know,
> But 'twas Divine.

In this fine stanza Traherne emphasizes metaphors of physical and emotional plasticity. "Health and Innocence" are not just "Native," they are alive, burgeoning like a plant within the hardest substances of the body. The very sense of life is entirely—"all"—"SPIRIT." But the "I" not only apprehends this "Vigour" within; in a marvelous shift Traherne stresses the malleable nature of the "I" by use of fluid imagery. The "I" moves within the infant self in the most elastic of all forms: with physical likeness to the irrepressible ocean tides, or with the unpredictable emotional effects of wine. Hence, the vitality of movement within corresponds to the Divinity pervading the macrocosm. In the following stanza the same theme is treated in antithetical terms; "Weeping Eyes" provide the only semblance of motion, as Traherne depicts the static, mundane world of adult commerce with "The State of Innocence." From the idyllic world of vital, liquid movement we are thrust into the restrained and dead world of the fallen senses.

In the remaining stanzas of "Wonder" the speaker describes this prelapsarian consciousness. On the one hand the world seemed like the Heavenly City, and it seemed also that the infant was the joyful possessor of all:

> The Streets were pavd with Golden Stones,
>   The Boys and Girles were mine,
> Oh how did all their Lovly faces shine!
>   The Sons of Men were Holy Ones.
> Joy, Beauty, Welfare did appear to me,
>   And evry Thing which here I found,
> While like an Angel I did see,
>   Adornd the Ground.

This stanza seems to blot out all possibility of evil. But as we read in stanza 7, the child fails to perceive the fallen world only because it literally flees from "the splendor of [his] Eys":

> Cursd and Devised Proprieties,
>   With Envy, Avarice
> And Fraud, those Feinds that Spoyl even Paradice,
>   Fled from the Splendor of mine Eys.
> And so did Hedges, Ditches, Limits, Bounds,
>   I dreamd not ought of those,
> But wanderd over all mens Grounds,
>   And found Repose.

174

In the final stanza the contrarieties set up in the poem (plenitude and deprivation, innocence and experience, Paradise and limitation, treasure and "ragged Objects") are drawn into accord. Even the figures of enclosure, which Traherne often uses with negative overtones ("Hedges . . . / Walls, Boxes, Coffers") "shine," like the faces of the children of Paradise. They shine because the infant fails to understand the human intentions underlying their functions in the "real" or adult world. The child projects his own sense of beauty outward: "Proprieties themselvs were mine." He invests the universe with the liberty of his own "Health and Innocence."

Like Milton, Traherne was a learned man. But like the Milton of *Paradise Regained*, he had grave doubts about the efficacy of knowledge, at least insofar as knowledge implied sophistication or disunity. The truth does not divide, but reconciles. The only residue of division in the poem is that between the fallen and Edenic visions. As in Thomas' "Fern Hill," or Blake's *Songs of Innocence*, Traherne's Eden is that blissful time before time-consciousness. The coffin represents limits only to one schooled in death. Pristine ignorance of time and mortality was the "Original Simplicitie" lost by Adam at the Fall: "Those Things which first his Eden did adorn, / My Infancy / Did crown. Simplicitie / Was my Protection when I first was born" ("Eden"). Structurally, "Eden" is like a parenthetical meditation on the "Happy Ignorance" which "Divided" the child from any sense of sin. As such, it is also a poem in praise of ignorance and naïveté. Traherne did not think of knowledge as the appropriate end of human life. Indeed, he shared with Montaigne and Pierre Charron a belief that knowledge was a potential source of danger and anxiety. Thus, in the opening suite of poems most frequently anthologized ("The Salutation," "Wonder," "Eden," "Innocence") Traherne examines the ideal sense of union between subject and object. He determines that the ideal perception is in the subject, and he is led to see the infant's ignorance as closely linked to innocence and security. Conversely, knowledge and complexity are features of the fallen, adult world. We need not construe this theme as anti-intellectual, however; it represents, instead, Tra-

175

herne's assumption that Truth and Goodness are identical. This was his theme in "Shadows in the Water": adult perceptions must not be insulated from the quickening illuminations of the child's vision, for where such fragmentation of viewpoint exists, an arbitrary limit has been mistakenly imposed, or the single part has been confused with the whole. The theme of unity, or of essentialism, is a clear expression of Traherne's Platonism: particularity and division are not consonant with perfection. Traherne would have agreed with Thomas Jackson's comment on God's perfection:

Wee must not conceipt a multitude or diversity of excellencies in his *Essence*, answering to the severall natures of things created: We must not imagine one excellencie sutable to *elementary bodies*, another to *mixt*, a third to *vegetables*, a fourth to *sense*, &c. one to humane nature, another to Angelicall.[5]

After a rather complicated discussion of the plural, the total, and the universal, Jackson concludes that the divine Essence precludes all quantification: hence,

Hee speakes more fully and more safely, that saith, *God is being itselfe, or perfection itselfe*. . . . So all *plurality* be excluded, we expresse his *being* and *perfection* best, by leaving them, as they truly are, without all quantity. [I,36]

The continual use of repetition, and the piling up of syntactic elements (especially of synonyms) appropriately conveys this Platonic sense of perfection by way of the inadequacy of language. Accordingly, Jackson explains, qualifiers which suggest "illimited Essence" are appropriate, "In that Hee [God] is without beginning [and] without end" (I, 37). So, we might point out, is the speaker of Traherne's poems. In this sense Traherne's conception and his dramatization of the inadequacies of language to express it meet happily in his love of abstract nouns and adjectives, a love shared by Jackson:

The indivisible unity of illimited *being* or *perfection*, is, in every respect imaginable, more excellent and soveraigne than all infinite *perfections*, by imagination possibly could be. . . . From this fundamentall truth of Gods absolute infinity by indivisible unity, we may inferre, He is *powerfull* above all conceit of infinite power, . . . *Wise He is*, beyond all conceit of infinite wisdom . . . *Good* likewise *He is* above all . . . Lastly, the immensity of his Majesty, and infinity of duration . . . infinitely exceed all conceipt of *infinite* succession or extension, whose parts cannot be actually and indivisibly the same, one with another, or with the whole. [I, 39-40]

In this context the very use of language at all becomes paradoxical, for the purport specifically negates the efficacy of language. Thus in the opening sequence of the Dobell *Poems* the speaker decides that the closest approximation of divine essence is the wordless "Serious Meditation" which occupies the child. What Jackson calls the "unity of illimited *being*" (I, 39) is like the self-contained eye of the child, into which "All Objects . . . feed" ("Innocence"). Just as "Eden" parenthetically focuses on the paradisical imagery of "Wonder," so is the thematic material of "Innocence" recursive: "But that which most I Wonder at." In effect, the speaker reiterates the reiterative substance of "Eden." The entire poem thematically parallels "Eden," and both are in syntactic apposition to "Wonder."

Part I ends with a resolve that is also a confession: "I must becom a Child again." Into the tensed world of experience the speaker has fallen from grace. His affirmation, drawn from a text in Matthew, presents the future as antidote to the present. Though as a child he was "A little Adam in a Sphere," now he must go forward by returning to the source. Thus "The Preparative" (pp. 12-14), which begins the second section of the sequence, returns to the very beginning, to the egoless nonbeing described in "The Salutation":

> My Body being Dead, my Lims unknown,
>> Before I skild to prize
>> Those living Stars mine Eys,
> Before my Tongue or Cheeks were to me shewn,
>> Before I knew my Hands were mine,
> Or that my Sinews did my Members joyn,
>> When neither Nostril, Foot, nor Ear,
> As yet was seen, or felt, or did appear;
>> I was within
> A House I knew not, newly clothd with Skin.

The last two lines here may remind us of the soul in Herbert's "The Flower," which during the long winter of afflictions withdraws to keep "house unknown" until the approach of spring. But they are more strongly reminiscent of Vaughan's "The Retreat":

> Happy those early dayes! when I
> Shin'd in my Angell-infancy.
> Before I understood this place
> Appointed for my second race,
> Or taught my soul to fancy ought
> But a white, Celestiall thought,
> When yet I had not walkt above
> A mile, or two, from my first love,
> And looking back (at this short space,)
> Could see a glimpse of his bright-face; ...
> Before I taught my tongue to wound
> My Conscience with a sinfull sound ...
> But felt through all this fleshly dresse
> Bright *shootes* of everlastingnesse.[6]

In both poems the diction and imagery stress the debilitating aspects of experience. But in "The Retreat" the child looks back at ever-increasing time intervals into the still glowing face of a personalized Deity, whose impression slowly disappears from the visible world; this process of attenuation is the outward sign of the speaker's self-inflicted punishment in the form of verbalized guilt. In Traherne, the child's sense of limitlessness derives from the fact that in the earliest moments of his life he can accord to the various parts of his body no specialized functions. With particularization come limits: the codifying of the human intellect.

In "The Preparative,"[7] again, we see the child's sense of reality as intrinsically godlike; he seems anesthetized to the perception of mundane differences which so pervade the adult and secular worlds. Only division of eternity into temporal units allows the child to distinguish his body from the world perceived. Earlier (before human time existed), the "I" was present, but in an unknown "House." In the Fall that followed, the seer was divorced from the scene. Characteristically, Traherne reaches back to the preceding poem for his imagery: "I was an Adam there, / A little Adam in a Sphere." The proper preparative is a reiteration of already stated and expanded motifs. The spheral imagery of the earlier poem contradicts the idea of movement and development suggested by the following poem's title. To reinforce this atemporality the world is again depicted virtually without a transitive verb:

> Then was my Soul my only All to me,
>   A Living Endless Ey,
>   Far wider then the Skie
> Whose Power, whose Act, whose Essence was to see.
>   I was an Inward *Sphere of Light,*
> Or an Interminable Orb of *Sight,*
>   An Endless and a Living Day,
> A *vital Sun* that round about did *ray*
>   All Life and Sence,
> A Naked Simple Pure *Intelligence.*
>
> [Stanza 2]

The infinite universe, the "All," is present to the child as his "Soul," which is a sphere. His being is represented by the emblem "A Living Endless Ey." The "Ey-I" perceives and encompasses the spatio-temporal world. The diction attempts to articulate the indefinable qualities of extension in time and space: "All," "Endless," "Wider," "Interminable," "Essence," "Pure." The "Sphere" of Adam takes on a new aspect: "I was an inward Sphere of Light." The "I" is either a microcosmic sphere of light (perceived), "Or" a universally extended "Ey." The two are one, for one place is like all space, and one present embraces eternity. God and the "I" are one, and only time and knowledge (being "shewn," becoming "skild") from the "Learned and Happy Ignorance" instilled at birth, dividing essence into power and act.

In *Christian Ethicks* Traherne associated the sphere with divine omnipresence,[8] and again, he may have had Thomas Jackson's *Treatise of the Divine Essence and Attributes* in mind: "God is a sphere, whose Center is everywhere, whose circumference is no where" (I, 55).[9] Jackson's discussion is tantalizing not only because we know that Traherne read it, but also because in it he uses many of Traherne's favorite abstract nouns. Thus, God is rightly compared to a sphere because "of all figures" the sphere is the most "capacious" (I, 56). The metaphor has perplexed certain men, apparently for two reasons. Most obviously, how can a circle's center be everywhere, and still remain the center? Secondly, in what sense is it appropriate to speak of God's presence as a center? According to Jackson, the answer involves a suprarational understanding of both space and time.

Both Jackson and Traherne try to make language express the unspeakable. In "The Preparative," the child is born to limits he at first does not or will not recognize. In a like manner the poet is forced into acceptance of an imprecise medium of expression: the emblem of fallen man, language. Ideally, both in experience and art, limits and differences do not exist. Yet the child without knowing it—and the poet too—have to some degree been compartmentalized and restricted almost from the beginning. Hence, the poet's use of paradox, whose function it is to violate the ordinary expectations and limits of commonsense experience. Thus Jackson writes, "Wheresoever *He* is (and *Hee* is every where,) *He* is *unity* it selfe, *infinity* it selfe, *immensity* it selfe, *perfection* it selfe, *power* it selfe" (I, 58). Except in the realm of fantasy, "place" logically excludes "every where"; and by the same token, "where" the speaker "is" or "was" when he perceived "an Inward *Sphere of Light*" becomes a set of atemporal and aspatial qualities. Further, if we take the "is" seriously we grasp the paradoxical function of piling up abstract nouns. If X *is* Y, and if Y is not the same as Z, how can X also *be* Z? The answer is that the mystic's declaration of equivalences is like the poet's reconciliation of the adult's analytical (if limited) view of reality with the unifying and charismatic qualities of the child's appreciative powers. The victim of this rhetorical thrust is the category "center." It is inappropriate and finally ineffective to apply too stringently a word which rightly is meant to approximate only one aspect of divinity. To insist upon this center as a literal point or "place" might suggest a denial of God's infinite extension by requiring simultaneously a conception of infinite movement from one place to another. And if God moves from place to place, he must exist temporally

as well as spatially, and consequently, he must change—clearly
an impossibility: "He is every where, because no body, no
space, or spirituall substance can exclude his presence, or avoid
penetration of his Essence" (I, 53). The qualifiers in "The
Preparative" consistently stress the inexplicable qualities of infinity: space without boundary, time without duration, subject
without object. The "Ey" does not see; it lives, and lives interminably—extended beyond all objects in space: "I / . . . was all
Sight, or Ey."

Not surprisingly, then, the entire poem develops paradoxically. Part of the soul's preparation is to recognize the speaker's
vision as not in the natural order of life, that order in which
"Iron Fate" and life's trivialities (intensely underlined in stanza
5 by the rhyme between "Dross" and "gross") impose upon the
early unity of the soul and the "All." The universe in which
the child dwelt is destroyed, and with it disappears the operative
unity between feeling and the self: "Vain Affections . . . Se-
duce" the soul from its earthly paradise, where *Feeling Feeling*
Wounds / With Pleasure and Delight." The catalog of senses
and their operations reiterates the Edenic qualities, particularly
unity in simplicity seen in the earlier poems. But the stanza does
more than reiterate this. Traherne tries to suggest the inexplicable identification of different objects or senses. Syntactically, *"Feeling,"* contiguous to *"Feeling"* in the sentence, becomes both subject and object of the verb "Wound," as if to
suggest that the poet would bind the two words while insisting
on their separateness and distinctness:

> For *Sight* inherits Beauty, *Hearing* Sounds,
>   The *Nostril* Sweet Perfumes,
>   All *Tastes* have hidden Rooms
> Within the *Tongue*; and *Feeling Feeling* Wounds
>   With Pleasure and Delight, but I
> Forgot the rest, and was all Sight, or Ey.
>   Unbodied and Devoid of Care,
> Just as in Heavn the Holy Angels are.
>   For Simple Sence
> Is Lord of all Created Excellence.
>
> [Stanza 4]

The intensity of this poem, one of Traherne's best, derives from an effective pathos. Since preparation of the soul depends on the recognition of the Fall, the speaker confronts again the image of a lost world:

> Divine Impressions when they came,
> Did quickly enter and my Soul inflame.
> Tis not the Object, but the Light
> That maketh Heaven; Tis a Purer Sight.
> Felicitie
> Appears to none but them that purely see.
>
> [Stanza 6]

Quickness here reminds the reader that the "Ey" lived, expelling light, like the cock in Vaughan's poem, whose "Sunnie seed" could not resist the magnetism of Paradise. But Traherne's poem does not end in prayer for spiritual union. Instead, the speaker addresses himself: "Get free, and so thou shalt even all Admire" (line 70). As in the garden of "Burnt Norton," here the lost and timeless world remains "a perpetual possibility." But the speaker by implication rehearses the true condition of man; in the tensed world of the English sentence, when the speaker expatiates on his past unfettered existence he implicitly introduces a future and potentially opposite possibility. "I was as free . . ." the speaker says in stanza 5; but this is the rhetorical "preparative" for his almost immediate resolve: "My Soul retire, / Get free."

The intensely chastening tone of "The Instruction" (pp. 14-15) must be understood in this light. The speaker has called to mind the pristine state, now lost. The nearly verbless stanzas of "The Preparation" are answered by the vigorous imperatives of the speaker, who now assumes the role of priest, of confessor and guide:

> Spue out thy filth, thy flesh abjure;
> Let not Contingents thee defile.
> For Transients only are impure,
> And Aery things thy soul beguil.

This stanza speaks directly to the temporal motif of "The Preparative," with its description of a being so attuned to life that it allows for no time lapse between stimulus and response, or between perception and enjoyment. Quickness refers not only to life (the quick as distinguished from the dead) but also to the time differential between subject and object, past and present, seeing and appreciation. "Transients" do not exist in the world of the child's original consciousness; succession is an inference learned from stultifying and divisive experience: "Custom, Action, or Desire." The shadow of duration between seen object and felt joy emerges through acquaintance with the adult world. In its tone "The Instruction" verges on self-accusation and approaches the mode of the penitential psalm. Verses very similar in theme and tone may be found in Richard Rowlands' *Seaven Penitential Psalmes* (1601):

> With savour view my soule deffects
>   In crymes I did begin,
> My nature bad, my mother fraile,
>   Conceav'd I was in sin.
>
>   Against my self I said wil I
> My wronges confesse and faultes defy,
> To thee o Lord, o Lord to thee
> That haest from all absolved mee.[10]

But the differences are as informative as the similarities. In Rowlands' poem the speaker's guilt is emphasized by the first person pronoun. In "The Instruction" the speaker never fully identifies himself as the subject for advice; he makes no confession of *his* sin. The confession is feigned, reenacted, like the experiences of the child's Edenic consciousness. Man's quotidian existence is the enemy of the child's vision, which reappears as the theme of the following poem.

As if in counterstatement to "The Instruction," which focused on the disunity of experience and on the learning and progress transpiring in the fallen world, "The Vision" begins, "Flight is but the Preparative." H. M. Margoliouth has noticed the similarity between the fifth stanza of "The Vision" (pp. 15-17) and the first of Marvell's "The Garden":[11]

> To see a Glorious Fountain and an End
>   To see all Creatures tend
> To thy Advancement, and so sweetly close
>   In thy Repose: To see them shine

> In Use in Worth in Service, and even Foes
>   Among the rest made thine.
> To see all these unite at once in Thee
>   Is to behold Felicitie.

Not only do the forms of nature "close," but in both poems we find an emphasis on the totality of nature's response to man. In Marvell, "All Trees and Flowers do close / To weave the garlands of repose," which are in signal contrast to the sparse adornments of laurel about the poet's brow. The merging forms of the garland are emblems of the fruitive virtues of solitude and innocence. Marvell's meditant has turned his back on the heats of competition and secular love. In "The Vision" the diction suggests something slightly different. "All Creatures . . . close," not as a reward for meditation and withdrawal but as a function of their existence: "All Creatures tend / To thy Advancement." Further, they "close" as if to manifest the unified perspective lost in the Fall, which now inheres "in" (as if inside) the speaker's "Repose," and that repose is the "experimental" aspect of the vision of "Felicitie." Appropriately, in the final stanza of the poem, the dominant figures suggest the merging, "conjoyned" quality of both the sight and seen universe:

> From One, to One, in one to see *All Things*
>   To see the King of Kings
> At once in two; to see his Endless Treasures
>   Made all mine own, my self the End
> Of all his Labors! Tis the Life of Pleasures!
>   To see my self His friend!
> Who all things finds conjoynd in Him alone,
>   Sees and Enjoys the Holy one.

Like "The Instruction," "The Rapture" (p. 17) functions in apposition to the preceding poem. In effect, it gives direct evidence of the feelings described more generally in "The Vision." Thus, its use of anaphora, of parallel phrases and synonyms, gives the reader the sense of a parenthetical exemplum, much like those found in *Centuries of Meditations*. Ideas of physical, temporal, or even moral development or progress disappear, and in their place we find the atemporal imagery of mysticism:

184

passions aflame, sacred illuminations, arms enfolding, heavenly delights. Even the title of the poem invites sensuous and erotic associations with such poems as "The Extasie" and "A Rapture."

> From GOD abov
> Being sent, the Heavens me enflame,
> To prais his Name.
> The Stars do move!
> The Burning Sun doth shew his Love.

Such ejaculations recur throughout the Dobell *Poems*. In the very next poem, for example, we read:

> O Rapture! Wonder! Extasie! Delight!
> How Great must then his *Glory* be, how Great
> Our *Blessedness*! How vast and Infinit
> Our *Pleasure*, how Transcendent, how compleat,
> If we the *Goodness* of our God possess,
> And all *His Joy* be in *our Blessedness*.

Here we see Traherne piling up abstract nouns and adjectives and omitting dependence on the verb. When the tensed verb does enter the sentence, it comes as the purveyor of inaction and stasis: "be," "possess," "be." If we look carefully at this passage we notice the typical tendency to repeat ideas in the form of synonyms: "Rapture," "Wonder," "Extasie," "Delight." But then, as if each word must be appreciated separately, he isolates them in the stanza and in the sentence, by insisting on the longest possible symbol of pause: the exclamation mark. The effect is a sense of expansion: one loses track of the ordering influence of rhyme; the orienting verb is submerged as we begin the stanza; and the repeated "How" reminds the reader of the frequency of such locutions and (implicitly) of how many more could be added without substantially altering the speaker's meaning. Each word, each iamb, of the first line is isolated in time and space, and yet all fuse in a universe of synonymy; and as the constraints of the sentence and of logic are thrown off, the residue of meaning is again one of endless possible ejaculations and paraphrases and synonyms: "how Transcendent, how compleat."

The stanza just quoted is from "The Improvment" which,

along with "The Approach," concludes the second section. As ecstasy leaves a residue of insight or recognition, these poems are like afterthoughts or reflections on "The Rapture." In "The Improvment" Traherne develops the triad of wisdom, power, and goodness which the speaker understands to be the source of "Felicitie" as well as the source of the entire sphere of the universe (which moves "*in one fair Order*"). In God's love lies the explanation of the central mystery: how the universe in its entirety is present in the point or minuscule center of the soul. The comprehensiveness of God's "*Marvelous Designe*" in the world reveals a correspondence with the state of bliss, the sphere of pleasure which is the essence of that still point. In childhood, and in the moment of spiritual union, we find the human counterpart of God's "*Wise Contrivance*" in the exterior world. The child "By Instinct *virtualy*" discerns the essential identity of the smaller and the larger sphere; his "Ey" and the "Divine Orb" were fashioned as one. Hence, in "The Approach" (pp. 21-22), we learn that recollection brings "Improvement." Memories of childhood have summoned forth a residue of truth:

> But now with New and Open Eys,
> I see beneath as if above the Skies;
> And as I Backward look again,
> See all his Thoughts and mine most Clear and Plain.
> He did Approach, he me did Woo
> I wonder that my God this thing would doe.

The speaker has begun to learn how he learned: with "curious Art" he was "Instructed" in childhood "by the Deitie"; taught and guided by the natural design of existence, he was "enveloped in more then Gold; / In deep Abysses of Delights" (lines 34-35). The "Ey" has begun to more perfectly understand its own unity. Peter Sterry likewise construed the awakening of the soul by degrees of expansion of this "Ey": "This (God's) Unity fills all, *is all in all*, the Eye, the Light, the Glass, the Object, or Image, the Union, the Light. This Unity is the *power* of sight in the eye, of shining, of uniting the Eye and the Object in the light."[12]

186

The entire development of soul toward perfection may be construed under the same figure. Sterry writes: "The Humane Soul, according to Philosophers, they say, rouleth it self into a four-fold Orb, or Globe; The Sensitive, Rational, Intellectual, or Angelical, its Divine Unity" (p. 107). Although any influence of Sterry's *Discourse* is impossible, it should be pointed out that something like Sterry's fourfold use of the sphere image operates in the Dobell *Poems*. We noticed in the four first poems the great emphasis on the sensors themselves, an emphasis which corresponds in some measure to this description:

1. The first, the *lowest Orb* of the Soul, is the *Sensitive*. The Soul in this part is all set and adorned with the sensitive and shadowy form of things, as a Meadow with the Trees, and Flowers by a Riverside, are seen, by their shadowy Figures, playing in the water. [P. 107]

In exactly the same way, tenuously and not fully recognizable, the soul possesses the "immortal Forms" of the visible world. This "Orb" differs from the second only in the increase of lucidity: "here the Angelic Forms and Essences of things are seen through the grosser and *cloudy medium*." Now the soul's orb sees not shadows in the water, but "the Face of Heaven, or the Trees and Flowers of the Neighbouring fields [as if] from beneath the water of an adjoyning River."

The third section, which runs from "Dumnesse" (pp. 22-24) through "Love" (pp. 60-61), is the longest, including nineteen poems. It begins by recursion to the theme of "The Salutation" (the body's silence), but the reiteration brings with it a sharpened analytical awareness. The speaker now thinks of his erstwhile "Silence" or "Non-Intelligence of Human Words" as an emblem of divine union. "Mixture," the element of discord, enters consciousness with the "Thoughts" or words of others, which close "the Holy Door" of the soul's "Temple." In "Silence" (pp. 25-27), the earth once viewed as "Tutor" and "Guid" performs "The office of a Priest"; the catechism taught is "Inward Work" of "Silence," a sphere and ocean of wordless feeling which is the earthly impression of Paradise. The sphere, the "Ey," the "Orb" of the speaker endures a recognizable

expansion; or, rather, the speaker's divine orb within achieves a
new perspective:

> A vast and Infinit Capacitie,
> Did make my Bosom like the Deitie,
> In Whose Mysterious and Celestial Mind
> All Ages and all Worlds together shind.
> Who tho he nothing said did always reign,
> And in Himself Eternitie contain.
> The World was more in me, then I in it.
> The King of Glory in my Soul did sit.
> And to Himself in me he always gave,
> All that he takes Delight to see me have.
> For so my Spirit was an Endless Sphere,
> Like God himself, and Heaven and Earth was there.
>
> [Lines 75-86]

Adam's "Original Simplicitie" endures an expanded definition:
"But being Simple like the Deitie / In its own Centre is a Sphere
/ Not shut up here, but evry Where" ("My Spirit," pp. 27-30).
The original sense of wonder rushes back, and with it, rapture:

> O Joy! O Wonder, and Delight!
>   O Sacred Mysterie!
> My Soul a Spirit infinit!
> An Image of the Deitie!
>   A pure Substantiall Light!
> That Being Greatest which doth Nothing seem!
> Why, twas my All, I nothing did esteem
> But that alone. A Strange Mysterious Sphere!
>
> [Stanza 5]

Here, an almost verbless passage culminates in an appositive
and verbless fragment, the rhetorical approximation of silence.
In this expanded "Ey" no distinction between subject and predi-
cate is possible, and so the poet meets the demands of language
by suggesting the simple, eternal presence of consciousness
itself. In this sphere there is no movement: "It Acts not from a
Centre to / Its Object as remote, / But present is" (lines 18-20).
For in this universe of feeling all motion—all physical and temporal expansion, is contained:

> A Strange Extended Orb of Joy,
>   Proceeding from within,

Which did on evry side convey
It self, and being nigh of Kin
    To God did evry Way
Dilate it self even in an Instant, and
Like an Indivisible Centre Stand
At once Surrounding all Eternitie.

[Stanza 6]

Though dilation implies movement, in this context it transpires as if without time. Though infinitely extended, yet eternity is surrounded by this sphere: infinite object coinciding with eternal response, a "Living Orb of Sight":

O Act, O Power infinit;
O Subtile, and unbounded Air!
    O Living Orb of Sight!
Thou which within me art, yet Me! Thou Ey,
And Temple of his Whole Infinitie!
O what a World art Thou! a World within!
    All Things appear,
    All Objects are
Alive in thee!

[Stanza 7]

In one sense, Traherne uses repetition as a metaphoric statement of consistency. But here, and often elsewhere, the rush of abstract nouns and adjectives includes contradictory figures and ideas. Opposites are thrust together as parallel appositives, thrust together in such a way as to syntactically declare their identity. Though a sphere is above all things fixed in shape, Traherne describes a sphere without boundaries; and as this and other boundaries blur they also fuse. As in this passage, appearance and reality fuse too; paradox provides for an enriched perspective on the truth, in that we have two or more (contradictory) ways of declaring a truth which accurately corresponds only to silence. In his original state man was born both deaf and dumb ("Dumnesse").

As the sequence continues to unfold, figures of the sphere and of expansion frequently recur. The "Universe" is "enclosed in Skin" ("Fullnesse"), and yet is in some way "not bounded with" the speaker's "Clothes or Skin" ("Nature"). As in Peter Sterry's third "Orb or Sphere" ("The Intellectual part of the

Soul"), the speaker's perceptions are informed in a more refined
manner; the outlines of creation appear more vividly. No longer
does the soul perceive the universe as from a bottom of a stream:
"3. The Intellectual part of the Soul, is the Orb or Sphere of
Angels. This is the Souls Angelical part. Here the Soul's *abstract*, and separate from the Body, (which is the *Divine Death*
of the Soul)" (p. 107). Similarly, in "Nature" (pp. 32-34), the
soul's "Orb" expands by "Dilating of it self." The soul's new
mark is the uttermost extent of "Wide Infinitie":

> But yet there were new Rooms, and Spaces more,
> Beyond all these, Wide Regions ore and ore,
> And into them my pent-up-Soul like fire
> Did break, Surmounting all I here admire.
> The Spaces fild were like a Cabinet
> Of Joys before me most Distinctly set:
> The Empty, like to large and Vacant Room
> For Fancy to enlarge in, and presume
> A Space for more, removd, but yet adorning
> These neer at hand, that pleasd me evry Morning.
> Here I was seated to behold New Things.
>
> [Lines 71-81]

Though in the reiterative pattern of the work the speaker returns occasionally to the heraldry of the body (as in "The
Person"), the dominant theme as this section unfolds concerns
the soul's expansion. The tone assumes a heightened sense of
ardor: the soul and God "burn" with mutual desire ("The
Estate"), and even the objects of nature take on erotic significance: "Men may delighted be with Springs, / While Trees and
Herbs their Sences pleas, / And taste even Nectar in the Seas"
("The Enquirie"). As once the "Spirit" flowed as an "Inward"
sea, now all earth flows with the "Lov" of God "Like Myrrh or
Incense," and the soul's "desire" is set by Love's "embrace."

Figures of expansion and stasis apply to the same spheral
objects in "The Circulation" (pp. 45-47), one of Traherne's
most interesting poems. In "The Circulation," which is fashioned as a gloss on "The Estate" and "The Enquirie," the "Ey"
apprehends the "fair Ideas from the Skie" in the same way that
a mirror reflects "The Face of Heaven." This would seem to

preclude ideas of the soul's expansion, for, implicitly, the soul returns only what first enters it, and so we might expect it to remain the same size. But Traherne treats the idea of "Circulation" in terms of his primary image (the "Ey"), and he does so by developing a simile between the "Ey" and a mirror. At first it all seems rather narcissistic in meaning; but as we have seen in Sterry's *Discourse*, in the estate of the third "Orb" the soul apprehends the "Intellectual Forms of things," walking in Paradise, viewing with both active and passive powers of the understanding, and because of this, perceiving with a heightened visual awareness:

As that above, like the living Face before the Glass, appears at the brink of the waters, upon the shore, with all its Angelical Glories round about it, in their Paradisical Region, which lies within the Soul it self. So the Soul beneath appears, looking up from its *pearly Cave*, at the bottom of the River, like the God of the River, answering and meeting it self above. [P. 107]

The motif is strikingly similar to that in "The Circulation" (pp. 45-47).

> As fair Ideas from the Skie,
> Or Images of Things,
> Unto a Spotless Mirror flie,
> On unperceived Wings;
> And lodging there affect the Sence,
> As if at first they came from thence;
> While being there, they richly Beautifie
> The Place they fill, and yet communicat
> Themselvs, reflecting to the Seers Ey,
> Just such is our Estate
> No Prais can we return again,
> No Glory in our selvs possess,
> But what derived from without we gain,
> From all the Mysteries of Blessedness.

As in the *Centuries*, here Traherne qualifies his images almost to the point of destroying them: the mirror image and the "Orb" both reflect and expand, receive and give, but they do not quantitatively alter the universal structure. Circulation and extension depend on proper absorption. The "Celestial Eys" of the expanded soul encompass both the source of light and its reflection:

> All Things to Circulations owe
> Themselvs; by which alone
> They do exist: They cannot shew
> A Sigh, a Word, a Groan,
> A Colour, or a Glimps of Light,
> The Sparcle of a Precious Stone,
> A virtue, or a Smell; a lovly Sight,
> A Fruit, a Beam, an Influence, a Tear;
> But they anothers Livery must Wear.
>
> [Stanza 3]

Again, the "Amendment":

> Am I a Glorious Spring
> Of Joys and Riches to my King?
> Are Men made Gods! And may they see
> So Wonderfull a Thing
> As GOD in me!
> And is my Soul a Mirror that must Shine
> Even like the Sun, and be far more Divine?
>
> [Stanza 5]

Thus, the figures of silence, of fountain, conduit, and mirror, stress cyclic temporal and spatial processes binding all circulations as a sphere.

The mirror image, in particular, is a convenient vehicle for Traherne's version of the correspondences. But for Traherne this principle of universal symmetry is a fact, not the end or aim of the physical world. The mirror not only reflects the light received, it presents an image of the viewer to the viewer which he could not otherwise enjoy. Just as the soul cannot fully understand its own existence "till the Ends of Things are seen," likewise the Deity depends on the mirror of man for eyes through which to enjoy himself. "The Demonstration" (pp. 49-52) takes for its subject the cause and purpose underlying the facts of correspondence treated in "The Circulation." Again, as in Peter Sterry, the soul must penetrate beyond "similitudes"

(Sterry, p. 108), through the clouds obscuring the Sun to Light
Incarnate: "As in the Air we see the Clouds / Like Winding
Sheets, or Shrouds; / Which tho they nearer are obscure / The
Sun, which Higher far, is far more Pure" (lines 7-10). The
purpose of the reflecting mirror is to penetrate all obfuscations,
and to perceive God's splendor directly, so that in this way God
may directly enjoy himself:

> And what then this can be more Plain and Clear
> What Truth then this more Evident appear!
> The GODHEAD cannot prize
> The Sun at all, nor yet the Skies,
> Or Air, or Earth, or Trees, or Seas,
> Or Stars, unless the Soul of Man they pleas.
> He neither sees with Humane Eys
> Nor needs Himself Seas Skies
> Or Earth, or any thing: He draws
> No Breath, nor Eats or Drinks by Natures Laws.
> [Stanza 5]

As in the *Centuries*, the cause and end of "Circulation" is self-
love: the universe emanates from divine narcissism, which is the
fountain of creation and enjoyment:

> In them [his creatures] he sees, and feels, and Smels, and Lives,
> In them Affected is to whom he gives:
> In them ten thousand Ways,
> He all his Works again enjoys,
> All things from Him to Him proceed
> By them; Are His in them: As if indeed
> His Godhead did it self exceed.
> To them He all Conveys;
> Nay even Himself: He is the End
> To whom in them Himself, and All things tend.
> [Stanza 8]

So as the author and end of all, God is viewer of the glass and
the glass too; His "Bosom is the Glass, / Wherin we all Things
Everlasting See" ("The Anticipation"). As the soul ascends, the
distinction between "Ey" and mirror collapses: "The End and
Fountain differ but in Name."

At this level of consciousness distinctions begin to collapse: "My Contemplation Dazles in the End / Of all I comprehend. / And soars abov all Heights." Means become ends; wants and pleasures merge as one. Human nature decrees that possession diminishes desire, but the opposite is true of divine Love: "Possession doth not Cloy, / Nor Sence of Want Destroy." God's love is total communication, "Act":

> His Essence is all Act: He did, that He
> All Act might always be.
> His Nature burns like fire;
> His Goodness infinitly doth desire,
> To be by all possest;
> His Love makes others Blest.
> It is the Glory of his High Estate,
> And that which I for ever more Admire,
> He is an Act that doth Communicate.
>
> ["The Anticipation," stanza 11]

Recognizing this identity of Essence and Act, the soul now enjoys a wholly increased perspective. Not only do the erotic overtones suggest increased excitement, but echoes from the Apocalypse invest these affective utterances with distinctly allegorical overtones. Sterry writes that the soul in this third stage of enlightenment is witness to the "Angelical Glories . . . in their own Paradisical Region," and, likewise, in stanza 13 of "The Anticipation" the speaker breaks forth in concert with the Cherubim: "And Holy, Holy, Holy, is his Name. / He is the Means both of Himself and all, / Whom we the Fountain Means and End do call" (lines 115-117). The end and operative principle of the universe—the maker of the mirror and the image in the glass—is the reconciliation between Essence and Act: Love.

Love realized is the openly stated theme of the remaining poems in Part III. In "The Recovery" and "Another" we find constant references to conjugal pleasures, these set in appropriately sensuous surroundings. "The Recovery" is a meditation on the value of the voluntary act in matters of the heart, and especially as they concern man's love toward God; and in a series of quatrains, "Another" reminds the reader that without God's love nothing would exist (*nihil ex nihilo*). In this relatively brief poem the word "love" appears twelve times, and the title of the final poem of the third movement further underlines this repetition: "Love" (pp. 60-61).[13]

This brilliant little poem opens with an intense direct address to Love, as if the speaker, caught up in his ardor, gropes for the proper descriptive metaphor, and the fourth stanza returns to the same mode. As its quadripartite suggests, "Love" is a self-contained hymn in praise of the divine Essence. The first and last stanzas are neatly paired in that both are marked by an ecstatic use of anaphora and asyndeton:

> O Nectar! O Delicious Stream!
> O ravishing and only Pleasure! Where
> Shall such another Theme
> Inspire my Tongue with Joys, or pleas mine Ear!
> Abridgement of Delights!
> And Queen of Sights!
> O Mine of Rarities! O Kingdom Wide!
> O more! O Caus of all! O Glorious Bride!
> O God! O Bride of God! O King!
> O Soul and Crown of evry Thing!
>
> His Ganimede! His Life! His Joy!
> Or he comes down to me, or takes me up
> That I might be his Boy,
> And fill, and taste, and give, and Drink the Cup.
> But these (tho great) are all
> Too short and small,
> To Weak and feeble Pictures to Express
> The true Mysterious Depths of Blessedness.
> I am his Image, and his Friend.
> His Son, Bride, Glory, Temple, End.

In both stanzas the separation and balancing of syntactic elements, large and small, suggest an agitated state of mind: the sentences break forth; their members seem to disengage, as if to signal a totally nonrational process.[14]

Similarly, stanzas 2 and 3 are closely parallel in strategy:

> Did not I covet to behold
> Som Endless Monarch, that did always live
> In Palaces of Gold

> Willing all Kingdoms Realms and Crowns to give
>   Unto my Soul! Whose Lov
>   A Spring might prov
> Of Endless Glories, Honors, friendships, Pleasures,
> Joys, Praises, Beauties and Celestial Treasures!
>   Lo, now I see there's such a King,
>   The fountain Head of evry Thing!
>
> Did my Ambition ever Dream
> Of such a Lord, of such a Love! Did I
>   Expect so Sweet a Stream
> As this at any time! Could any Ey
>   Believ it? Why all Power
>   Is used here
> Joys down from Heaven on my Head to shower
> And Jove beyond the Fiction doth appear
>   Once more in Golden Rain to come.
>   To Danae's Pleasing Fruitfull Womb.

Both stanzas are composed of extended rhetorical questions, and both dramatically juxtapose states past and present. But this linkage is enriched by subtle thematic contrasts: "Did not I covet?" (stanza 2) becomes "Did my ambition ever Dream?" (stanza 3), with the subtle shift providing contrast between the longings of desire and the pleasures of fulfillment. Then, too, the repetition in stanza 4 of the third person genitive (in the first stanza, statement of the theme of possession is muted) frames the reflective material of stanzas 2 and 3 so as to greatly amplify the theme. The soul desires both a king and spouse, and—yes— a father too. The shifts in gender intensify the passage by suggesting that the normal expectations of human contact, sexual as well as all other, can merely hint at the delights of "Felicitie": "A garden inclosed is my sister, my spouse." In this communication we find a confusion of sexual roles; the speaker not only tastes but gives "The Cup." He is both giver and receiver of total gratification. As such, the speaker is both male and female. The reference to the chalice is hardly casual, but an appropriate representation of the erotic enjoyments which are the subject of this stanza and of the poem: "He brought me to the banqueting house, and his banner over me was love. Stay me with flagons, comfort me with apples: for I am sick of love"

(Cant. 2:4-5). As the last line of the poem makes clear, the theme of fulness in love includes not only a merging of sexual roles but annihilation of temporal boundaries. The cup of spiritual union represents eternal communion between God and man; and in the last line of the poem we have a miniature movement encompassing life's cycle (birth, marriage, death), a movement involving all humanness (male and female) in transport through glory in the earthly Church and in the Church Triumphant, to divinity: "His Son, Bride, Glory, Temple, End."

Structurally, the closing couplet of the poem broadly hints at a major break in the sequence, but it is one for which the reader has been prepared. Thematically, it represents a shift in perspective from earth to heaven, in itself a completed journey. But a second metaphoric layer concerns the psychic equivalent of this progress, the soul's preparation for entry into the terrestrial paradise. Thus, the word "End" appears as the final foot in a line of parallel and abstract nouns. Each of these is isolated as a discrete phrase by the hiatus of a comma, and, in turn, arranged to approximate this union by an ascending scale of metaphor. Finally, this sequence of nouns is recursive in that it refers to psychological material of stanza 1, and more generally to hints and starts and sudden recognitions throughout the third part of the Dobell *Poems*, these concerning the "End" or ultimate aim of man's existence: "Felicitie." Even though this "End" presupposes a heightened awareness of times present and past (in its recognition of the steps from instruction to illumination), still its perfect experience requires that the time-sense be obliterated. The two middle, "narrative" stanzas are enclosed by two others whose verbless syntax plunges the reader into an actionless universe of union with God, a "Mysterious" enjoyment for which words are only "Weak and feeble Pictures."

This final representation of a timeless experience whose subject is not words but "Thoughts" (the essence of the act of language) has been fully prepared for by the preceding sequence. The soul has now transcended the "Intellectual Orb of Sphere of Angels" ("How like an angel came I down"), following Traherne's theodicy which posits a higher union than the child can intuit: a fortunate fall into alienation from the world as a prelude to total absorption in the divine Essence. This union is the fourth and final stage, "the highest Point," the *"Divine Orb"* toward which the soul's longing and progress have inclined. As Peter Sterry describes it, "The last, and *Divine Orb,* the highest Point, and amplest Circuit of the Soul, is its *Unity.* In this it hath the most immediate resemblance to, and *Conjunction* with the supream Unity, the *Divine Nature"* (p. 107). It is in this stage that language is most apt to prove an unreliable expressive vehicle.[15] It has been said that the mystical poet is one who tries to make language do the impossible. If this is so, then the Traherne of the Dobell *Poems* qualifies as a mystical poet, for certainly he tries to depict the qualities of stasis and timelessness in the radically tensed medium of syntactic structures. He attempts to make the figure of "transparent Words" apply literally; his rhetorical drift is to equate the words themselves with the substratum—the "simple Light"—of the universe. For this reason, in the ecstatic portions of "Love" the grammatical integrity of the sentence itself begins to falter, leaving the words themselves—nouns without past or future—to carry the sense. Similarly, in Part IV the continuing "Thoughts" are interrupted by short, exultant, paired poems: "Blisse," "Ye hidden Nectars," "Desire," "Goodness." The second of these could appropriately be called "Joy" or "Ecstasy," for much of the poem is an apostrophe to the "Pleasant Thoughts" of the preceding poem. The speaker characterizes his "Thoughts" as "Images of Joy," and, again, as "Living Pictures [of] all Joys."

As in "Blisse" and "Desire," so in "Ye hidden Nectars" the diction and syntax suggest the immediate presence of paradisaical wonders, and all four interruptive lyrics are exceedingly rich in sensuous detail, particularly the garden imagery suggested as early as "Eden." In these closing poems Traherne draws upon the iconographic and literary associations of *hortus conclusus* and the New Jerusalem. At last the soul's "Ey" apprehends the golden city of the Apocalypse ("Thoughts. III"), and this glimpse poetically joins the end of the sequence to the beginning. From its earliest salute to the body ("The Salutation") the soul has passed to a serene and timeless love ("Goodnesse") and is no longer able to distinguish the self from others. Other men's bliss is the same as one's own, and in the same way and simultaneously all other apparent contrariety has been transcended. Again, Peter Sterry:

This is that *new Jerusalem*, where the street, the lowest form of things, is as Gold and Glass. The pure Glory of the eternal Spirit, as the finest Gold, shineth in each Creature, like the Cherubim, or the Angels standing up out of the Mercy-Seat, made of the *same piece* of massy Gold together with it. The lowest Creature here is an Angel of Glory, the street that sustains us is as *composed* of Angels, Angelical Glories. In every Angel as a particular Glory, all the Angels with their several Varieties of Glory; the Glory of Christ, and all the Saints, which is the full, the Universal Glories of the Divine and Humane Nature, the Original, and its best beloved Image in Union. The Glory of God, as the Father, in its simplicity, in its paternity and transcendency over all; *meet all in one*. This Unity of the Spirit in each Creature renders it *divinely transparent*, like the finest glass. In the beauty of every Face, we have the *prospect* of Eternity . . . with an endless Variety opening themselves one *within* another, *one beyond* another, all equally clear, present, and pleasant in every one. [P. 132]

Like Sterry, Traherne represents this fourth and final stage with language suggesting physical expansion as well as contraction; the soul's "Thoughts," though "pent within [the] Brest, / Yet rove at large from East to West" ("Thoughts. I," pp. 61-64). His theme now is the total disintegration of common-sense categories of time and space:

> The Ey's confind, the Body's pent
> In narrow Room: Lims are of small Extent.
> But Thoughts are always free.
> And as they're best,
> So can they even in the Brest,
> Rove ore the World with Libertie:
> Can Enter Ages, Present be
> In any Kingdom, into Bosoms see.
> Thoughts, Thoughts can come to Things, and view,
> What Bodies cant approach unto.
> They know no Bar, Denial, Limit, Wall:
> But have a Liberty to look on all.
>
> [Stanza 6]

199

The condition of this freedom is the emotional substance elaborated in "Blisse," in effect a parenthetical interruption of "Thoughts. I." The speaker understands now in the "experimental" manner that to be like Adam is "To do as Adam did" ("Blisse"); and, further, to do this is exactly what David "did intend" when he constructed a "Temple" of the mind. Accordingly, this vision or state of mind is the reification of all imagined and real parts of time and space. "This Sight . . . doth comprehend / Eternity, and Time, and Space" ("Thoughts. II"). In the second interruptive poem the focus is on this visual perspective; as the speaker searches for the exact locution ("Ye rich Ideas . . . Ye Living Pictures . . . Ye Spirits that do bring . . ."), a flood of pure emotion bursts forth:

> O what Incredible Delights, What Fires,
> What Appetites, what Joys do ye
>   Occasion, what Desires,
> What Heavenly Praises! While we see
> What evry Seraphim above admires!
>   Your Jubilee and Trade
> Ye are so Strangely, and Divinely made,
>   Shall never, never fade.
> Ye ravish all my Soul, Of you I twice
> Will speak. For in the Dark y'are Paradice.
>   ["Ye hidden Nectars," pp. 66-67]

"Thoughts are the Angels which we send abroad" in the way that God sent the soul to the body ("How like an Angel"). The theme of free spatial movement explains much about the rhetorical strategy of the "Thoughts" section. On the one hand, we find the language of fire and heat as well as of conjugal love, figures implying a fusion of objects: "This Soaring Sacred Thirst / . . . The Living Flowing Inward Melting, Bright" ("Desire"). On the other, in "Thoughts. III" (pp. 67-69) we notice the imagery of spatial expansion:

> They [Thoughts] bear the Image of their father's face,
> And Beautifie even all his Dwelling Place:
> So Nimble and Volatile, unconfind,
> Illimited, to which no Form's assignd,
> So Changeable, Capacious, Easy, free,

That what it self doth pleas a Thought may be.
From Nothing to Infinitie it turns,
Even in a Moment: Now like fire it burns,
Now's frozen Ice: Now shapes the Glorious Sun,
Now Darkness in a Moment doth become,
Now all at once: Now crowded in a sand,
Now fils the Hemisphere, and sees a Land.

[Lines 31-42]

As in *Centuries of Meditations*, Traherne uses paradox to destroy the concepts or categories he has generated. As I have already suggested, the rhetorical aim of this strategy is to reconcile the irreconcilable: to reconcile the idea of infinity with the figure of the sphere:

The Best of Thoughts is yet a thing unknown,
But when tis Perfect it is like his Own:
Intelligible, Endless, yet a Sphere
Substantial too: In which all Things appear.
All Worlds, all Excellences, Sences, Graces,
Joys, Pleasures, Creatures, and the Angels Faces.
It shall be Married ever unto all:
And all Embrace, tho now it seemeth Small.
A Thought my Soul may Omnipresent be.
For all it toucheth which a Thought can see.
O that Mysterious Being!

[Lines 67-77]

The style of the "Thoughts" section is subtly different from that of the earlier three. It is marked by a hesitancy or discontinuity, such as we find, say, both before and after "Blisse." "Thoughts. I" ends almost where "Thoughts. II" begins, with "Blisse" spliced in, like a frame or two in a cinema sequence. Yet the tangential quality of "Blisse" functions as a fragmentary hint at the underlying mental process at play in the larger poetic scheme. Similarly, even the tenuous demarcation between "Thoughts. II" and the following poem suggested by the absent title implies a sense of attenuated order, a sense heightened by the form as well as the substance of "Thoughts. II." In the same way "Thoughts. III" seems to revert back to the material interrupted by the end of "Thoughts. II." Yet the two poems are very different. The later poem is eruptive in quality; its iambic

pentameter couplets frequently seem to diverge completely
from each other:

> A Thought can Clothe it self with all the Treasures
> Of GOD, and be the Greatest of his Pleasures.
> It all his Laws, and Glorious Works, and Ways,
> And Attributs, and Counsels; all his Praise
> It can conceiv, and Imitate, and give:
> It is the only Being that doth live.
> Tis Capable of all Perfection here,
> Of all his Love and Joy and Glory there.
> It is the only Beauty that doth Shine,
> Most Great, Transcendent, Heavnly and Divine.
> The very Best or Worst of Things it is,
> The Basis of all Misery or Bliss.
> Its Measures and Capacities are such,
> Their utmost Measure we can never touch.
>
> [Lines 49-62]

The proverbial or axiomatic quality of the couplets heightens
the eruptive sense of the poem. The couplets function in much
the same way as parallel nouns and verbless phrases do so often
in Traherne—to convey a sense of discontinuity and excitement,
but more important, to insinuate a meaning not amenable to
language. Hence, the transparent aspect of "Transparent
words."

The fourth and last "Thoughts" poem is the speaker's poetic
answer to the psalmist, whose words provide the epigraph (and
Thomas's title) to the poem (pp. 72-74): "In thy Presence there
is fulness of Joy, and at thy right hand there are Pleasures for
ever more." In the living mind the imitator of David fashions a
temple without walls; the poet's method is to arrange a collocation of images (in an almost kaleidoscopic manner) intended to
elucidate the soul's unitive stage. Traherne stresses a fusing of
already established figures; "Thoughts" are represented as
"Messengers" soaring through the universe. They are "Privileged Posts that Soar" to the throne of God:

> Thoughts are the Wings on which the Soul doth flie,
> The Messengers which soar abov the Skie,
> Elijahs firey Charet, that conveys
> The Soul, even here, to those Eternal Joys.

Thoughts are the privileged Posts that Soar
Unto his Throne, and there appear before
Our selvs approach. These may at any time
Abov the Clouds, abov the Stars may clime.
The Soul is present by a Thought; and sees
The New Jerusalem. . . .

Spatial transport combines with Traherne's theme of communication, and the allusion to Elijah's (and later to Elisha's)
transfiguration suggests communication between the farthest
worlds, the worlds of spirit and of flesh. The speaker reasserts
the expansive spirit of the work, depicting the myriad "Hosts of
Angels" who join with him in communion. Surrounding God's
throne are "All Ages," "all Kingdoms," "all Creatures," "All . . .
Benefits"; "all Worlds" exist, and they exist within a sphere. Infinity reveals its spheral form: "His Omnipresence is an Endless
Sphere, / Wherin all Worlds as his Delights appear" (lines 29-
30). Figures of flight and distance stress the theme of miracu-
lous translation from one world to another. The speaker *is*
Elijah and Elisha in his freedom of spatial movement.

Nevertheless, with all its emphasis on outward movement, the
poem insists upon the spheral form of eternity, which is enclosed like the earth:

As Mountains, Charets, Horsemen all on fire,
To guard Elisha did of old conspire,
Which yet his Servant could not see, being blind,
Ourselvs environd with his Joys we find.
Eternity it self is that true Light,
That doth enclose us being infinite.
The very Seas do overflow and Swim
With Precious Nectars as they flow from him.
The Stable Earth which we beneath behold,
Is far more precious then if made of Gold.
Fowls Fishes Beasts, Trees Herbs and precious flowers,
Seeds Spices Gums and Aromatick Bowers,
Wherwith we are enclos'd and servd, each day
By his Appointment do their Tributes pay. . . .
                                    [Lines 37-51]

Whereas on earth the appreciative eye beholds and enjoys all
that it beholds, now all the parts of the universe itself delight

"the [soul's] Ey with their Magnificence." In a marvelously
symmetrical fashion, the speaker's "Thoughts" fly out in the
same way that the "Living Waters" of God's "Lov" emanate
from his throne. The reader is reminded by the imagery of
"Aromatick Bowers" that the speaker's vision has its sacramental application, adumbrated by the figure of the chalice:
"We drink our fill, and take their Beauty in, / While Jesus
Blood refines the Soul from Sin" (lines 74-75). In this ineffable
communion of souls, the speaker's quickened "Sight" merges
with "Love," and the two become the same. The object of man's
affections ("His Grievous Cross") suffices to empower man's
fashioning of a temple, "a Living one within the Mind." The
poem ends on a note of finality, with prayerful petition and
resolve:

> O give me Grace to see thy face, and be
> A constant Mirror of Eternitie.
> Let my pure Soul, transformed to a Thought,
> Attend upon thy Throne, and as it ought
> Spend all its Time in feeding on thy Lov,
> And never from thy Sacred presence mov.
> So shall my Conversation ever be
> In Heaven, and I O Lord my GOD with Thee!
>
> [Lines 95-102]

The various figures of conveyance have prepared the reader for
this direct statement of intimate address. The soul, "transformed
to a Thought," is actually present at the throne of God.
Throughout the poem the speaker has tried finally to define his
"Thoughts," and he has done so by generating numerous references to flight and transport, especially that involving communication. The shift at the end of the poem implies that he has
reached the desired goal of travel, and that he now enjoys the
consequent physical presence and rewarding "Conversation" of
God. I think we must read the final poem of the sequence as if
spoken by the speaker from this newly-attained physical and
spiritual perspective.

As Margoliouth suggests (II, 396), the proper gloss on the
concluding poem, "Goodnesse" (pp. 75-77), is the eleventh
chapter of *Christian Ethicks*, "Of Goodness Natural, Moral and

Divine." This chapter is part of a sequence of chapters dedicated to the manifestations of the three divine virtues, goodness, righteousness, and holiness, which Traherne treats instead of their "Heathenish *Heroical*" counterparts. These virtues possess the power to change men into the "same Image" as their "Object and End, namely, God" (pp. 25-26). This is an important point, carefully elaborated later on, and one bearing on the abruptness of the opening line of "Goodnesse": "The Bliss of other Men is my Delight." According to Traherne, goodness is "an infinite and Eternal Act . . . An Act whose Essence is seated in the Preparation of all Delights and the Communication of all its Glories" (pp. 147-148). "Communication" is the operative word here, for in "Goodness" one deals with a paradox: "It is *Invisible* in its Essence, but *Apparent* in its effects." Goodness must be seen—"Communicated"—in order to *be*, for it is both essence *and* act, invisible *and* apparent: "Its Felicity is Eternal and Infinite, yet seated intirely in the Felicity of others."

Partly, this idea plays on Traherne's theme of disintegration, as the boundaries of self and other, of subject and object, become more and more attenuated. Now the speaker is in love with himself *in* others; he is the anti-Narcissus, whose love is like the self-immolating love of Christ. At last, in the Wedding Supper of Apocalypse, the speaker sees in the faces of other men the radiance of his own "Felicity"; he sees the face of divinity. "Goodnesse" is an attempt at a final unthreading of the Gordian knot of creation: "THIS *Divine* Goodness is . . . the efficient Cause of the Worlds Creation." In stanza 2 of the poem Traherne reminds the reader of how the paradox of "Goodness" works. It seems as if the more faces there are that shine, the greater the evidence that the universe exists only for the speaker. In each discrete object, the goodness of divinity "is multiplied and magnified . . . as the same Object is in several Mirrors" (p. 151). Traherne has come again to his idea of God's self-love. By attending to the goodness in others, man recognizes a universal law: "For we all desire to be seen, and Known, and Beloved, and for that Cause, without Living Agents, should be very Desolate and discontented" (p. 155). This fact explains why God created more than one man, and more than a single species. "Eternity and Immensity" would otherwise have been emptied of certain treasures. Along this line, the same figures appear in both "Goodnesse" and *Christian Ethicks*: "The Stars are no hindrance to our Enjoyment of the Skie, but the Light and Beauty of the place which we contemplate. Were they all annihilated, the Heavens would be obscure" (p. 154). Likewise, as we read in stanzas 3 and 4, the multiplicity of human eyes is emblematic of the infinity of the human soul, which fills all time and space with itself, just as does the Almighty. One soul communicates itself to itself:

It is our Interests, that the Eys should be innumerable, that see and admire the Glory which we had with the Father in some Sense before the World was; that they should see (I mean) how much we are Beloved of GOD from all Eternity; that there should be Millions of Blessed Persons to whom we may communicate our selves, concerns our Glory, as it doth also that, that they should be Great and Perfect, that are made to Admire and Delight in us.

[P. 157]

This equation of delight in the other and delight in self is, in part, an expression of the truth of Scripture: "*Inasmuch as thou hast done all this to the least of these my Brethren, thou hast done it to me.*" But above all, it is a form of self-love: in loving the reflection, one loves the self (p. 153).

The two last stanzas of "Goodnesse" emphasize figures of ripeness, of satiety and liveliness. Grapes swell, the sun warms, the stars salute, wine flows, and lips are soft. All earth is filled with the warmth and smell of love. The pungent eroticism of these closing lines suggests a final apotheosis; harvest figures signal a temporal end but also, in their abundance, an opulence of emotional response in this new and satisfying world. Like *Meditations on the Six Days of the Creation*, the sequence ends with verses inviting visions of Apocalypse:

> The Soft and Swelling Grapes that on their Vines
>   Receiv the Lively Warmth that Shines
>   Upon them, ripen there for me:
>   Or Drink they be
> Or Meat. The Stars salute my pleased Sence
> With a Derivd and borrowed Influence
>   But better Vines do Grow
>   Far Better Wines do flow

206

Above, and while
The Sun doth Smile
Upon the Lillies there, and all things warme
Their pleasant Odors do my Spirit charm.

Their rich Affections do like precious Seas
   Of Nectar and Ambrosia pleas.
    Their Eys are Stars, or more Divine:
     And Brighter Shine
Their Lips are soft and Swelling Grapes, their Tongues
A Quire of Blessed and Harmonious Songs.
    Their Bosoms fraught with Love
   Are Heavens all Heavens above
And being Images of GOD, they are
The Highest Joys his Goodness did prepare.

In the beginning the speaker (as the emerging consciousness of
the child) heralded his salute to the body. Now the cosmos
salutes the united spirit whose expansive view and voice remind
the reader of St. John at Patmos. Present to the speaker's view
is a new "Heaven and Earth," extending and multiplying beyond the skies (stanza 4). The poem is not so much concerned
with mystical transport as with the speaker's expanded voice:
"A Quire of Blessed and Harmonious Songs." In "The Salutation" the speaker asked: "Where was? in what Abyss, my
Speaking Tongue?" Now the answer plummets from the timeless sphere of the "Divine Orb," which the "Infant-Ey" has
expanded to fill. Enclosing all time and space, the "Endless
sphere" encompasses also the singing tongues of Cherubim and
Seraphim.

CONCLUDING
REMARKS

VIII

O sages,
standing in God's holy fire
As in the gold mosaic
of a wall,
Come from the holy fire,
perne in a gyre,
And be the singing-masters
of my soul.
Consume my heart away;
sick with desire
And fastened
to a dying animal
It knows not what it is;
and gather me
Into the artifice of eternity.
—"Sailing to Byzantium"

No empty Space;
it is all full of Sight,
All Soul and Life,
an Ey most bright,
All Light and Lov;
Which doth at once
all things possess and giv,
Heven and Earth,
with All that therin liv;
It rests at quiet,
and doth mov;
Eternal is,
yet Time includes;
A Scene abov,
All Interludes.
—"Felicity"

In his own time those who remembered or had heard of Thomas Traherne thought of him first as a scholar, and after that as a seriously devout man. When Anthony à Wood accorded him his place among the luminaries of Oxford, he made no mention of Traherne's talent as a prose writer, let alone as a poet. If Wood's account no longer satisfies the interested reader, it is, nonetheless, one that must be kept in mind in any attempt to evaluate Traherne's achievement. Too many imaginary portraits describe Traherne as a rather quaint but harmlessly devout and simple man who enjoyed a modest success with the unadorned style. Intellectual historians think of him as a naïve mystic whose writings celebrate the wonders of the new science. It may be that the audience of a scholarly work is small, and I venture to say that *Roman Forgeries* will not likely find a secure place in seventeenth-century anthologies, much less in collections of "Masterworks of Western Civilization." But as a scholarly work *Roman Forgeries* must be judged in comparison with other works like it. We must remember that Traherne chose to make his public debut with this work, and that *Roman Forgeries* captured sufficient attention in its own time to assure its author of a place among the distinguished graduates of Oxford. Though the work may never gain a wide audience, it does deserve attention for what it tells us about the methods of a young scholar at mid-century. And it tells us much about the emotional furor generated on the campus by the "Catholic question." The rhetorical weaknesses of the work are evident. Traherne himself appears to have wearied of his theme, as his trimming of the later sections suggests. The chapters grow thin as the book progresses, and the reader is hurried to the next rehearsal of the same paradox. But with all of its flaws *Roman Forgeries* has its moments of intensity and flourish too.

With the new Marks and Guffey edition, *Christian Ethicks* seems likely to achieve due recognition. Unlike *Roman Forgeries*, the *Ethicks* has been an unjustly forgotten work. It deserves close study by critics and historians of ideas, not only as a document of the neo-Platonic revival but also for its literary merit. Certainly students of Traherne cannot afford to be ignorant of the rhetorical stance employed in this work; and the strategy of the *Ethicks* must be seen as part of the epistemological issues which are its main concern. Cast as a handbook of devotional and reflective pieces, *Christian Ethicks* depicts a speaker who has ventured beyond the sublunary interests of moral conduct. We have seen how Traherne's strategy differs from that of Pierre Charron, but also that method is intended to resolve the doubts unattended in the systems of Charron and Descartes. Other neo-Platonists dealt with the subjects of ethics and virtue; for example, we think of Henry More's *An Account of Virtue*. But comparison between these two works shows the effectiveness of Traherne's approach; in *Christian Ethicks* the point of view and the major thematic developments function to intensify a metaphoric conception of the subject matter, ethics. The "I" has been freed from the restrictions of the moral sphere; free will and "Felicity" coincide by way of structural and imagistic similarities. The will and the speaker's spirit expand, like the sentences and the chapters (and the book itself)—beyond the norms of ethical discourse, even beyond the limits set by the speaker at the inception of the work.

The drift of Traherne's technique is toward an "open" form, representing a process of association, like reverie. As we see in many of his other works, inconsistency is not only a structural feature but a distinguishing mark of the speaker's temperament. Entries in the Commonplace Book are long or short, depending on the values of the antiquarian compositor, but also on so simple a matter as the allocation of space left on the partially filled page. Perspectives, persons, passages are added, and spaces of the book remain to be filled. Similarly, in *Centuries of Meditations*, clearly Traherne's major prose work, the speaker breaks off with a veritable eternity of blank pages to spare. He is able to add another meditation, another decade of meditations, or (as "Select Meditations" seems to suggest) another "century" in the language of another person. Authorship as well as syntax is a matter of the utmost flexibility; in Traherne's mature prose style "openness" is the defining characteristic of the speaker's point of view. The dominant voice is that of an anti-character, an egoless being whose soul expands by a process of perfect narcissism, one who, like the loose syntax of the work itself, bears no limits of space or time. Hence, the author tries to erode the expected distinction between author and audience, just as he tries to destroy the integrity of beginning, middle, and end. I think he is most effective at this technique in the *Centuries* and in *Meditations on the Six Days of the Creation*. In both these works, by fictionalizing time Traherne is able to destroy the overarching figures of the week and the century. The same erosion operates in the discrete meditations, too: Traherne adds, adds even what has already been said, and quotes; in the process he disintegrates the landscape, the settings of place and time, attenuating the means by which readers ordinarily orient themselves to follow action and character development.

As a prose writer, Traherne must rank high had he written no other work than *Centuries of Meditations*. I have tried to show that other prose works—certainly "Select Meditations" and *Meditations on the Six Days*—also possess merit. As the shape of this book indicates, I have tried also to suggest that critics have tended quite wrongly to slight Traherne's poetry. It seems to me that many of the harsh critical judgments stem from confusions about what Traherne is doing, confusions often deepened by Philip's contamination of the texts. For even more important than Philip's emendations (some of these can

be corrected) are the effects of his collation of "Divine Reflections" with the poems in the Dobell manuscript. If we disen-
tangle the web spun by the poet's brother, we end up with two
sequences, parallel in structure, and similar in many ways to
the *Centuries* in their use of imagery and syntax. Perhaps another manuscript containing a second volume of "Divine Reflections" may yet come to light. But even now the complex
artistry can be seen: we have two intensely concentrated poetic
developments, beginning with chaos and ending with an apocalyptic vision of the New Jerusalem. This was a theme dominant also in the *Centuries*:

Eternity retains the Moments of their Beginning and Ending within
it self: and from Everlasting to Everlasting those Things were in
their Times and Places before God, and in all their Circumstances
Eternaly will be, serving him in those Moments . . . the Creation
and the Day of Judgement. . . . [V. 8]

The two poetic sequences are intense and rich in their treatment
of such themes, as fine as any poetry of its kind written in the
period. The problem is that critics have too frequently limited
good poetry to that which is precise in its imagery. Clearly this
is not a meaningful critical principle but fashionable dogma—
dogma, one might add, which would condemn, along with much
of Traherne, many of the best passages from Yeats and Eliot as
well. It is not difficult to imagine a universe of value in which a
poetry of abstractions has found its place in the affections of
discriminating readers. Such an audience would recognize the
intensity of stanzas like this:

> O Nectar! O Delicious Stream!
> O ravishing and only Pleasure! Where
>   Shall such another Theme
> Inspire my Tongue with Joys, or pleas mine Ear!
>   Abridgement of Delights!
>   And Queen of Sights!
> O Mine of Rarities! O Kingdom Wide!
> O more! O Caus of all! O Glorious Bride!
>   O God! O Bride of God! O King!
>   O Soul and Crown of evry Thing!

> ["Love"]

And this intensity, effective in itself, would be recognized as part of the complex development of the poetic sequence. For in Traherne the patterns of ebb and flow, rise and fall, expatiation and summing up work by a process of accretion. Objects and categories are annihilated only by this process of expansion, qualification, restatement, and further qualification.

On the other hand, Traherne hardly excludes particulars, but rather makes use of them with considerable effect—as, for example, in the landscape description in "Wonder." The careful reader will look for the way abstractions as well as concrete figures are used to forward Traherne's attempts at radical destruction of limits and boundaries. Hence, the treatment of spherical imagery in Traherne is paradoxical: the "Orb" of the soul both is and is not a sphere ("My Spirit"). This quite typical method of undermining the categories and figures set out earlier may be seen in his use, also, of the dominant figure in the poems: the "Infant-Ey." Accordingly, Traherne sees paradox as the natural answer to the false dilemma posed by appearance and reality, a split caused by an unnecessary breach between the child's and the adult's conceptions of the world. Child's vision merges with its opposite in the apocalyptic epiphany of "Goodnesse"; the text from Matthew is not Traherne's defense of infantilism, but a poetic invitation into the "Kingdom." We live in a period in which "Custom" decrees a fashionable recognition of a split between generations. Admired thinkers have gone so far as to insist that such a split is rooted in man's nature, that it is "necessary."[1] Traherne was most impatient with the determinism of his time; and he believed that if a view had become customary, then it must be wrongheaded. For "Custom" imposes limits: reason versus intuition, freedom versus responsibility, knowledge versus feeling. But Traherne's theme is not invidious; he would not likely join in the fatuous worship of pubescence one may observe in certain writers. He does not take sides; he tries to destroy them by including the adult truth with the sweetness of the child's mistake in a wider, more complete view. Truer than either partial conception is that amalgam of the adult's intellect and practicality with the child's spontaneity and openness.

To the child seemingly useless or unimportant objects are

worthy of his complete attention. He becomes absorbed, trans-
fixed, gazing on a tiny object of no apparent "value"—so completely rapt, in fact, that the entire universe may seem to
collapse into this single appreciative act. Such a spirit and power
of concentration need not exist mutually exclusive of the principles of reason and common sense. Traherne's theme of re-
concilation is not the naïve product of mindless enthusiasm. Nor
is it necessarily a product of "mysticism." To be sure, Traherne
occasionally echoes the language of mysticism, but it seems to
me quite wrong to think that he intended to limit "Felicity" to
a particular kind of feeling (nor would he likely consider excluding psychological ecstasy either). It seems to me, rather,
that he draws attention to an important fact of nature, long
before Freud or Jung or Marcuse brought such views to the
popular audience of Sunday supplements and women's maga-
zines: civilization seems to extinguish something of value in the
child's freedom and love of life in the very process of educating
him. Traherne is on the side of those who insist that such an
extinction is not inevitable. Appreciation as a condition of life—
as an attitude inextricably entwined with the child's very sense
perceptions—is not irretrievably lost through the development
of experience and judgment. Intellect and feeling are only
apparent opposites; it can do no harm to recognize, with Keats,
the intense satisfaction experienced by the mathematician who
has solved a difficult problem, or of the man of science at the
moment when through his experiment or insightful formula one
of nature's puzzles suddenly unravels:

> Then felt I like some watcher of the skies
>   When a new planet swims into his ken;
> Or like stout Cortez when with eagle eyes
>   He star'd at the Pacific—and all his men
> Look'd at each other with a wild surmise—
>   Silent, upon a peak in Darien.
>   ["On First Looking into Chapman's Homer"]

Traherne aims at the same sense of wonder, of splendor captured through an intense capacity to appreciate the objects of
nature. Intellect and feeling are temporally identical in the experience—the overwhelming experience—of love and wonder.

Traherne's poetry attempts to capture and to celebrate the world as perceived directly, in a way unsullied by the anesthetizing qualities of convention, guilt, or sophistication. Both sequences depict an open response to the objects of creation as an Eden from which man falls; man is not born in sin, he stumbles into it without knowing how or why, by teaching himself to intellectualize about the world independently from enjoying it. The result is a block to pure and intense apprehension of the objects of nature and, what is more important, to the spontaneous appreciation of other men. Man's ultimate alienation from the world is felt most tragically in the loss of the sense of his identity with others. From such a death in life man can and must be resurrected: the poetic sequences culminate in visionary glimpses of the kingdom in which man's reconciliation to the world is complete. The soul is transfigured by a process of divine narcissism into a being able to love himself—his humanity —in others; the speaker is able to see in the glow of other men's faces the reflection of his own and God's love. And such a lover's glance is appropriately accompanied by an expanded poetic voice, "A Quire of Blessed and Harmonious Songs":

> And Holy, Holy, Holy, is his Name.
> He is the Means both of Himself and all,
> Whom we the Fountain Means and End do call.
>   ["The Anticipation"]

In this paraphrase of Revelation 4:8 Traherne restates his theme of anticipation, a theme directly related to the apocalyptic note on which the poems end. It is a theme running through most of his best work, but one which he never handles with greater intensity or craft than in the Burney and Dobell poems. Even in a period as incredibly rich in minor poetry as the seventeenth century, these poems deserve an honored place.

NOTES

Unless otherwise noted, all books published before 1700 bear a London imprint. Throughout the text and notes, in quotations from manuscripts and early printed books, I have regularized the use of *i* and *j* and *u* and *v* and have expanded contractions. Where an entire poem originally appeared in italics, I have eliminated the italics completely.

CHAPTER I: INTRODUCTION

[1]The standard critical biography is Gladys I. Wade's *Thomas Traherne* (Princeton, 1944), Pts. I & II, but most of what is actually known about Traherne's life appears in the summary biography in Thomas Traherne, *Centuries, Poems, and Thanksgivings*, ed. H. M. Margoliouth, 2 vols. (Oxford, 1958), I, xxxvii; see Margoliouth's "Traherne's Ordination and Birth-Date," *Notes and Queries*, n.s. I (1954), 408.

[2]"Correspondence," *TLS*, Sept. 29, 1927, p. 667.

[3]Arthur W. Hopkinson, "Correspondence," *TLS*, Oct. 6, 1927, p. 694.

[4]*Athenae Oxonienses* (1691-92), II, 388.

[5]John Aubrey, *Miscellanies* (1696), p. 77.

[6]See Wade, *Thomas Traherne*, pp. 5-10, and Bertram Dobell's "An Unknown Seventeenth Century Poet," *Athenaeum*, VII (1900), 433-435, 466.

[7]*A Serious and Pathetical Contemplation of the Mercies of God, in Several Most Devout and Sublime Thanksgivings for the Same* (1699), "To the Reader," sig. A4ᵛ.

[8]Wade, *Thomas Traherne*, p. 15.

[9]Ibid., p. 27.

[10]Ibid., p. 3; see also p. 105.

[11]Alfred Watkins, "Thomas Traherne," *TLS*, Oct. 20, 1927, p. 743. Traherne contributed to the Brasenose College Fund in 1664; see J. A. W. Bennett, "Traherne and Brasenose," *N&Q*, CLXXIX (1945), 84. Brasenose was designed for commoners, and almost every student received a stipend. Noblemen needed special allowance for admission; see John Buchan, *Brasenose College* (London, 1898), pp. 16-19.

[12]Miss Wade turned up a copy of the record of Traherne's admission to Oxford (p. 15), which corroborates Wood's account in *Athenae Oxonienses* and provides the main clue to the poet's birth date ("between March 1, 1637 and February 28, 1639").

[13]My remarks on Oxford and Cambridge universities draw upon several fine historical studies: Charles Edward Mallet, *A History of the University of Oxford*, 3 vols. (London, 1924-27); Mark H. Curtis, *Oxford and Cambridge in Transition: 1558-1642* (Oxford, 1959); James Bass Mullinger, *The University of Cambridge from the Earliest Times*, 3 vols. (London, 1873-1911); William T. Costello, S.J., *The Scholastic Curriculum at Early Seventeenth-Century Cambridge* (Cambridge, Mass., 1958).

[14]Northern connections made Brasenose violently Royalist; in 1648 two thirds of the College signed in opposition to Parliament, and in 1673 a major riot erupted (Buchan, pp. 22-23); see also John Steegmann, *Cambridge* (New York, 1941), p. 30, and Mallet, II, 360. The town itself was intensely Royalist (Mallet, II, 364-365).

[15]For a thorough account of Pious V's Bull, *Regnans in excelsis*, see Arnold Oscar Meyer, *England and the Catholic Church under Queen Elizabeth*, tr. J. R. McKee (New York, 1967), pp. 76-82.

[16]Curtis, p. 189.

[17]See J. W. C. Wand, *Anglicanism in History and Today* (London, 1963), pp. 99, 138, 194, 218.

[18]Ibid., pp. 170, 195-196.

[19]Mallet, II, 82, 104-105, 418; Curtis, pp. 171-175, 188; for an absorbing account of the Fifth Monarchy Men, see P. G. Rogers, *The Fifth Monarchy Men* (London, 1966).

[20]*The Booke of the Common Prayer* (1549), sig. Xiiv.

[21]In the earlier decades of the century, university fellows were called to account for disputing Calvin's view of the will. Only a royal edict ended the furious debate; the Thirty-nine Articles left the matter unresolved. See Mallet, II, 237; Curtis, pp. 177, 188, 225.

[22]Oxford produced many of the great Jesuits (Robert Parsons, Edmund Campion), and Cambridge graduated numerous Puritan reformers; see Curtis, pp. 191, 193.

[23]Curtis, pp. 189-190, 195-197.

[24]See ch. 3.

[25]This point is clearly made by Costello, ch. 1.

[26]Curtis, pp. 88-89.

[27]Ibid., p. 90; see also Mallet, II, 323-328.

[28]Curtis, p. 232, and Costello, pp. 49-50.

[29]Curtis, p. 5.

[30]Costello, pp. 30, 35.

[31]René Descartes, *Discourse on Method*, tr. Laurence J. Lafleur (Indianapolis, 1956), pp. 10-11; this fine translation is readily available in the Library of Liberal Arts series, but cf. *The Philosophical Works of Descartes*, tr. Elizabeth S. Haldane and G. R. T. Ross (London, 1934), I, 90.

[32]*Discourse on Method*, p. 11; cf. *Works*, I, 91.

[33]*Complete Poems and Major Prose*, ed. Merritt Y. Hughes (New York, 1957), p. 632. For a thorough account of Milton's attitude toward the received curriculum, see *Complete Prose Works of John Milton* (New Haven, 1959), II, 374.

[34]*Art of Logic* (1672), ed. and tr. Allan H. Gilbert, in *The Works of John Milton* (New York, 1931), XI, 13—hereafter referred to as *Columbia Milton*. In this context of repression, student and faculty interest in Ramus took on a rhetorical function. Ramus was a great favorite of the Calvinists at Cambridge.

[35]*Columbia Milton*, XI, 13, 15.

[36]Ibid., p. 7.

[37]Charles Homer Haskins, *The Rise of Universities* (Ithaca, N.Y., 1957), p. 29.

[38]Curtis, pp. 86-88 et passim.

[39]Ibid., pp. 86-87, 102; Mallet, II, 244.

[40]For a thorough discussion of the scholastic structure of 17th-century curriculum at Cambridge, see Costello, pp. 7-35, esp. pp. 11-19.

[41]Curtis, p. 131.

[42]For an admirable discussion of Traherne's Platonism, see Carol L. Marks, "Thomas Traherne and Cambridge Platonism," *PMLA*, LXXXI (1966), 521-534.

[43]Marjorie Nicolson, *The Breaking of the Circle: Studies in the Effect of the "New Science" upon Seventeenth Century Poetry* (Evanston, 1950), pp. 173-179.

[44]Wade, p. 86.

[45]*Thanksgivings*, sig. A4.

[46]Ibid., sig. A4 and A4v.

[47]Ibid., sig. A3v.

[48]*Athenae Oxonienses*, II, 388.

CHAPTER II: THE RHETORIC OF *ROMAN FORGERIES*

[1]Wade, *Thomas Traherne*, pp. 63-68.

[2]Thomas Traherne, *Roman Forgeries* (1673), sig. B7v.

[3]See Mark Curtis, *Oxford and Cambridge in Transition: 1558-1642* (Oxford, 1959), pp. 6-16, 30-32.

[4]The following general remarks on the Council of Trent are drawn from *Encyclopaedia of Religion and Ethics*, ed. James Hastings (New York, 1925), and from *The Catholic Encyclopedia*, ed. Charles G. Herbermann et al. (New York, 1912).

[5]Curtis, p. 104.

[6]John Jewel, *A Defence of the Apologie of the Churche of Englande* (1567), sig. Aiiv-Aiii.

[7]Thomas Harding was Jewel's contemporary at Oxford, and a prebendary of Salisbury, when Jewel made his first visitation, at which time Harding refused to take the oath of supremacy and, after being removed from his position, fled to the Continent, where he immediately set to attacking Jewel (*DNB*).

[8]John Jewel, "A Sermon Preached . . . at Pauls Crosse," in *The Works of the Very Learned . . . John Jewel* (1609), I, 58.

[9]*Nouvelle Biographie Generale* (Paris, 1858).

[10]*Letters of Sir Thomas Bodley to Thomas James: First Keeper of the*

Bodleian Library, ed. G. W. Wheeler (Oxford, 1926), pp. 187-188, 191-193. Fifteen years later Dr. James was still trying to gain support for his endeavor; he made an appeal in 1625 at a convocation at Oxford for the establishment of a commission to examine patristic documents (*DNB*).

[11]Thomas James, *The Humble Supplication of Thomas James Student in Divinitie, and Keeper of the Publike Librarie at Oxford, for the Reformation of the Ancient Fathers Workes, by Papists Sundrie Wayes Depraved* [1614?].

[12]See n. 10 above.

[13]Thomas James, *A Treatise of the Corruption of Scripture, Councels, and Fathers, by the Prelats, Pastors, and Pillars of the Church of Rome, for Maintenance of Popery and Irreligion* (1611), sig. *2v.

[14]"Mr. Dr. Ward Mr. of Sydney-Sussex Colledge in Cambridge." This marginal note seems to refer to Samuel Ward, master of Sidney-Sussex College, who was involved in the translation of the Authorized Version, but whose work with Bishop Ussher on patristic writings seems never to have reached print (*DNB*).

CHAPTER III: *CHRISTIAN ETHICKS*: PHILOSOPHY AND FORM

[1]Mark H. Curtis, *Oxford and Cambridge in Transition: 1558-1642* (Oxford, 1959), pp. 111, 115.

[2]The following remarks on the Commonplace Book owe much to Carol Marks's admirable article, "Thomas Traherne's Commonplace Book," *Papers of the Bibliographical Society of America*, LVIII (1964), 458-465.

[3]Speculation began with Grosart, whose opinions along with Dobell's dissent appear on the flyleaf of the Dobell Folio; see also Wade, *Thomas Traherne*, pp. 250-255.

[4]As on Bodleian MS. Eng. poet. c. 42, fol. 87v.2, around "Seed."

[5]Traherne seems to subsume astronomy under the heading of astrology: "The Astronomie and Astrologie, which the Chaldeans (according to the common presumption) received from Abraham" (fol. 17.1).

[6]"Freedom" would have to fit into a rather small space on fol. 45v.1, unless (as with "Deitie") the entry were to continue after the immediately following brief entry, "Fruit," after which an entire page is available (fol. 47).

[7]Fol. 83. "Reasen" occupies both columns of fol. 82v, but a column on the recto of that leaf follows "Punishment."

[8]Fol. 26v.

[9]"Thomas Traherne's Commonplace Book," p. 462.

[10]Ibid., p. 464.

[11]Early Notebook, Bodleian MS. Lat. Misc. f. 45, pp. 7-21.

[12]All references to *Christian Ethicks* in this chapter have been changed from page numbers of the first edition to correspond with page numbers of Cornell Studies in English, XLIII: Thomas Traherne, *Christian Ethicks*, General Introd. and Commentary by Carol L. Marks, Textual Introd. by George Robert Guffey (Ithaca, 1968). Unfortunately, the present study was completed before publication of this fine edition, so I could not make use of the

NOTES TO PAGES 49-56

very complete commentary. Miss Marks graciously placed finished material, including her most helpful Introduction, at my disposal.

13Sig. a4 et passim. Coke stresses the atheistic implications of all three men, and in particular he is at pains to argue against any societal explanation of virtue and vice. See especially chapters entitled "Of Virtue," "Of Particular Moral Virtues," "Moral Virtues are commanded by God in the Holy Scripture," and "Of Justice," in "Elements of Power and Subjection," pp. 13-20, 121-132. Traherne may have known Henry More's discussion of the "Divine Life" as distinguished from the secular and rational "Middle Life," with its consideration of Obedience, Humility, Charity, Justice, Purity (Temperance and Fortitude), and Prudence. See Henry More, *An Explanation of the Grand Mystery of Godliness* (1660), pp. 52-56.

14John Donne, *The Anniversaries*, ed. Frank Manley (Baltimore, 1963), pp. 73-74.

15In the Early Notebook Traherne includes a lengthy extract from Bacon's *De Augmentis Scientiarum*, pp. 71 ff.

16[Richard Allestree], *The Whole Duty of Man* (1677), p. 417: "AS *thou art putting off thy clothes, think with thy self that the time approaches that thou must put off thy body also.*"

17*Of the Vanitie and Uncertaintie of Artes and Sciences*, tr. James Sanford, p. 1.

18Ibid., p. 4.

19The following remarks on the Pyrrhonian crisis owe much to Richard Popkin, *The History of Scepticism from Erasmus to Descartes* (Assen, Netherlands, 1964).

20*Outlines of Pyrrhonism*, in *Sextus Empiricus*, tr. R. G. Bury (London, 1961), I, 115 [I. 196-197].

21See the discussion of this sketch in ch. 1. Miss Wade's view is typical: "The poet was, it is plain, one of those rare and enviable individuals in whom no jarring element is present, who came into the world as into their rightful inheritance, and whose whole life is a song of thankfulness for the happiness which they enjoy in it" (Gladys I. Wade, ed., *The Poetical Works of Thomas Traherne* [London, 1932], p. lvi).

22Popkin, *Scepticism*, pp. 57-63, but esp. p. 63.

23Pierre Charron, *Of Wisdom: Three Bookes*, tr. Samson Lennard [1612], p. 123. *De la Sagesse* was first published in 1601, and the *STC* lists nine separate editions published in England by 1700.

24Charron (1612), sig. A4.

25Ibid., pp. 39-42.

26Ibid., pp. 47-62.

27Ibid., pp. 61-62.

28Ibid., p. 41.

29"Scepticisme," in the Commonplace Book, Bodleian MS. Eng. poet. c. 42, foll. 87-87v. I do not know Traherne's exact sources here, but he seems to quote and to intersperse his own remarks.

30Ibid., fol. 87ᵛ.1.

31Ibid., fol. 87.1.

32Ibid., fol. 87ᵛ.1.

33See my "Romeo and Necessity," in *Pacific Coast Studies in Shakespeare*, ed. Waldo F. McNeir and Thelma N. Greenfield (Eugene, Ore., 1966), pp. 47-67.

34Jean Calvin, *Institutes of the Christian Religion*, tr. John Allen (Philadelphia, 1936), I, 287 [I. 15].

35Robert Burton, *The Anatomy of Melancholy*, ed. Holbrook Jackson (London, 1961), I, 167.

36See, for example, K. W. Salter, *Thomas Traherne: Mystic and Poet* (New York, 1964), pp. 130-135. John Malcolm Wallace considers Traherne a Pelagian; see his review of Louis L. Martz, *The Paradise Within* (New Haven, 1964), in *Journal of English and Germanic Philology*, LXIV (1965), 732-738. Wallace may be right in recognizing Augustine and Pelagius as polar opposites; they are so in the issue of the will. But insofar as the term "Pelagian" implies that Traherne explicitly rejects the concept of original sin, or the efficacy of continuing acts of grace, it seems inaccurate. Like the humanism of the Renaissance generally, Traherne's work emphasizes free will. But this emphasis need not imply the proposition that continuing grace is not necessary to salvation. It seems to me that Traherne never actually confronts the logical issues raised by this most important of all controversies within the Christian Church. But if such terms apply to him at all, he seems closer to Arminius than to Pelagius. Like Arminius, Traherne is impatient with the neo-Augustinianism of Calvin; but we find evidence also of his belief in congenital sinfulness and in the efficacy of the sacrament, both in the *Ethicks* and in the First Century. See "Pelagianism and Semi-Pelagianism," in Hastings, *Encyclopaedia of Religion and Ethics*. J. B. Leishman seems to hint in this direction when he says that Traherne never actually confronts the problem of evil; see his *The Metaphysical Poets, Donne, Herbert, Vaughan, Traherne* (New York, 1963), pp. 188-224, but esp. pp. 194-198. In other matters—in his conception of time, for instance—Traherne may be legitimately described as an Augustinian.

37The idea is all but ubiquitous in Traherne, but see *Christian Ethicks*, pp. 25, 31-35, 78-79, 85, 90-93, 148-150; it is especially important in the Fourth Century (see ch. 5), and see also *Meditations on the Six Days of the Creation* (1717), introd. George Robert Guffey, Augustan Reprint Soc. Pub. no. 119 (Los Angeles, 1966), pp. 78, 83-84.

38*Leviathan* (1651), pp. 8-9.

39Richard Allestree, the generally acknowledged author of *The Whole Duty of Man* [1658], provides a perfect contrast to Traherne in his method of organization, which is oppressively logical. The paragraphs are numbered, and typical transitions throughout the work are: "There is a two fold enjoying of God"; "first, . . .; secondly"; "A second sort of submission to His will"; "The third part of TEMPERANCE," and so on (pp. 19, 35, 37, 203). This rigorous manner fits the aim of the work, which is to teach the "meanest Readers, *to behave themselves . . . in this world.*" Hence, the emphasis on "Particulars," "*the* Practice" of piety (sig. A3), which Traherne excludes from consideration.

[40]Northrop Frye, *A Study of English Romanticism* (New York, 1968), esp. ch. 1.

CHAPTER IV: TRAHERNE AND THE MEDITATIVE MODE

[1]Jackson I. Cope, *The Metaphoric Structure of Paradise Lost* (Baltimore, 1962), esp. ch. 3.

[2]Stanley Stewart, "Time and *The Temple*," *Studies in English Literature*, VI (1966), 97-110.

[3]See ch. 3 above.

[4]Michel de Montaigne, *The Essayes: Or Morall, Politike and Millitairie Discourses*, tr. John Florio (1603), p. 386. The present discussion owes much to Joan Webber's perceptive study, *The Eloquent "I": Style and Self in Seventeenth-Century Prose* (Madison, 1968), ch. 8; her remark about Montaigne appears on p. 5.

[5]Thomas Traherne, *Christian Ethicks* (1675), pp. 62-63.

[6]A good literary example of the practice is Sir Henry Hubert's "Golden Harpe," in which a textual reference follows virtually every line.

[7]Thomas Traherne, *Meditations on the Six Days of the Creation* (1717), introd. George Robert Guffey, Augustan Reprint Soc. Pub. no. 119 (Los Angeles, 1966), p. 1. Traherne's authorship of *Meditations on the Six Days of the Creation* has been questioned, in particular, by Helen White, in *The Metaphysical Poets: A Study in Religious Experience* (New York, 1936), pp. 323-324. Cogent arguments for Traherne's authorship have appeared in Catherine A. Owen, "The Authorship of the 'Meditations on the Six Days of the Creation' and the 'Meditations and Devotions on the Life of Christ'," *Modern Language Review*, LVI (1961), 1-12, and in Mr. Guffey's Introduction to the Augustan Reprint edition. I think *Meditations on the Six Days* is unquestionably the work of Traherne.

[8]*The Works of Joseph Hall* (1625), p. 810.

[9]*Annotations upon the Five Bookes of Moses, the Booke of the Psalmes, and the Song of Songs, or Canticles* (1627), I, 3-4.

[10]See Vincent Hopper, *Medieval Number Symbolism* (New York, 1938), pp. 23, 36.

[11]St. Bonaventure, *The Mind's Road to God*, tr. George Boas (New York, 1953), p. 9.

[12]See Stanley Stewart, *The Enclosed Garden: The Tradition and the Image in Seventeenth-Century Poetry* (Madison, 1966), p. 18.

[13]"The H. Scriptures, II," in *The Works of George Herbert*, ed. F. E. Hutchinson (Oxford, 1953), p. 58.

[14]*Order and Disorder: Or, The World Made and Undone. Being Meditations upon the Creation and the Fall; As It Is Recorded in the Beginning of Genesis* (1679), sig. *2.

[15]See Lily B. Campbell, *Divine Poetry and Drama in Sixteenth-Century England* (London, 1959), ch. 1; Stewart, *Enclosed Garden*, pp. 1-10.

[16]See Miss Webber's discussion in *The Eloquent "I,"* pp. 19-20.

[17]*The Annotated Book of Common Prayer*, ed. John Blunt (London, 1866), p. 26.

[18]Bodleian MS. Eng. th. e. 51, flyleaf.

[19]My remarks on the Church's Year-Book owe much to Carol L. Marks's admirable discussion, "Traherne's 'Church's Year-Book'," *Papers of the Bibliographical Society of America*, LX (1966), 31-72.

[20]Cited in H. Inigo Triggs, *Formal Gardens in England and Scotland* (London, 1902), II, 6. In the miscellanies and commonplace books the theme is all but ubiquitous: "Time flyes away fast; / Our houres doe waste . . ." (Thomas Grocer, "Dayly Observations Both Divine and Morall," Huntington MS. 93, p. 17, but see also pp. 5, 9, 28, 168).

[21]*Centuries, Poems, and Thanksgivings*, ed. H. M. Margoliouth (Oxford, 1958), II, 208; unless otherwise noted, further citations from Traherne in this chapter will be from this edition.

[22]Bodleian MS. Eng. th. e. 51, fol. 113.

[23]*Christian Ethicks*, p. 78.

[24]See the section entitled "The Technique of Repetition" in Louis L. Martz, *The Paradise Within: Studies in Vaughan, Traherne, and Milton* (New Haven, 1964), pp. 43-54, 23-27.

[25]For a provocative discussion of the idea of apocalypse and its importance to the development of literary forms, see Frank Kermode, *The Sense of an Ending: Studies in the Theory of Fiction* (New York, 1967).

[26]*A Serious and Pathetical Contemplation of the Mercies of God, in Several Most Devout and Sublime Thanksgivings for the Same, Published by the Reverend Doctor Hicks, At the Request of a Friend of the Authors* (1699), sig. A3.

[27]See Louis L. Martz, *The Poetry of Meditation* (New Haven, 1954), ch. 1.

[28]*A Rationale upon the Book of Common Prayer* (1655), pp. 9-10.

[29]Loredano, *The Ascents of the Soul: Or, David's Mount Towards God's House. Being Paraphrases on the Fifteen Psalms of Degrees*, tr. Henry Lord Coleraine (1681), sig. a1.

[30]Becon, foll. 76-76v.

[31]*La Scala Santa: Or, A Scale of Devotions Musical and Gradual Being Descants on the Fifteen Psalms of Degrees* (1681), frontispiece; this work is bound with *The Ascents of the Soul* (1681).

CHAPTER V: "A MYSTERIOUS ABSENCE OF TIMES": THE
CENTURIES

[1]*Centuries, Poems, and Thanksgivings*, ed. H. M. Margoliouth (Oxford, 1958), I. 2; all citations from the *Centuries* in my text are from this edition.

[2]Miss Wade writes, "In tracing this personal history, I am accepting as literal facts Traherne's own references and allusions in his *Centuries of Meditations* and in the two autobiographical cycles in his poems" (Gladys I. Wade, *Thomas Traherne* [Princeton, 1944], p. 27); this method is evident throughout the book, but see esp. pp. 43-44. For a comment on Miss Wade's method, see René Wellek and Austin Warren, *Theory of Literature* (New York, 1949), pp. 214-215.

[3]Wade, *Thomas Traherne*, p. 184.

[4]Richard Baxter, *Reliquiae Baxterianae: Or, Mr. Richard Baxter's Narrative . . . of His Life and Times* (1691), p. 1.

[5]*The Journal of George Fox*, ed. John L. Nickalls (Cambridge, 1952), p. 1; see also John Bunyan, *Grace Abounding to the Chief of Sinners*, ed. Roger Sharrock (Oxford, 1962), p. 5.

[6]*The Diary of John Evelyn*, ed. E. S. de Beer (London, 1959), p. 1.

[7]Jean Calvin, *Commentary on a Harmony of the Evangelists, Matthew, Mark, and Luke*, tr. and ed. William Pringle (Edinburgh, 1845), II, 129.

[8]Baxter, p. 12.

[9]*Roman Forgeries* (1673), sigs. B7v-B8.

[10]For an illuminating discussion of Traherne's use of the first person pronoun, see Joan Webber, *The Eloquent "I": Style and Self in Seventeenth-Century Prose* (Madison, 1968), ch. 8; an earlier version of this chapter, " 'I and Thou' in the Prose of Thomas Traherne," appeared in *Papers on Language and Literature*, II (1966), 258-264.

[11]*The Differences of the Ages of Mans Life* (1607), p. 115, sigs. B6, B1-B1v; see also John Swan, *Speculum Mundi* (Cambridge, 1635), p. 6.

[12]See Carol Marks's General Introduction and Commentary in *Christian Ethicks*, ed. Carol L. Marks and George Robert Guffey (Ithaca, 1968).

[13]*A Treatise of the Divine Essence and Attributes*, Part I (1628), p. 53.

[14]For a thorough discussion of this point, see G. J. Whitrow, *The Natural Philosophy of Time* (New York, 1963), pp. 1-5. See also Richard M. Gale, "The Static Versus the Dynamic Temporal," in *The Philosophy of Time: A Collection of Essays*, ed. Richard M. Gale (New York, 1967), pp. 65-85 and Section II generally.

[15]See ch. 4; Traherne's "mitigated skepticism" emphasizes the contingent value of the normal curriculum, and in this sense departs from the views of Agrippa and Montaigne. Knowledge in the form of certainty is the inner quality of experience which he calls "Felicity."

[16]Thomas Wilson, *Theologicall Rules* (1615), title page and sigs. A2v, A4.

[17]Ross's earlier work is in verse and treats of a variety of subjects; *A Centurie of Divine Meditations upon Predestination, and Its Adjuncts: Wherein Are Shewed the Comfortable Uses of This Doctrine* (1646) is a prose work, and the full title explains much about its substance; but appended to the century are two sequences of eight meditations each on God's justice and mercy.

[18]The usage has been noted by Ernst Robert Curtius, *European Literature and the Latin Middle Ages*, tr. Willard R. Trask (New York, 1953), p. 255n.

[19]The contrast between the rectilinear (animal) and cyclic (divine) movements of the soul is discussed in John Freccero's interesting essay, "Donne's 'Valediction Forbidding Mourning,' " *Journal of English Literary History*, XXX (1963), 335-376.

[20]In "Select Meditations" Traherne writes of "an Ey without walls; All unlimited & Endless Sight" (I.91); and in *Christian Ethicks* (1675) all of time

is present to the soul in the way that all the world is present "in the Eye" (p. 88). The soul's "Eye" seeks a view of space and time where "there be no walls to exclude, or Skreens to hide" (p. 91). This expansive potentiality in man is his conceptual as distinct from the animals' conceptual capacities: see p. 78.

21I am indebted to Mr. James M. Osborn of Yale University, who generously allowed me to consult and to quote from the newly-discovered manuscript of "Select Meditations." For an account of the discovery of "Select Meditations," see James M. Osborn, "A New Traherne Manuscript," *Times Literary Supplement*, Oct. 8, 1964, p. 928.

22I refer to the usage in Sigmund Freud, *Civilization and Its Discontents*, in *The Complete Psychological Works of Sigmund Freud*, tr. and ed. James Strachey with Anna Freud (London, 1964), XXI, 64-65.

23Bodleian MS. Eng. th. e. 51, fol. 51.

24*Christian Ethicks* (1675), p. 60; see also p. 88.

25See Oscar Cullman, *Christ and Time: The Primitive Christian Conception of Time and History*, tr. Floyd J. Filson (Philadelphia, 1964), esp. Pt. II, ch. 1.

26*The Divine Pymander*, tr. Dr. Everard (1649), p. 211.

27In this way, each individual is joined in the unified act of God's self-love; see *Christian Ethicks*, p. 151; see also note 28 below.

28The idea is almost ubiquitous, but see Marsilio Ficino, *Commentary on Plato's Symposium*, tr. Sears Reynold Jayne (Columbia, Mo., 1944), pp. 141, 144; Johann Gerhard, *Meditationes Sacrae* (1635), p. 48; William Gouge, *The Saints Sacrifice* (1632), pp. 9-11. Traherne writes: "O Let me so long Eye Thee, till I be turned into Thee" (I.87).

29*Christian Ethicks*, pp. 97-99, 199-200; Gerhard, pp. 48, 87; Ficino, p. 144.

30*Christian Ethicks*, p. 34.

31Vincent Foster Hopper, *Medieval Number Symbolism* (New York, 1938), pp. 42, 73, 90, 150, 165-168, 178, 194.

32Plotinus, *The Enneads*, tr. Stephen MacKenna (New York, 1962), III.vii.

33*The Comings Forth of Christ* (1650), sig. A4ᵛ.

34*Christian Ethicks*, passim, but esp. pp. 18-19.

35See Helen Gardner, "The Argument about 'The Ecstasy,'" in *Elizabethan and Jacobean Studies Presented to Frank Percy Wilson*, ed. Herbert Davis and Helen Gardner (Oxford, 1959), pp. 279-306. Peter Sterry uses very similar language to describe the unity of the soul's understanding, in which the soul "contemplates it self within it self": "The Will is the essential, the intellectual, and adequate Union of these two [Father and Son], with the most full communion and highest complacency, by which they propagate and multiply themselves within themselves" (*A Discourse of the Freedom of the Will* [1675], p. 67).

36John Donne, *The Elegies and the Songs and Sonnets of John Donne*, ed. Helen Gardner (Oxford, 1965), p. 60.

37George Kubler, *The Shape of Time: Remarks on the History of Things*

(New Haven, 1962), p. 55; Peter Sterry writes: "Time is defined to be the number of motion, in an orderly Priority and Posterity" (*Discourse*, p. 91).

³⁸In his insightful chapter, "Thomas Traherne, Confessions of Paradise," Louis L. Martz emphasizes Traherne's use of synonyms as part of his ruminative "Technique of Repetition" (*The Paradise Within: Studies in Vaughan, Traherne, and Milton* [New Haven, 1964], ch. 2, esp. pp. 43-54).

³⁹This paradoxical idea is one means of negating the tensed quality of existence or, as Traherne would think of it, the distinction between essence and act. The English verb is an emblem of human time.

⁴⁰"But he that created summer and winter, knoweth the congruity of times" (John Wall, *Jacobs Ladder* [Oxford, 1626], p. 46).

⁴¹Miss Wade's phrase is "straightforward simplicity" (*Thomas Traherne*, p. 208).

⁴²Margoliouth ed., I, 291.

⁴³From James Shirley, *The Contention of Ajax and Ulysses*, in *The Dramatic Works and Poems of James Shirley*, ed. William Gifford and Alexander Dyce (London, 1833), VI, 396-397.

⁴⁴Sir Thomas Browne, *Hydriotaphia: Urne-Buriall* in *The Works of Sir Thomas Browne*, ed. Geoffrey Keynes (Chicago, 1964), I, 169.

CHAPTER VI: "INFINITE CENTER": THE LYRIC VOICE

¹The consensus is summarized by Douglas Bush, *English Literary Criticism in the Earlier Seventeenth Century: 1600-1660* (New York, 1952), pp. 148-149, but the phrase belongs to John Malcolm Wallace.

²*Centuries*, III.60, 65, 66. All citations from the *Centuries of Meditations* in my text are from Thomas Traherne, *Centuries, Poems, and Thanksgivings*, ed. H. M. Margoliouth (Oxford, 1958).

³*Poems, Centuries and Three Thanksgivings*, ed. Anne Ridler (London, 1966), p. 163. All citations from Traherne's poetry in my text are from this edition, hereafter cited as Ridler.

⁴Ridler, p. 162*n*.

⁵Bodleian MS. Lat. Misc. 45, p. 199.

⁶Ovidius Naso, *Metamorphoses*, with tr. by Frank Justus Miller (London, 1916), I, 148-161; for a thorough discussion of this motif, see Frederick Goldin, *The Mirror of Narcissus in the Courtly Love Lyric* (Ithaca, 1967), esp. pp. 1-68.

⁷Ovidius Naso, *The Fable of Ovid Treting of Narcissus, Translated Out of Latin into Englysh Mytre, with a Moral Therunto, Very Pleasante to Rede* (1560), title page, sig. D4^v, respectively.

⁸Brendan O Hehir, *Expans'd Hieroglyphics: A Critical Edition of Sir John Denham's Coopers Hill* (Berkeley, 1969), pp. 150-151, 152.

⁹See, for example, Susanne Langer, *Philosophy in a New Key* (Cambridge, Mass., 1948), ch. 6.

¹⁰*The Poems of Saint John of the Cross*, tr. Willis Barnstone (Bloomington, Ind., 1968), p. 47; cf. *The Complete Works of Saint John of the Cross: Doctor of the Church*, tr. and ed. E. Allison Peers (Westminster, Md., 1949), II, 444.

[11]Louis L. Martz has, of course, provided an admirable discussion of this general meditative movement (memory, understanding, will) in his important study, *The Poetry of Meditation* (New Haven, 1954), esp. ch. 1.

[12]The Church's Year-Book, Bodleian MS. Eng. th. e. 51, fol. 51.

[13]Thomas Traherne, *Christian Ethicks* (1675), pp. 78, 87.

[14]British Museum MS. Burney 392, foll. 3-4.

[15]John Malcolm Wallace, "Thomas Traherne and the Structure of Meditation," *Journal of English Literary History*, XXV (1958), 78-89. See ch. 7 below.

[16]The issue of the missing MS has not yet been fully explored. If, as Margoliouth implies, Philip used the Dobell Folio in compiling the *Poems of Felicity*, it follows that this other MS would be the source of the Burney MS poems. But what of the poems *not* included from Dobell? If Philip did not have *D* or a facsimile of *D*, he must have had a MS with at least *D* minus the 15 poems left out of *F*, plus either a fair copy of the poems included only in *F* or one including *D*-15 + (*F*-[*D*-15]). In any case, we must posit some basis for the implied aim of a second volume of *Poems of Felicity*. It seems to me that the most economical hypothesis would include the likelihood of a missing MS containing a third sequence, which Philip planned also to contaminate with the remaining 15 poems from *D*. It seems unlikely that a fair copy in Traherne's hand of *F* will ever show up. (Why would Thomas Traherne recopy the poems he had so carefully inscribed in *D*?) If we assume that *F* is Philip's attempt to reduce three sequences which he only partly understood to only two, we need not explain the existence of still another volume, containing *D*-15, which Philip then used in compiling *F*.

[17]British Museum MS. Burney 392, p. 24. The same shift may be involved in the change on pp. 22-23 from "Misapprehension" to "Adam's Fall." I follow the Oxford editions in using "Adam" as the title of the poem on p. 23 of the MS, but I must admit my reservations about Margoliouth's argument for the priority of the catchword on p. 22. We have the discrepancy between the catchword and the corrected title, but the shift parallels that on pp. 24-25. "Adam's Fall" is neatly drawn in on p. 23, and the text of the poem by no means precludes the subject implied by the title "Adam's Fall." As for catchwords, they are of dubious reliability in such cases; see Ronald B. McKerrow, *An Introduction to Bibliography* (Oxford, 1951), pp. 82-84.

[18]British Museum MS. Burney 392, fol. 2.

[19]In 1910, Dr. Bell published *Poems of Felicity*, introducing Philip's contaminations from the Dobell Folio, and though Wade correctly published the Dobell *Poems* separately (*The Poetical Works of Thomas Traherne . . . together with Poems of Felicity* [London, 1932]), she reprinted the Burney MS poems without excising those in Dobell. Hence, *Poems of Felicity* would be for our purposes an ambiguous title, referring to the suite of poems as compiled by Philip, rather than to the sequence of poems in the Burney MS which emerges when Philip's additions are withdrawn. I have therefore selected the subtitle to refer to those poems found only in the Burney MS. Perhaps *Poems of Felicity* might refer to the two sequences, to which another might well be added, should the missing MS turn up.

[20]George Puttenham, *The Arte of English Poesy* (1589), pp. 197-198.

CHAPTER VII: THE EXPANDED VOICE: THE DOBELL *POEMS*

[1]"Thomas Traherne and the Structure of Meditation," *Journal of English Literary History*, XXV (1958), 79-89.

[2]Gladys I. Wade, *Thomas Traherne* (Princeton, 1944), p. 169.

[3]All citations from Traherne's poetry in this chapter are from *Poems, Centuries and Three Thanksgivings*, ed. Anne Ridler (London, 1966).

[4]"Traherne and the Doctrine of Pre-existence," *Studies in Philology*, LXV (1968), 81-97.

[5]*A Treatise of the Divine Essence and Attributes* (1628), I, 34.

[6]*The Works of Henry Vaughan*, ed. L. C. Martin (Oxford, 1957), p. 419. *Silex Scintillans* appeared in 1650, and so was available to Traherne, who may have meant openly to echo "The Retreat."

[7]For an admirable analysis of "The Preparative," see A. L. Clements, "On the Mode and Meaning of Traherne's Mystical Poetry: 'The Preparative'," *Studies in Philology*, LXI (1964), 500-521.

[8]*Christian Ethicks* (1675), pp. 18-20, 60-62, and esp. 448-449.

[9]The figure itself goes far back in the mystical tradition; Georges Poulet traces this particular phrase to a twelfth-century source, but the idea in one form or another is at least as old as *Timaeus: The Dialogues of Plato*, tr. B. Jowett (Oxford, 1871), II, 528 [33], 538 [44]. For a few of the many pertinent discussions of the figure, especially as it applies to Dante's *La Vita Nuova*, see Poulet, *The Metamorphoses of the Circle*, tr. Carley Dawson and Elliott Coleman (Baltimore, 1966); Robert Fleissner, "Donne and Dante: The Compass Figure Reinterpreted," *Modern Language Notes*, LXXVI (1961), 315-320; John Freccero, "Dante's Pilgrim in a Gyre," *PMLA*, LXXVI (1961), 168-181; Freccero, "Donne's 'Valediction Forbidding Mourning'," *Journal of English History*, XXX (1963), 335-376.

[10]*Odes: In Imitation of the Seaven Penitential Psalmes*, pp. 10, 4.

[11]Thomas Traherne, *Centuries, Poems and Thanksgivings*, ed. H. M. Margoliouth (Oxford, 1958), II, 343.

[12]*A Discourse of the Freedom of the Will* (1675), p. 106.

[13]John Malcolm Wallace sees "Love" as the first poem in the last part of the quinquipartite Jesuitical exercises. Though his argument is cogent, my own view is that the *Poems* have a somewhat more "open" form than Wallace suggests, and that this loose form corresponds in some measure to the four levels of awareness described by Sterry as "Orbs." Nevertheless, my debt to Wallace's discussion should be clear.

[14]For a more detailed discussion of Traherne's use of the "heaping figure," see ch. 6.

[15]Philip's numbering of the "Thoughts" poems tends to obscure the continuity of the section.

CHAPTER VIII: CONCLUDING REMARKS

[1]Herbert Marcuse, *Eros and Civilization: A Philosophical Inquiry into Freud* (London, 1956), ch. 3. The idea is ubiquitous in the writings of Norman O. Brown and Paul Goodman. For a history of the idea, see George Boas, *The Cult of Childhood* (London, 1966). According to Boas, "No account of the literary history of this idea would be complete" without some mention of Thomas Traherne. But the Pelagian bias of Traherne's view would not fit the neo-Calvinist determinism of such thinkers as Marcuse.

INDEX